THE DEVELOPMENT
OF FRENCH ROMANTICISM

THE DEVELOPMENT
OF FRENCH ROMANTICISM

*The Impact of the Industrial Revolution
on Literature*

ALBERT JOSEPH GEORGE

GREENWOOD PRESS, PUBLISHERS
WESTPORT, CONNECTICUT

Library of Congress Cataloging in Publication Data

George, Albert Joseph, 1913-
    The development of French romanticism.

    Reprint of the 1955 ed. published by Syracuse
University Press, Syracus, N. Y.
    1. Romanticism--France. 2. French literature--
19th century--History and criticism. 3. France--
Economic conditions. I. Title.
[PQ287.G4 1977]   840'.9'14   77-10903
ISBN 0-8371-9806-2

Originally published in 1955 by Syracuse University Press,
Syracuse, New York

Reprinted with the permission of Syracuse University Press

Reprinted in 1977 by Greenwood Press, Inc.

Library of Congress Catalog Card Number 77-10903

ISBN 0-8371-9806-2

Printed in the United States of America

ACKNOWLEDGEMENTS

SINCE A BOOK MATURES slowly over a long period of time, a writer necessarily incurs a great many debts of gratitude before he finishes his manuscript. This one is no exception to the rule. Syracuse University granted the author a leave of absence while both the Institute of International Education and the Department of State made the research possible, the first through an appointment to the office of Director of its Paris bureau, the second through a Fulbright Research Grant for study in France. Former professors lent their wisdom and support, Professor Pierre Moreau of the Sorbonne, and Professor Jean-Albert Bédé of Columbia, always kind, ever thoughtful and lavish with their time for a former student. Colleagues from my own and other universities painstakingly read the manuscript, Professor Henri Peyre, of Yale, and Professors Edwin H. Cady and Winthrop H. Rice, both of Syracuse University. And, of course, Miss Dorothy Rivers typed countless revisions and offered many a valuable suggestion. To all of these my deepest gratitude for helping polish and improve the present study.

CONTENTS

INTRODUCTION

THE STUDY OF French romanticism has provided scholars with one of the most entertaining and irritating of literary puzzles. For generations they have vainly tried to reduce a complex series of disparate elements to a brief but satisfactory definition. Periodically one writer or another has blackened hundreds of pages in attempts to find a phrase which might function as mental calipers for measuring the exact degree of a writer's romanticism. Whenever such a definition has been proposed, critics have cheerfully listed sins of omission, tearing down carefully-prepared arguments or offering substitute interpretations. But still other optimists have always risen to the challenge, sure that they could solve the riddle —and so goes the game.

Scholars being among the most contrary of men, the net result has been a wealth of contradictory statements. And the situation has not been improved by the fact that historically the romanticists themselves were not sure how to explain their work. The 1835 edition of the dictionary of the French Academy noted that " Romantique se dit des écrivains qui affectent de s'affranchir des règles de composition et de style établies par l'exemple des auteurs classiques." From the well-known " libéralisme en littérature " of Hugo, to the famous quip of Stendhal on the modernity of romanticism, the writers varied in interpreting their own ideas. Consequently, it is no wonder that the Baron Seillière saw in romanticism a kind of naturistic mysticism, while Auguste Viatte traced it back to the occult and illuministic philosophies of the 18th century. On the other hand, a chauvinistic Louis Reynaud considered it the result of the evil influence of foreign cultures, although Pierre Moreau understood it as a vast reaching for the infinite and a concern for the relative. Irving Babbitt sneered at romanticism as an undue insistence on individualism, but Roger Picard has found it to be a main source of socialism. Maurice Souriau wrote of it vaguely as " la collaboration de quelques génies avec la tristesse de l'âme française." More recently, Adrien de Meeüs simplified the problem by calling " romantic " everything in man which is opposed to reason, that which seeps from the mysterious and secret corners of the soul.

Contemporary usage of the word presents further difficulties. Romanticism and romanticism exist side by side, with entirely different meanings. For some, romanticism denotes a state of mind that may be contrasted with the precise, regulated symmetry of classicism. Therefore, it is legitimate for them to write on the romanticism of the *Chanson de Roland*, of Pascal, or Voltaire. On the other hand, Romanticism signifies to most people a definite period of history during which specific writers accepted the name to differentiate their particular kind of literature from all others. It is in this sense that the word is used herein, though without benefit of capitalization.

II

This book does not contain the solution of a problem that has so long perplexed so many. Its intent is simply to introduce a new factor for consideration as an important determinant in the development of romanticism : the Industrial Revolution. The impact of mechanization and the shift to industrial capitalism are phenomena which have been greatly neglected as influences on literature, although they have been universally acknowledged as major creators of social change. The machine, the growth of the urban proletariat and the social consequences of the factory system have, in general, been overlooked in favor of problems of aesthetics.

To be sure, the field is not brand new. Elliot Grant has investigated the machine age as a theme in the work of the romanticists. D. W. Owen, in both the *Socialisme des romantiques* and *Le Roman social sous la monarchie de juillet*, has written extensively of the relationship of this movement to the forerunners of modern socialism, themselves a product of the industrialization of society. Roger Picard's *Le Romantisme social* touches upon some phases of the Industrial Revolution, notably the preoccupation of the early 19th-century writers with social problems. More recently (1948), the leftist periodical *Europe* has dedicated a number in celebration of the " Centenaire de la révolution de 48," all of its articles in praise of the " people."

The work of these scholars, and many others, must, of course, be taken into consideration. But the direction of the present discussion lies along another road. The fundamental thesis here is that the Industrial Revolution functioned as one of the prime sources of romanticism, and, simultaneously, became a principal force in transforming the initial character of that literature. Replies are sought to such questions as : why did romanticism change so fundamentally about 1830; why did it break into splinter movements; and why these particular movements? Some of the answers can be found by studying both the effect of the Industrial Revolution on society and its influence on the political and literary philosophies of the writers of the period.

III

In this work romanticism has been treated as a phenomenon covering roughly the period 1800-1852, to give it the greatest latitude. To be sure, the historical view of romanticism entails close consideration of an age that saw a fantastic succession of governments, religious cults, economic saviors, and dabblers in the delights of ecstatic mysticism. The various short-lived regimes of the Revolution made way for the Consulate, the Empire, and the Restoration, which in turn culminated in the Orléans Monarchy and the Second Republic. During this era, Saint-Simonism and Fourierism vied with the New Jerusalem; Enfantin paraded in splendid costume while his followers were seeking the *femme-messie* in the East; Pierre Leroux and Jean Reynaud disagreed sharply on the interplanetary migration of souls. Simultaneously, a Catholicism outlawed during the Revolution blossomed in rich renascence and writers like Ballanche and Lamartine stirred uneasily, conscious of the way time erodes all institutions. French authors finally rejected most of the tired tenets of the classical aesthetics, while modern history struggled for attention against a popular taste for Gothicism. The age seems one of incredible complexity, with little or no continuity.

One fact, however, does stand out amidst all the chaos. France, blocked from the Industrial Revolution by a great political revolt, the Imperial wars, and the apathy of the Bourbons, suddenly began to feel the shock of industrialization, at about the time when the French romanticists were winning their argument with the neo-classicists.

The effects of the Industrial Revolution were not long in appearing. Romanticism prior to 1830 had been mostly negative in nature, concerned primarily with refuting the claims of classical dicta. By 1830 its supporters had made their point but their very victory created for them the problem of establishing a positive creed if they hoped to keep the attention of the public. And it was the Industrial Revolution which, in part, furnished the new school with the materials it was seeking; new plots, new characters, new images, even a new purpose for writing, came from this great age of major social change.

Not only did the Industrial Revolution yield the reasons and means for revising the content of literature, it also contributed to the establishment of new approaches to art. Writers who, for the first time, faced a mass audience without benefit of patrons, and who were forced to please potential buyers, necessarily had to modify techniques established for communication with an elite. The novel in particular felt this transformation. Hitherto an unimportant genre, it rapidly came to dominate the literary scene and, where once few had given heed to its form, the art of the prose narrative began more and more to concern the majority of writers. Furthermore, authors increasingly felt the need for a new set of symbols and myths to synthesize the beliefs and aspirations of their age, as they attempted to express the feelings of contemporary society. They set to work to fill this gap and, by 1840, romanticism had created a new mythology of its own, a handy frame of reference for the problems of the period.

This, then, is the general thesis. But one word of warning. It should not be assumed that the Industrial Revolution was the only factor governing the development of romanticism, nor that it regulated the growth of the new literature according to a kind of determinism. It should be clearly kept in mind that the events which conspired to push romanticism in the direction it took occurred from historical coincidence. And although 1830 seems to be a magic year, a division line in the development of French literature of the 19th century, it should be remembered that the date is here used primarily as a handy reference and should actually be read as " about 1830." In any case the concurrence at that time of the phenomena under discussion cannot in any way be attributed to inexorable cause and effect. Chance played the strongest part in the turn of events.

IV

A word concerning the presentation of the material seems advisable. In general, the number of footnotes has been kept to a minimum, though some scholars may object. The principle has been followed that there is no need to give the bibliographical sources of common and undisputed knowledge. Hence, in Part I, which is primarily a synthesis of well-established facts, only the major works on the subject at hand are indicated and these are given simply to indicate the kind of authority on which the account is based. Many more notations could have been made, but the expense of type-setting has presented a practical difficulty, the solution of which takes precedence over any desire to impress with a display of scholarly fireworks. Therefore, only Part II will contain a large number of footnotes to indicate the source of unusual material or to identify rare or little-read books and, even here, the notations have been sharply curtailed.

PART ONE

THE BACKGROUND

CHAPTER 1
DEVELOPMENT OF EARLY
ROMANTICISM

COINCIDENTALLY WITH THE first stumbling steps France took into the 19th century, a great change became noticeable on the literary scene when romanticism made its timid appearance, unnamed and unrecognized.

It is difficult to fix a beginning for what was to become a major literary movement.[1] The transformation came through slow progression as a nation with a new political and social set of mind began to grope for values befitting an age of hope. France haltingly turned from an era of literary conservativism to hesitant experimentation with new means of expression. Yet, so cautiously was innovation approached that in 1800 one of the first calls for change, Mme de Staël's *De la littérature,* raised no shouts of alarm from the ever-present, self-appointed protectors of the national heritage. To be sure, Madame de Staël was merely following a distinguished line of predecessors in proclaiming the perfectibility of the literary man but she established for the critics two handy pairs of opposites : the North versus the South, modernism versus classicism. Basically she was only suggesting that writers broaden French taste by borrowing judiciously from other literatures, a happy idea which had never seemed revolutionary. Even her association of literature and human institutions raised no critical eyebrows. Not even the publication of *Atala* or the *Génie du Christianisme* made conservatives suspect that Chateaubriand would become the grand sachem of a new movement. At the time, they considered him only a successful writer of royalist persuasion who had not strayed very far from the socially acceptable.

In fact, prior to 1810 few critics viewed literature with alarm. In 1804 a writer for the *Débats* noted acidly that melodramas like the *Français en Alger* could become a menace to tragedy, but he did not foresee how dark would be his prophesy when the melodrama was cast in verse. A colleague on the *Mercure de France*, Charles Durdent, took a more suspicious attitude when he reviewed Delille's translation of *Paradise Lost* on February 16, 1805. He, too, voiced grave doubts about the modern penchant for giving imagination free rein, and he advised his colleagues to curb young writers for the good of the national literature.

Nevertheless, stubborn French admiration for the perfection of the past lessened rapidly from 1804 to 1810, and such a minor literary quibble appeared ridiculously esoteric to most readers. True, in 1808, Wilhelm Schlegel's comments on the classical aesthetics had provoked Dussault, dramatic critic of the *Journal de l'Empire*, into three sharp articles on the former's uncomplimentary *Comparaison entre la Phèdre de Racine et celle d'Euripide*. But such manifestions of chauvinism were rare because the rapidly expanding Liberal party approved of reform, even advocated the use of foreign material on the grounds that tradition acted as the narcotic of talent. Stapfer, Benjamin Constant and Mme de Staël heartily backed this opinion. One writer, Sébastien Mercier, even dared publish the audacious *Satires contre Boileau et Racine* (1808), but he was treated as a minor idiot by almost all readers. Benjamin Constant, however, received more serious attention for his introduction to *Wallenstein* (1809), in which he compared the German theater to French tragedy, to conclude that the French might well study foreign drama for hints on a more modern conception of tragedy.

By 1809, France was reacting sluggishly to the debate over modernism. Constant's *Wallenstein* provoked Viollet-le-Duc to answer with his *Nouvel Art poétique*, a bitter satire on the excesses of foreigners and the decadence of the 19th-century intellect. Even the prudent Népomucène Lemercier braved the teapot tempest with *Christophe Colomb, comédie shakespearienne*, a flagrant violation of the unities and the rule forbidding the mixing of genres. A cautious man with an eye on Academic immortality, he wisely disclaimed his own work the night before its opening, but the first performance nonetheless treated Paris to one of its famous riots, with indiscriminate fist fights and canings. Neutral spectators, who had naïvely paid to see a play, were forced to seek shelter on the stage until the police cleared the hall. Modernism had become obvious enough in 1809 to irritate the fustiest of classicists.

Between 1810 and 1813 the debate quieted, perhaps because the gravity of political events made literary squabbles seem relatively unimportant; but, by 1813, proponents of the present had plucked up new courage. Mme Necker de Saussure translated Schlegel's *Cours de littérature dramatique;* Sismonde de Sismondi's *De la littérature du Midi de l'Europe* appeared; and Madame de Staël's *De l'Allemagne* was published in London. Of the three, Mme de Staël wielded the greatest influence. Just when the emigrés were returning home with some knowledge of foreign writings, she repeated her thesis of 1800 : that the North and the South existed in literary opposition. But now she preached the substitution for classicism of a national, popular, Christian, and chevaleresque literature. To accomplish this, she again suggested the acceptance of foreign influences to the detriment of the sacred rules.

By now sensitive to any hint of literary heresy, the classicists immediately flew to arms. Dussault of the *Débats* led a counterattack on Schlegel's Germanism and Mme de Staël's cosmopolitanism, backed by Hoffman, Auger, and the acid-tongued Féletz. A young writer named Charles Nodier accepted the unenviable position of conciliator and tried in vain to soothe the antagonists by suggesting that romanticism was merely a variety of classicism, but neither side felt in a mood for charitable concessions.

Between 1816 and 1819, the sniping produced only further stalemate, though the modernists managed to score a few minor successes, even finding friendly newspapers and magazines. The war of pamphlets continued unabated, especially since the classicists now realized how much lay at stake. The Vicomte de Saint-Chamans, a tired old classicist, equated romanticism with unrestrained genius in his partisan *Anti-romantique ou examen de quelques ouvrages nouveaux* (1816); Népomu-cène Lemercier, always on the side of the strongest, aided the classicists with a public recantation of previous literary sins. He fully recognized that nascent romanticism contained practically everything the ruling critics disliked.

By 1816 the issues had become clearer, though romanticism still remained a vague menace to most observers. The word itself, hitherto little known, began more and more to creep into print. As a complicating factor, the nationalism rampant after Waterloo introduced a new note of discord into the debate. Sensitive patriots vaunted the

superiority of French literature over foreign products at the very time
when Byron, Scott, Schiller, Shakespeare, and Goethe were competing
seriously with French classical literature for popular support. Thus,
when Lady Morgan published her impressions of France in 1817,
the groundwork had been laid for a violent argument. Nothing could
have been more unfortunately timed than her remarks on the absurdity
of the classical dramatic system. Howling nationalists reacted as
though she had denied the existence of God.

Until the publication of Mme de Staël's *Considérations sur la révolution française* (1818), romanticism had been considered primarily a
foreign import. Now it became something more profound : a consequence of the Revolution, and a struggle between two generations
separated by a great social upheaval. Once again the 18th century's
thesis of the perfectibility of man began to attract attention, and some
classicists even grudgingly acknowledged the need for the renewal
of literary inspiration. By 1819 the problem seemed obvious enough
for the Académie des Jeux Floraux at Toulouse to propose as the
topic of a prize competition : " Quels sont les caractères distinctifs
de la littérature à laquelle on a donné le nom de *Romantique*, et quelles
ressources pourrait-elle offrir à la littérature classique ? " As in all
similar contests, nobody could supply an answer acceptable to any
but the unhappy judges. The classicists could still point out stiffly
that modernism had not yet produced any work of consequence but,
on the contrary, had sponsored innumerable translations from barbaric
cultures, dipped the melodrama in gore, and cluttered literature with
vampires. So many romantic zombies crowded into plays and novels,
vied for public favor with bloody nuns and lusty renegade priests,
that even the universities took cognizance of the trend.

By 1820, the balance of power began to shift slightly in favor of
the proponents of the new. As yet this group lacked any of the five
requisites for the success of a literary group in Paris : a clear doctrine;
a recognized chief; a meeting place; some medium for propagandizing
new ideas; and at least one successful product of its doctrine. But
the romanticists were busy translating their aspirations into works,
slowly attaining the measure of cohesion necessary for the formation
of a unified group.

It fell to Lamartine to provide one of the necessities, an outstanding
success. In March 1820, public reception of the *Méditations* showed

clearly that former greats like Delille, Le Brun, and Parny had been surpassed. Utilizing Delille's technique of word painting and Parny's use of sensuous reaction, Lamartine revolutionized French poetry with the soft fluidity of his verse. A new set of values came to replace those worn threadbare by almost two centuries of hard use when, for the first time since Malherbe, a book of French verse explored the lyrical possibilities of an unrestrained sense of freedom and inspiration. The poetry rolled forth in such powerful waves that the classicists felt overwhelmed, though not alarmed. Critics demonstrated a complete inability to discuss Lamartine's art and ineptly explained it as a manifestation of religiosity. To be sure, other poets had expired in verse, though none had displayed such skill in so doing. But, despite the novelty of the poetry, it provoked only a nominal amount of adverse criticism. Close observers noted that Lamartine strayed little from the tradition of Baour Lormian or Millevoye, and that the structure of his poems remained true to older models.

With a resounding success to their credit, the new generation worked to fulfill the second condition for survival. The first *cénacle* achieved coherence around Emile Deschamps at his home on the rue Saint Florentin. Here even some of the elders deigned to appear; Baour Lormian and Chênedollé mingled with the Gay sisters, the royalistically-inclined Alfred de Vigny and Victor Hugo. Only a loose friendship cemented the strange political mixture, but it meant progress in the right direction. Almost all the romanticists huddled together sympathetically for mutual protection as they sought to explain their brave new world.

For the time being, too, it seemed that the dissidents might have access to a newspaper, the *Conservateur littéraire*. The Hugo brothers had dominated the periodical since its founding in December, 1819, and though supposedly conservative royalists, they had displayed a slight show of independence. Ambitious Victor prudently placed his faith in Boileau rather than in the new heresy but, after the collapse of the journal in March, 1821, most of his collaborators willingly accepted the leadership of the rebel Soumet.

By 1821-1822 camps had begun to form on a political rather than a literary basis, royalist versus liberal. Each faction contained a weird conglomeration of literary creeds, with little attempt made to reconcile

contradictory ideas. The quarrel over romanticism led to bitter
antagonism between, and within, the parties, with the resultant creation
of two branches of modernism, one liberal, encyclopedic in origin,
the other royalist, dedicated to the worship of the 17th century.

The latter group scored a series of notable successes when several
of its members broke into print. Hugo published the first volume
of the *Odes*, Vigny his *Poèmes*. On the stage Guiraud placed the
Macchabées at the Odéon, while Soumet scored doubly with *Cly-
temnestre* at the Comédie Française and *Saül* at the Odéon. Though
each of these earned some measure of popular success, the critics
refused to admit the validity of their literary premises. Hugo, himself,
despite a petulant statement that he saw no fundamental difference
between the two factions, smarted under the critical lash. But the
sneers of their caustic elders only forced the modernists to unite more
strongly around Soumet. By now, too, they had formulated a vague
doctrine that included a plea for the renewal of literary forms, plus
a return to the political and religious inspiration of the Middle Ages.
Still fervently royalist, they scorned the liberal vulgarity of the crowd.

The incessant polemics continued without decision through 1823
and 1824. The word romanticism meant so little that the first volume
of the *Mercure du 19e siècle* (1823) complained of the vagueness of
the term. Nevertheless, young writers felt they had a cause, and by
1824 Emile Deschamps had assumed the position of spokesman for
the younger romanticists. In May, 1824, he published in the *Muse
Française* the first draft of a manifesto entitled *La Guerre en temps
de paix*, which bitterly denounced the classicist plot to stifle the new
and the different. The essay vigorously excoriated the opposition
for publishing false accusations and charged the classicists with writing
new books from memories of the old without any regard for inspiration. Yet, ironically, Deschamps still found it possible to kill the
Muse Française, the leading organ of romanticism, when its existence
threatened to compromise the chances of his friend, Soumet, for
election to the Academy, even though Soumet had already abjectly
begged forgiveness for his literary sins.

The defection did little harm to the movement. The rebels reformed
around Nodier, though only as a social group. Hugo's influence
grew steadily, now that he had the prestige of a considerable bibliography. Tirelessly and ambitiously he worked to become the recog-

nized chief of all romanticists of Catholic, royalist persuasion. Simultaneously, the liberal romanticists established their own salons at the home of Stapfer, Viollet-le-Duc, or Delécluze. And, most important of all, Paul Dubois founded the *Globe* in September, 1824, as a newspaper dedicated to the unification of liberalism and the new literature. The *Globe* never functioned as the mouthpiece of any faction, yet it did recognize romanticism as a continuation of the Revolution, " le protestantisme dans les lettres et les arts." A brilliant group of collaborators, among them Sainte-Beuve, insured the dissidents of powerful allies during the crucial years of their struggle.

Despite all these favorable signs, a romantic literature was tardy in appearing. In 1826 it still consisted primarily of translations of Scott, Byron, Schiller, Goethe, and Shakespeare, intermingled with an over-supply of melodrama and examples of the *genre frénétique*. A few volumes of poetry showed promise, greatest among them Lamartine's *Méditations*. But most important, the group had frightened off most of the semi-classicists, and Hugo reigned contentedly as unchallenged leader, directing operations and soliciting supporters with amazing energy. Conscious of his position, he prefaced the third volume of the *Odes* with a belligerent demand for artistic freedom that foreshadowed the *Préface de Cromwell*. He moved closer to the *Globe*, effecting a merger of the various factions of romanticism under his guidance. Thus, by the critical year 1827, the new school could boast of an active chief, a center of operations, friendly papers and critics, and some conception of a doctrine.

II

The years 1827-1828 marked an important phase in the development of romanticism with the appearance of three manifestoes : Sainte-Beuve's *Tableau historique et critique*, Emile Deschamps' introduction to the *Études françaises et étrangères*, and Hugo's preface to *Cromwell*.

The function of Sainte-Beuve's *Tableau* was principally to build a romantic defense against the jibes of the classicists. It had long been a sore point with young writers that they could lay little claim to any connection with French tradition. Their opponents labelled them imitators of foreigners, copyists of ideologies inimical to the best interests of the nation. On the other hand, the classicists pointed with pride to a long succession of great predecessors, revered in academic circles as the founding fathers of their particular republic of letters. With this point of great propaganda value to aid them in the battle for public support, they could always turn literary arguments into easily-won discussions of patriotism.

The *Tableau* gave the romanticists the ancesters they yearned for and a means of turning the tables on the enemy. Sainte-Beuve explained the 16th century to a France which had forgotten the age, binding the work to the author and the author to his times. Moreover, he established a continuity of tradition from the Pléiade to the romanticists which enabled the new school to claim forerunners of great stature who ante-dated the classical age. Consequently, the romanticists could proudly proclaim themselves more French than Racine; Boileau they treated as a bewigged pettifogger.

Like Sainte-Beuve, Deschamps preached the doctrine of slow, continuous evolution. More moderate than some of his colleagues, he nonetheless defended the thesis that modernism should replace classicism. Deschamps vigorously defended the 19th century against its detractors, enthusiastically called for more translations of foreign authors, a rejuvenated theater and freer verse forms. Lyric poetry, especially, seemed to him a weak point in the national literature, stifled as it was by classicists unworthy of having their names mentioned in the same breath with Lamartine, Hugo, or Vigny.

As a manifesto, the preface to *Cromwell* ranks ahead of the *Tableau* and the *Études françaises*, though it offers little more of a positive nature. Hugo, too, preached rebellion against the restrictions of the past and the tyranny of a group that pretended to judge everything according to " reason." To him, the unities of time and place seemed nonsensical; he asked for the " real," for the liberation of imagination and sensibility, but for the most part he inveighed lengthily against the famous " principes invariables " or the " immuable beau." What the classicists had done was wrong and France needed to wipe the cobwebs from its aesthetics.

On the positive side, Hugo sketched a theory of the romantic drama later to be realized in *Hernani* and *Ruy Blas*, a new kind of play independent of all rules, passing in pseudo-Shakespearian fashion from the tragic to the comic, full of antitheses, and supposedly crammed with the complexities of life. Secondly, he replied to the anti-poetic theories which Stendhal had expounded in two pamphlets on Racine and Shakespeare. Here Hugo gave specific recommendations regarding the form of romantic verse. By displacing the caesura, employing enjambement rather than inversion, avoiding the tirade and making verse more supple, poetry could benefit from all the qualities of prose, yet surpass it in emotional expression. It could be as simple as daily speech, or rhythmic and complicated. Beyond a few further recommendations on the theater, Hugo indulged primarily in defying the classicists and in outlining a peculiar philosophy of history. The preface, where it included positive suggestions for change, dealt mostly with questions of form since the young men for whom Hugo spoke were interested almost exclusively in abolishing the old restrictions.

Thus, by 1828, romanticism had tried to justify itself, had chosen literarily acceptable ancestors, and had proclaimed itself a new poetic art based on modern " realism." It revolutionized the Alexandrine and extended lyricism to the indistinct and the unformulated. And as proof of the vitality of his group, Hugo published more *Odes et Ballades*, full of audacious rhymes, and the *Orientales*, a radical departure from previous French versification which flung down the gauntlet to the critics.

III

As yet, however, the romanticists had not carried their point. Although the classicists continually criticized new works, the freedom of the poet had been accepted without undue excitement. In the realm of prose there had been no debate. But France considered the theater, particularly when in verse, to constitute its chief glory, and on this ground the classicists had successfully maintained their standards. It was obvious to both sides that whoever controlled the stage not only had access to public opinion but could also earn a decent return on his intellectual investment. As long as the older generation could limit the younger to poetry and to the unrecognized and deprecated field of prose, classicism still reigned supreme. Recognizing this, the romanticists had long tried to worm their way onto the stage, but a tight phalanx of classically-minded directors had implacably rejected their plays.

Therefore it was over the question of the theater that the final battle for romanticism was to be fought. Not until 1825, when Baron Taylor became Royal Commissioner for the Comédie Française, did there seem to be any hope; even then, the young writers had to wait several years for their triumph. Meanwhile, fully appreciative of their position, the romanticists raced for the glory of being first to receive the plaudits of theater-goers. In this they agreed with Emile Deschamps' contention for the need of a drama founded on the national history, copied neither from Shakespeare nor Racine. Stendhal had also made this point, but he was discredited as a heretic who advocated the use of prose.

From 1828 forward, the romanticists rushed toward glory, though simultaneously they had to compete with their enemies and with the lure of the melodrama, now almost the standard literary fare of the middle class. To the observant it had become obvious that the application of verse to the melodrama, with a plot well-steeped in local color, stood a good chance of success. Mindful of this, Hugo presented in *Amy Robsart* (October, 1828) an idea borrowed from *Kenilworth* but felt so uncertain of himself that he cautiously ascribed the drama to his brother-in-law, Paul Foucher. The play failed, but this did not deter Dumas from staging *Henri III et sa cour*, a travesty of history which earned popular acclaim despite its inaccuracies. The romanticists promptly claimed Dumas as one of their own but continued to work on their own manuscripts, persuaded that *Henri III* lay too close to the melodrama to represent a true example of their doctrine.

By 1829 the debate had entered its stormiest period. When Hugo finished *Marion Delorme* only to have the censor table the play, others leaped to the breach with creations of their own. A kind of fever seized these aspirants to fame as they worked madly to replace Racine. Soulié tried to score first with *Christine*, Vigny next with a translation of *Othello*. Soulié's play failed before a hostile audience that whistled, screamed, and hooted so loudly that few heard any of the lines. Alfred de Vigny felt more secure as the translator of a great work, but when women fainted at his delicate use of the word *mouchoir*, to avoid the implication of the word *sheets*, it provided the classicists with an excuse to riot over the " obscenity " of *Othello*. Shakespeare and Vigny managed to outlast the tumult but the victory remained dubious. Neither side rejoiced, and the critics limited themselves for the most part to debating, not Shakespeare, but the new dramatic style. Actually the classicists seemed ready to accept most of the points made by the romanticists except the matter of a change in the style of tragedy. They could not as yet stomach either the vocabulary or the colorful writing of the rebels.

Hugo, meanwhile, patiently awaited his great moment. For a time he had considered racing Vigny for the honor of being first to achieve success on the stage, but careful thought and a great sense of timing persuaded him to allow *Othello* to pave the way for his own play, even at the risk of its infuriating the conservatives. Thus it was in a decidedly hostile climate that he first laid plans for presenting *Hernani*. Both sides sensed that the final decision was at hand and, consequently, prepared their defenses. There is little need to recount the unbelievable story of *Hernani*, with its secret rehearsals, literary espionage, and hostile actors. The fantastic première has been described often enough, with its parade of weirdly-dressed combatants, its violent arguments, and loud bursts of partisan expression, even on the part of the actors. But when the newspapers of 1830 came to assess the evening's entertainment, they reluctantly admitted that the new school had won. For the first five days the shouting had continued, but the real decision was given when the man in the street, with the price of admission in his pocket, cast the deciding vote. Both sides might rant at each other, but they recognized that the public on which they now depended had settled their conflict. The classicists retired to lick their wounds. Temporarily they abdicated their power, though they would continue harassing tactics for a long time to come.

As for the romanticists, they could cheer momentarily in the pride of their accomplishments. In a few years they had created a new lyric poetry, renewed the conception of the beautiful and smashed the antiquated and restrictive forms of verse which the past had thrust upon them. Unnoticed, they had also enlarged the idea of the novel by utilizing popular taste for history, though this last achievement remained for long obscured by the fact that they had replaced tragedy with the *drame* and rejuvenated French poetic style through a new use of imagery.

NOTES

1. The history of French romanticism has been well established. There exists, in fact, a multitude of books, all of which could be cited, but mention need only to be made here of a sample of the kind of standard text from which the following information is drawn: Pierre Moreau, *Le Romantisme*, Paris, De Gigord, 1932; René Bray, *Chronologie du romantisme*, Paris, Boivin, 1932; and Maurice Souriau, *Histoire du romantisme*, Paris, Spes, 1927.

CHAPTER 2

DETERMINANTS OF ROMANTICISM

AT THE MOMENT romanticism triumphed, France was simultaneously feeling the initial impact of a number of phenomena far removed from the world of books, which nonetheless were drastically to affect the budding literary movement. Around 1830, France began to distinguish the first astonishing effects of the mechanization brought by its own Industrial Revolution; coincidentally, only by then did the nation have a large reading public and the means of production to give a mass literature to that audience. When the romanticists finally grasped these two facts, the course of their development underwent a sudden and violent shift of emphasis. But to understand this change a complex series of factors must be taken into consideration.

I

By the end of the Revolution, France had not experienced any of the effects of the Industrial Revolution. The country still functioned on a system of commercial capitalism, with most of the population concerned primarily with agriculture. A few men worked as artisans, but France lagged far behind England in exploiting the possibilities of the machine. Some primitive engines were employed in mining, but they were practically unknown in other industries. In the few cases where machines were utilized, the workers regarded them suspiciously in fear of the possible consequences of the use of such monsters. In 1802, the ribbon makers of Paris demanded from the National Assembly the suppression of all mechanized trades. The spinners of Lille rioted in the year XIII when they discovered that English machines had been ordered for the factory; and, in 1803,

workers at Sedan frightened their employers into cancelling an order
for mechanical shearers.[1]

War, however, had even more effectively blocked France from
undergoing the Industrial Revolution that was transforming England.
The turmoil of political revolution had so upset the nation that any
possibility of industrialization disappeared. France careened dizzily
from one form of government to another, each more inept at solving
current problems than its inglorious predecessor. With the removal
of the artificial stimuli that came from privileges, shops were abandoned
and factories closed. Economic chaos followed so closely in the wake
of political turbulence that in 1797 France fell into the chill hands
of a depression from which a futile Directory could not rescue it.
What little industrial expansion had begun in the Ancien Régime
smothered in the fumbling hands of neophyte politicians. Napoleon
stabilized the economy of the country but refused to permit trade
with England for military reasons. When he forbade the importation
of British goods in 1803, his action effectively sealed off France from
the advantages of industrialization. Then, in 1806 and 1807, the
decrees of Berlin and Milan completed the country's isolation. France
continued to remain solidly an agricultural nation, populated mostly
with peasants who tilled ancestral slopes by antiquated methods. By
1815, France could boast only 15 steam engines of a total horsepower
of 230, these used principally in mining. With large numbers of
men in uniform, Napoleon had recognized the necessity of inventions
for increasing the potential of a reduced number of workers, but
French scientists could not possibly meet the urgency of his demands.

Yet, despite this, Napoleon actually set the stage for the change
to industrialization. In a desperate attempt to compensate for the
lack of English goods, the Emperor founded a school of mines and
dyes, established prizes and competitions in the areas he thought
needed most attention. In some respects he succeeded; thanks to
the Douglas, Cockerill, Ternaux, and Jacquard machines, the textile
industries boomed, with wool, cotton, and silk selling at prices to
delight the manufacturers' hearts. The chemical industry took its
first, hesitant steps into a promising future. To facilitate this and
other new enterprises, Bonaparte established the Bank of France to
develop the credit needed for the tremendous expansion required by
the government. His efforts resulted in setting the conditions requisite

for the coming Industrial Revolution : 1) French manufacturers realized what great profits could be gained from mechanization; and 2) large amounts of capital finally accumulated in the hands of the men supplying the armies.

Up to this time, none of the unpleasant features of the change in the economic system had appeared. Salaries rose; the number of women and children employed in industry increased, though not enough to create major social problems. France needed hands to keep her factories going, and no manufacturer worried about the moral problems implicit in the employment of women and children.

II

With the Restoration, industrial transformation continued at a slightly faster pace along the lines set during the Napoleonic age. Although France had now started toward mechanization, she had to waste much of her amazing vitality in recovering lost ground. Since millions of men had died in battle, there existed a critical shortage of skilled labor, and industry in general needed reorganization to match the advances England had made.

Nevertheless, France enjoyed the financial security required for such a step. Napoleon had reorganized the currency and founded a national bank that functioned well even after Waterloo. Consequently, the production of wool, silk, and cotton continued to climb, while the chemical industry expanded even more vigorously. In some areas, as in the spinning of wool, hand labor disappeared entirely. The 15 steam engines available in 1815 had become 625 in 1830, with 10,000 horse power. French metallurgy was slowly remodeled along English lines, though a lack of coke long restricted operations.[2]

By about 1825, it was becoming apparent that the face of France was changing slowly but inexorably. The economy had recovered sufficiently to permit considerable industrial expansion. The machine had come to stay and it eliminated many of the problems of hired hands; more work produced in a shorter time meant more profits. By the end of the Restoration the first railroads began to spread their webs over small sections of France. In fact, in 1827, the first locomotive with a tubular boiler puffed noisily along the Saint-Etienne-Lyon line. Some measure of the transformation may be reckoned from the rate of urban population growth, which Clapham calls the best general test of a nation's industrialization. Paris jumped from 588,000 in 1801 to 890,000 in 1826; Lyon and its suburbs grew from 109,000 to 170,000; Marseille, Bordeaux, Rouen, and Nantes followed the same pattern.

Nevertheless, France shifted her center of economic gravity very cautiously. In 1826 some 22,000,000 of a total population of about 31,000,000 still clung to agriculture. Certain factors mitigated against any quick success in overtaking England. For one thing, immediately after 1814 the English had flooded France with goods against the cost of which the French could scarcely compete. Not only that, but the influx of foreign goods and the upsurge of home production soon glutted the market. Prices of manufactured articles sagged at a time when industrialists had committed large amounts of capital for the first establishment of factories. To make matters worse, cheap as they were, these goods languished on counters because salaries dropped 22 per cent, while the cost of living rose 60 per cent between 1800-1830.[3] And, finally, lack of coal prevented the French from mechanizing quickly and, since hand labor worked so cheaply, manufacturers generally persisted in thinking in the same terms as their grandfathers. French markets were expanding far more slowly than the means of production and the result was a series of hampering depressions during 1816, 1818-1819, and 1826-1827.

By 1830 the pace of the Industrial Revolution had so quickened in France that even the unobservant noticed that the basic structure of the economic system was changing. The shift to industrial capitalism had even produced a new class, the *grande bourgeoisie manufacturière*, to which Louis Philippe willingly lent the prestige of his government. Production increased enormously; large industry began to concentrate; and the machine became commonplace. Free enterprise reigned in a manner calculated to delight the heart of Adam Smith, principally at the expense of the underprivileged.

The advances made under Napoleon and the Restoration now began to pay full dividends. By 1830, France had about 600 steam engines in operation. The cotton industry had adopted the power loom even more quickly than Lancashire with the result that 2000 were in use by 1830, some 10,000 by 1846. Between 1828-1847 the output of pig iron more than doubled; in 1832 important iron-ore deposites were discovered near Boulogne and the development of the coal beds of the Nord and the Pas de Calais began about the same time. Simultaneously, the government embarked on a program of canal construction to insure the even distribution of finished goods.[4]

Most exciting of all, however, was the spread of the railroads. Toward the decline of the Restoration, France had debated their value but had only tentatively decided to use them. But after 1828, locomotives began to crawl slowly over the countryside, frightening peasants and their animals, but tightening the hold of the machine on the economy. Manufacturers especially felt happy whenever the rails passed near their factories. At first only idealists and dreamers dared envision the day when the puffing horrors would transport people, but at least they could drag goods behind them. Then, after 1832, when the railroads began to carry passengers, they captured the imagination of admirers of a machine age even though, in 1836, the nation could only boast of 270 kilometers of line open to the public.[5] Truly France was at last beginning to catch up with England in the matter of industrialization.

III

The machine made other changes, particularly in the domain of printing, where the same backwardness had existed prior to 1830 as in all other industries. Technologically, the art of printing had not progressed much beyond the days of Gutenberg, and only the large urban centers could boast firms capable of publishing books.

For one thing, there existed in France no factory for the industrial production of ink until Pierre Lorilleux of the Imprimerie Nationale created such an enterprise at Paris in 1808. Up to this date, the manufacture of printer's ink had existed on a personal basis. Though a minor item, the establishment of this industry was necessary for the large-scale operations required to produce a mass literature.

More important, however, is the fact that prior to the 19th century France had no means of making quantities of paper in any format. Especially lacking were the large sizes required by newspapers. Actually, all paper was handmade by a slow and primitive process until the early years of the 19th century. A skilled worker dipped a sieve-like mould into a vat of fibers suspended in water. Lifting this, he brought forth a thin matted layer which, when dried, furnished printing stock. Obviously, the dimensions of the largest sheets were limited to the small tray a man could conveniently balance. Moreover, so few factories existed that not enough paper could be produced to supply France's needs.[6] Thus, the methods of printing were controlled by the arm-length of skilled artisans and the speed at which a limited number of them could produce. And to make matters worse, at the end of the 18th century France possessed only 33 dipping vats and 25 mills.[7]

This situation continued until Nicolas-Louis Robert was literally driven to invent the paper-making machine. Furious at the constant bickering between the workers he supervised at the Didot paper mill, he bent all his energies to replacing the men he hated. On September 9, 1798, he requested a patent for a machine that produced paper larger and faster than ever before, but because of disturbed conditions little could be done with his idea. When Robert became too heavily involved financially, he abandoned his discovery to Didot for 25,000 francs, but the purchaser failed to make the payments and Robert resumed the patent in 1801. Meanwhile, however, Didot had informed his brother-in-law, John Gamble, the English paper maker, of the new invention and, in a fine bit of double-dealing, he asked if foreign capital could be raised to build a model from Robert's plans. At the suggestion of Dryan Donkin, an engineer, two English manufacturers, Henry and Sealy Foudrinier, undertook to build the machine and, by 1803, Donkin had finished an apparatus that made acceptable paper.

But the French were not to enjoy the results of their invention for some time. The first machine in France was built in 1811, though it did not start operating commercially until January of the following year. Even then, the process meant little to publishers since one pilot model could scarcely produce enough paper to make possible larger, or more frequent, editions. By 1827, there were only four such machines in France, enough to permit increased publication, and not until 1833 had that number increased to 12.[8]

Even had sufficient paper been available, the state of printing technology restricted production to what was produced for a small, highly-educated class. As late as 1800, printers persisted in considering themselves primarily craftsmen as they operated presses essentially the same as those used by Gutenberg. A printer's devil still meticulously swabbed type with a tampon of wool dipped in thick ink. Not until 1818 was the Stanhope press introduced from England, a machine similar in principle to the old wooden ones, but utilizing a lever for turning the screw. This simple change drastically reduced press time and made publishing cheaper and faster. Two years later America exported the iron Clymer press, operated completely by levers and capable of producing far more books per working hour than any other press then known. And, finally, more labor was saved in 1817 by Ganal's invention of a roller for the speedy inking of type.

All these improvements did not immediately result in a complete technological change. Though manufacturers produced better presses about 1820, not enough of them appeared to remove previous restrictions until five years later. By then France was just groping her way out of her papermaking difficulties. Thus, only about 1830 did the factors necessary for a mass literature appear, all of them the result of the first stirrings of the Industrial Revolution.

IV

Apart from mechanical restrictions, France did not possess the final requisite for a modern literature until long after 1815. The nation could boast of one of Europe's greatest literatures, particularly a highly sophisticated prosody; but an appalling rate of illiteracy kept most Frenchmen in ignorance of the subtleties of the Alexandrine or the delicate manipulations of the caesura. The country folk, particularly, were to experience a dark age until well into the 19th century. What few statistics exist on literacy prior to 1815 are scarcely trustworthy, yet they indicate a pathetic situation. Up to 1789, little effort had been made to spread education except haphazardly. Under the old regime, institutions of higher education existed only for the privileged, and curricula never strayed from the domain of letters. In the early days of the Revolution, there were only 72,747 students in the collèges,[9] a fact which aroused the ire of the Constituent Assembly, though its fumbling action produced nothing to ease the situation. On September 3, 1793, the Convention voted to take drastic action. It decreed the immediate establishment of a common, free public instruction, equitably distributed over the entire nation. Then it contradicted itself in March by voting the sale of the property of all endowed schools, the proceeds to revert to the state. Seven months later it successfully ruined what few schools remained by abolishing all existing universities and faculties.

When Napoleon assumed power, he realized that secondary education urgently needed rescuing to insure the schooling of the classes on whom the Emperor counted for a stable society. Fourcroy, a State Councillor, called this to his attention, with the notation that country dwellers existed almost without instruction. Thus, two generations of children were menaced with illiteracy. Napoleon acted quickly but with grandiose futility. A series of laws attested only to his intentions since no funds were provided to carry out their intentions.

A report issued by the prefect of the Vaucluse, showed no change from 1801 : nearly half the communes slept in blissful illiteracy. Where schools did exist, most of the teachers were old and infirm, and when they left no replacements were named. By 1808, only 25,575 students attended the lycées and the communal collèges.[10] Six years later the combined faculties of letters of French universities could claim a total enrollment of only 1210.[11] As one last distinction for the Emperor, it can be noted that during his entire reign a sum of only 4250 francs was granted for primary schooling.[12]

Education fared little better under the Restoration. An ordinance of February 29, 1816, decreed the establishment of elementary instruction in every commune—but there the matter rested. By 1821, there existed only 28,000 primary schools, 30,000 in 1829. In 1819, the combined enrollment of all free elementary schools in Paris amounted to 15,433, slightly more than one-fifth of the city's children between the ages of 5 to 12.[13] That same year, it is estimated, 15,000,000 of 25,000,000 adults could neither read nor write.[14]

In some ways, the Bourbons even managed to retrogress, though primary education spread during their reign. The situation under Napoleon had been somewhat ameliorated by the rise of mutual schooling and various lycées, athénées, musées, or institutes. Actually, by 1802, some 100 of these " auberges académiques " attempted practical schooling.[15] Mutualism grew steadily until the Restoration, when the royalists, never forgetting, but never learning, bitterly fought the movement. Although 990 such groups existed in 1821, only 254 remained five years later.[16] And in the faculties of letters of the universities, the number of students declined even below that enrolled during the Empire. Somewhat tardily the Restoration tried to make amends. Charles X established the office of Minister of Public Instruction in 1828, a political sinecure, and then, on February 14, 1830, ordered the communes to consider means of raising funds for school support. But the royal command came only as a gesture because the July uprisings put an end to any plans.

After the Revolution the most notable advances in education had taken place in the lower middle classes, but when the July Monarchy applied itself to the development of public instruction, the great expansion it fostered was confined almost exclusively to primary education. In 1833 Guizot reported a deplorable state of ignorance both in teachers and population. Despite an ordinance of 1816, which made mandatory a school for every commune, France had not made any great attack on illiteracy.

Nevertheless, France was one of the most educated nations of Europe. The ignorance of peasant and artisan had diminished considerably since the Restoration. And with the law of 1833, a whole rash of schools sprouted over the nation. One year after the promulgation of the decree, 2,275 new schools opened their doors. Fifteen normal schools were added to the 47 already in existence and the number of elementary schools jumped by 2,000. During the amazing upsurge of educational opportunity during the period 1830-1848, some three and a half million children, or about one tenth of the population, were to receive at least a basic education. To be added to this number is the group of adults who reached literacy through the system of mutual education which had continued from the time of the Empire. More people than ever before could read and write, though, in terms of literature, the ability of the average Frenchman to understand and appreciate poetry and prose was indeed low. Primary schooling might endow a large number of citizens with the ability to count and to decipher simple sentences, but it almost eliminated readers of any material demanding acquaintance with tradition or sensitivity to the subtleties of the written word.

NOTES

1. Henri Sée, *Histoire économique de la France*, Paris, Colin, 1942, II, 102-3.

2. J. H. Clapham, *Economic Development of France and England*, Cambridge, University Press, 1921.

3. Jean Montreuil, *Le Mouvement ouvrier en France*, Paris, Aubier, 1946, p. 56.

4. Clapham, *op. cit.*, pp. 62-66.

5. S. Charléty, *La Monarchie de Juillet*, Paris, Hachette, 1921, pp. 198-99, 204.

6. In this respect, it is to be noted that even in England, a country mechanically far more advanced than France, as late as 1818 it was a punishable offense to produce a newspaper exceeding 22 by 32 inches.

7. Charles Ballot, *L'Introduction du machinisme dans l'industrie française*, Paris, Rieder, 1923, p. 555.

8. Dard Hunter, *Papermaking*, New York, Knopf, 1943, pp. 257, 264-5, 350.

9. Frederic Farrington, *French secondary schools*, New York, Longmans, Green, 1910, p. 70.

10. *Ibid.*, p. 70.

11. Frederick Artz, *France under the Bourbon Restoration*, Cambridge, Harvard University Press, 1931, p. 136.

12. Matthew Arnold, *Popular education of France*, London, 1861, p. 39.

13. S. Charléty, *La Restauration*, Paris, Hachette, 1921, p. 319.

14. Artz, *op. cit.*, p. 283.

15. G. Pariset, *Le Consulat et l'Empire*, Paris, Hachette, 1921, p. 319.

16. Charléty, *op. cit.*, p. 319.

CHAPTER 3

SEARCH FOR NEW CONTENT

SUCH WAS THE SITUATION facing the romanticists when, after 1830, they teetered dizzily on the peak of success. They had conquered the ogres, refuted the detested rules and proclaimed the freedom of art. But they had forgotten one frightening question : freedom for what ? That they lacked a positive credo had as yet occurred to few. Like Jérome Paturot in search of a social position, they had persisted in assuming that the triumph of *Hernani* somehow sanctified their position until the terrible truth dawned on them. Now that they had convinced France of the necessity for a new way of writing, they had to have something to write about. History, Christianity, the chills of the terror novel, all these might suffice momentarily, but the romanticists soon recognized the need to take fundamental positions, to match their new forms with a new content for a new public. In their search for the different, they obeyed the injunction of Mme de Staël and sought aid from the past and from abroad.

I

At first the romanticists had paid little heed to the problem of content. Being " moderns " they had used many of the themes tabooed by the classicists, but strictly as a revolt against their elders. Thus the romanticists had returned to the Middle Ages in imitation of Chateaubriand. They practiced the troubadour genre assiduously, aped the long-lost chords of Provençal or those of the trouvères from the colder north. In the beginning, the young revolutionists contented themselves with borrowing helter-skelter from all available sources in the hope of finding exciting topics for a public increasingly disdainful of the old.

Prior to 1830, the national history had furnished the new school with many a plot. France had just passed through a great moment of history; that everyone knew. But nobody understood clearly why a country steeped in monarchist traditions had so suddenly and violently forsaken its past. In quick succession came the bloodbath of the Revolution, a fantastic succession of fumbling governments, and then the advent of the strong man who led France to the conquest of all Europe, only to fall, rise, and sink again after a series of epic struggles. The nation, like its young writers, sought an explanation for the present in the past. It became conscious of a history long forgotten and, while scholars busily exhumed dusty documents, writers borrowed from the same material for poems, short stories, or novels. From 1820 to 1830 France was flooded with historical novels. But the craze died down quickly, albeit in a blaze of glory. Hugo's *Notre-Dame de Paris* represents the last great historical novel à la Walter Scott to be produced in France. Dumas' *Isabel de Bavière* would turn the genre toward the melodramatically sensational; historical in name only, it practiced the doctrine of local color only in the interests of a disguised novel of terror.[1]

Inevitably scholars reached back into the past to the Middle Ages for the threads of cause and effect with which to weave their philosophies of history. Following their lead, writers accepted medieval themes for two reasons : first, the classicists had set them beyond the literary pale and, second, medieval themes attached the new school to a historical entity as yet little understood but which offered rebels a measure of the respectability they had been seeking. In the race for ancestors, romanticism gladly welcomed the epic or any other tales that pre-dated the 17th century. And such a move was good politics. To choose the medieval meant siding with the Bourbons, and the romanticists were at first glad to crouch in the protecting shadow of the recently returned rulers, like themselves a minority in need of succor from all available sources.

For some of the early romanticists, Christianity seemed to promise a wealth of material since Chateaubriand and Lamartine had risen to fame by exploiting themes from the national religion. Chateaubriand, however, had luckily made use of the subject just when a Catholic renaissance was bringing the Church victorious from underground. Lamartine had published during the early days of the Restoration, when the monarchists were at their strongest. The many imitators of these men soon reduced their themes to clichés barren for further exploitation. Moreover, the Church set sharp limits to what authors could safely do with religion. In the early moments of the revival, the ecclesiastical authorities had welcomed all aid and comfort but, even then, they had recognized the danger of letting amateurs dabble in theology. Though the Church might trust Ballanche, it became alarmed at the shaky doctrine of Chateaubriand and despaired of Lamartine's vague religiosity. Then, as the Restoration wore on, religion less and less interested writers, who considered it sucked dry by a plague of copyists.

Both the themes of Christianity and of the Middle Ages led the new school to a dead end. Soon the writings of the young men all displayed a dreary similarity. Blonde pages, courageous knights, beautiful queens, fair maids from Avalon, all danced across pages of poetry or prose to the beat of a versification modernized in defiance of the classic rules. The troubadour songs of Provençal echoed in the lyrical effusions of the new school; reminiscences of an *aube* or an *estompie* reappeared hundreds of years after their first presentation.

But the troubadour genre was destined to remain timid, romances for almanacs or keepsakes. In the novel, the vogue spread principally through the diligent labors of contemporary authors like Mme de Beauharnais, Mme Cottin, or Mme de Beaufort d'Hautpoul. Despite the ladies' penchant for troubadours, the genre reached its apogee during the Empire and by 1830 the mode had passed. Gautier noted in the preface of *Mlle de Maupin* (1834) that this aspect of the Middle Ages had become fit only for the Opera. To be sure, scholars would continue to study the period, but its success as a literary theme actually ended about 1820.[2]

Since the medieval period alone could not fill the needs of romanticism, other aid had to be sought. For a while the terror novel, a late 18th-century import from England, gave additional support. Close in spirit to the melodrama that lured crowds to the boulevards, Gothic novels had met with great success in France. The works of Monk Lewis and Mrs. Radcliffe not only found hordes of readers but encouraged an imitation that verged on lunacy. For a time, Restoration literature swarmed with wicked uncles who pursued virgins through dank dungeons only to be foiled by the blundering efforts of not-overly-intelligent but fantastically virtuous heroes. The Bloody Nun stalked cruelly into many a room, to thrill seekers after the sensational and, for the more philosophically bent, there was Ahasvérus, condemned to stumble sadly over the earth for all eternity.   Nodier established the blood-sucking vampire beside the deformed ogre, offering the possibility of a different series of vicarious and ghoulish adventures. But, as in the case of the troubadour genre, the terror novel and its spawn lost popularity by 1830.[3] Even at its height, it had never been taken seriously by the modernists, since most of them were firmly convinced of the sanctity of poetry.

To some extent the romanticists even dipped back into the 18th century for material.   Nature continued to inspire writers, though all too frequently they fell back on their memories of the graveyard school of poetry.   The ruin became a favorite trysting place; pale, tubercular lovers met beside a lightning-struck oak to dangle their hands in a foaming torrent.   Primitivism still affected a few, and a surprisingly large number seemed acquainted with the occult and illuministic theorists of the late 18th century.   But, again, most of these themes went out of fashion before 1827.   They quickly became shopworn, unable to satisfy the needs and desires of later generations.

II

As part of their great search, the romanticists tried to widen their literary horizons by venturing abroad.   To that end, the young men explored the literatures of a number of countries, ranging as far as the New World and the Orient.

The New World actually contributed little to the nascent movement. Some had heard vaguely of Irving, more of James Fenimore Cooper. The latter exercised a moderate influence on France between 1824 and 1828, then dropped from public notice.   Only Balzac seems to have paid him much attention at first, though later Eugène Sue, Edouard Corbière, Auguste Jal, and Jules Lecomte would come to know his work.   In the last analysis, Cooper's influence on Balzac was slight and did not last much after *Les Chouans*.[4]

Portugal, too, gave sparingly.   The great Camões had long been known, though rarely at first hand, and only the strange episode of Inez de Castro seems to have attracted the French.   The early days of romanticism saw many a rendition of the scene in which the skeleton

of Inez is crowned queen of Portugal by her faithful lover, a popularity
perhaps due to the same grisly reasons that made best sellers of terror
literature. At all events, Portugal's contribution to French romanticism
cannot be considered either great or lasting.[5]

Germany fared better, because her writers enjoyed greater European
renown. Some, like Herder, found a meager intellectual fortune in
France, despite the efforts of Quinet.[6] But Bürger's *Lenore*, on the
other hand, clearly helped incline French romanticism to the fantastic.
Between 1820 and 1830, the apogee of this genre, the themes of love
beyond death, or of phantom knights, titillated many a reader, despite
the fact that *Lenore* was not successfully translated until 1830, by
Gerard de Nerval.[7]

Goethe's influence spread even more, though in a curious way.
Between 1807-1820 the great German author was known almost solely
as the creator of Werther. At that last date, the appearance of Constant's
Adolphe killed the vogue for imitation of the melancholy hero. Not
that he disappeared completely, but after that time he was to be set
in such gems as Mme Cottin's *Claire d'Abbe* or buried in the vaudeville.
At the height of his popularity Werther became almost a symbol
of the early romantic, not man in revolt against civilization, but a
model lover. Young writers liked the idea of melancholy, of associating
sentiment with death, and teen-age rebels admired a man who defied
a society in which his place was not clearly defined. Later, by 1828,
Goethe's reputation managed to escape from under the burden of
Werther when opinion focused on *Faust*. But *Faust* left far less a
mark on French literature than *Werther*. Though the play was cited
as a powerful argument against the classical doctrine, even despite
Werther, the romanticists never considered Goethe one of their gods.
A generation educated to Catholicism failed to appreciate his pantheism
or mystic symbolism; his use of legends lay beyond their capacity
to understand. For them, the picturesque, the marvelous, and the
fantastic in *Faust* seemed more attractive.[8]

Of all the Germans, Schiller succeeded best in impressing the
French, though prior to 1815 he had been known only to a select
few. Then Mme de Staël launched a vogue for his books that resulted
in 30 to 40 translations during the Restoration alone. For fifteen
years he personified the Anglo-German theater, and so many were
the adaptations or transpositions of his work that he left romanticism

a rich legacy : the heroic and adored bandit, the courtesan regenerated by love, and the intolerant, corrupt priest.   Certain favorite scenes can be traced directly back to him : the revolt of the people for liberty, the deadly hate between two brothers, and the forgotten fateful oath. Since he generously daubed on local color, the romanticists borrowed for their own the use of barred doors, astrology, and horoscopes, as well as certain psychological situations : the nostalgia of an exiled queen, the anguish of ambition, and the betrayal of a woman by one who loves her.   But in 1830, when the *drame* successfully won its place on the stage, Schiller dropped from favor because he seemed a bit too classical for successful revolutionaries.[9]

No one could say this of the great Hoffmann, however. Unfortunately, he remained unknown until 1823 and, even then, the romanticists were confused about his work until Renduel published Loève-Weimars' 20-volume translation in 1829.   Then the master of the marvelous and the horrible exported legends, apparitions, sorcerers, and devils to France after Nodier had made the gruesome popular. Actually Hoffmann, along with Tieck, Novalis, and Chamiso, the creator of the shadowless Peter Schlemihl, merely strengthened a tendency in French literature that had existed since the 18th century. He and his confrères enhanced the vogue for the fantastic to the point of exciting almost blind admiration until Edgar Allan Poe displaced them in the public favor in 1855.   But despite minor influence on some of the major figures of romanticism, Borel in *Champavert*, Balzac in the *Peau de chagrin*, Sand in *La Petite Fadette*, Hoffmann never affected any but the lesser lights, the imitators and the lunatic fringe.   What he had to offer already existed in the national heritage, and his recipe for mixing the real and the supernatural offered little for the young men to copy.[10]

England, despite political and military differences with her neighbor, still managed to export more literature than Germany.   France had long been in touch with new trends in English literature, though the strength of late 18th-century neo-classicism had prevented any great cross-channel influence. In his day Ossian had transcended Napoleon's hate for things British, to became a royal favorite even on crucial campaigns.   During the Consulate and the Empire, careless critics ranked him with Homer, thus leading to a rash of imitations full of heroes with a marked predilection for climbing mountain peaks in stormy weather. However, by 1817, Ossian had been demoted to the position of ancestor, with little effect on nascent romanticism. All paid him the courtesy of recognition but, since MacPherson was not a colorist, they preferred to seek their gods elsewhere.[11]

The harsh, cold Milton found few disciples because of his closeness to classicism. His influence seems mostly restricted to the decoration of the living quarters of the " true " romanticist. According to the *Figaro* of 1832 it was almost required for a self-respecting Jeune-France to have on his walls a picture of Milton's Satan in black and white.[12]

The great Shakespeare fared better though, try as they might, the romanticists had difficulty understanding him. Nevertheless, his name became a rallying cry during the Restoration, an insult to any convinced classicist. Rebels cited the traditions of the Shakespearian drama in support of the argument for a free, historical drama liberated from ancient rules. The bard's cause was aided by the arrival of a troupe of English actors in 1823, then again in 1827 and 1828, giving the romanticists an opportunity to extol what unhampered genius could produce. Both the proponents of prose drama and those who worshipped poetry could agree on the greatness of Shakespeare. From his work they could cite instances of the value of a variety of forms, the use of local color or of history. But they never borrowed more than superficially. He, too, was an ancestor, gigantic in stature and difficult to comprehend. Once the romanticists had established the principle of theatrical liberty, they preferred to treat Shakespeare as the symbol of a creator freed from rules. The age of Elizabeth had little in common with that of Louis-Philippe.[13]

Byron, the handsome defender of Greece, really did capture the fancy of the romanticists, something which Shelley never accomplished.[14] Young Frenchmen early transformed him into a legend that maintained his influence until about 1835 and, for a time, at least, between 1820 and 1830, he furnished most of their themes, encouraged their search for new forms and images. He taught them to sing of solitude, of nature and liberty, to celebrate the independence of peoples and the greatness of Napoleon, and to look to the Orient for inspiration. From him emanated a savage melancholy that made the romanticists shiver with delight over the anguish of thought and feel fiercely proud of their own revolt. More influential than Werther or Ossian, Childe Harold, Lara, and Manfred came to personify despair and melancholy pessimism, and by 1825 Byron ranked as the recognized chieftain of French lyricism.

Yet it must be acknowledged that Byron did not shape the romanticism that pre-dates *Hernani*. What he brought simply reinforced existing influences. Furthermore, his star began to wane about 1830 when the romanticists tired of sadness and doubt. Perpetual meditation and lamentation no longer seemed suitable for the conquerors of a literary world. The new rulers of art passed on to the making of themselves as gods, leaving Byron for the Jeunes-France and the *bousingos* of the next generation. Musset and the dandies copied his cynical irony and aped his persiflage, but his work became principally the Bible of second-rate poets who longed for Satanic revolts and somber anguish. Finally, Byron passed into literary history by 1835, a great name, but no longer an influence.[15]

In prose, Byron's influence could be matched only by that of Scott on the novel. During the last ten years of the Restoration, Scott's historical romances became almost an obsession, thereby establishing for him a place almost as great in French literature as in his own. During that period booksellers like Pigoreau had to publish special catalogues to keep buyers acquainted with the mass of historical novels that rolled off the presses. Some owners of lending libraries even swore to purge their shelves of the new works, all dim carbon copies of *Quentin Durward* or *Ivanhoe*.

Such an important ally received a hearty welcome from young men eager to use any handy weapon against their elders. Scott loved history; he was a foreigner, and he made lavish use of exotic local color; therefore he became an aid to their cause. But only an aid, for his writings were never socially accepted. As poets, the romanticists felt prose beneath their dignity. The novel as yet had not risen from the position of inferior genre, good for upstairs maids or for momentarily diverting a languid mind. Respectable people hid in corners to read them, ashamed to admit indulgence of their desire for exciting plots.

Spain, always known to the French, made a strong re-entry into French literature with Chateaubriand, who needed its sumptuous settings for his melancholy. With the vogue for the troubadour, the romanticists as a whole came face to face with a country overflowing with lore, heroic and still medieval. The colorful legends of violent passions led them to add to the misconceptions of Spanish life which the nation had inherited from the past. Actually, most of what they knew came from three books : Bouterwek's *Histoire de la littérature espagnole* (1812), Schlegel's *Cours de littérature dramatique* (1814), and Sismondi's *De la littérature du Midi et de l'Europe* (1813), the veracity of which they never doubted. With such meager sources of suspect information, it is no wonder that French romanticists so completely misunderstood Spain.

It was mostly the younger men who used " Spanish " themes in the theater, and these quite inexpertly. Like Shakespeare, Lope de Vega and Calderon were cited as unrestricted geniuses, but the romanticists found to their surprise that some foreign masterpieces were hard to import. They genuflected before Cervantes, but they could not imitate. Hence, they restricted their borrowing of things Spanish to a few clichés, exotic backgrounds, and the names of special characters. What themes they did accept usually drowned in a flood of melodrama. Spanish literature, then, can be said to have given little that was definite to French romanticism, much less than came from mistaken notions of the country itself.[16]

Last, but far from least, Italy made her contribution. The literary giants of her past bewitched more than one writer, though actually it was Italy itself which seduced most of them. Tasso, for instance, the romanticists knew for his tormented and pathetic life. They welcomed the victim of any tyrant, the target of pedants, and he symbolized their cherished notion of the misunderstood poet. But they preferred to use his life as subject matter, not to imitate his manner.[17]

As in the case of Spain, renewed interest in Italy came through Chateaubriand, aided by Mme de Staël and Lamartine. Almost all the other romanticists, Musset, Deschamps, Hugo, Brizeux, and Gautier helped enrich French literature with their memories. Yet, as the Italians complained, they failed to picture the " true " Italy, since they unanimously described the unhappy natives as complete profligates, faithless lovers, or hapless warriors. Each romanticist apparently drew on the country according to his personal needs : Chateaubriand saw Rome as a refuge from care; Lamartine remembered Naples as the scene of his great vision; Mme de Staël praised a land of breath-taking scenery; while Stendhal always associated the Italians with music and unbridled passion. In general, Italy was pictured as a land of dreams, of the poetry and vigorous crime of the Renaissance, and no French author seems to have understood her political problems. Of her modern writers, Santarosa, Pellico, Luisa San Felice, Mazzini, and Garibaldi received the most plaudits, principally because their lives presented great acts of selfless patriotism.

As in the case of Spain, however, Italy, more than its literature, attracted the French. No Italian won a vogue comparable to that of Byron, Goethe, or Schiller, although Poliziano, Cellini, Machiavelli, Bruno, and Goldoni were well known. Alfieri hated France, an attitude that caused the touchy French to avoid him; Monti exerted little influence even on the group of his friends surrounding Mme de Staël; and the great Leopardi did not find recognition until after 1850.[18] To be sure, Manzoni attracted considerable attention between 1820 and 1827 as a theorist of the drama, but he contributed primarily to catalyzing imaginations eager for the new. As a poet he had little success in France, and the *Promessi Sposi* found few disciples.[19]

Other nations might be consulted for their contributions, but compared to those already mentioned no one could call them anything but minor. In any case, the same story is repeated : prior to 1830, at the very moment the romanticists were battling over questions of form, they preferred to take themes, characters, and plots where they could find them. Nonetheless, it would be wrong to assume that this borrowing represents a foreign invasion that created French romanticism. As Fernand Baldensperger wrote : " il est bien certain qu'une époque littéraire, lorsqu'elle découvre et qu'elle annexe des idées ou des formes exotiques, ne goûte et ne retient que les éléments dont elle porte, par suite de sa propre évolution organique, l'intuition et le désir en elle-même."[20]

Before 1830, the romanticists had been more preoccupied with form than content, and above all the form of poetry. Hence their need for borrowing, especially since they rejected much of the national tradition. But after *Hernani* the victors found themselves able to write almost anything in any way they pleased. The trouble was that they had little of their own to say and they finally came to understand that imitation was clearly not the answer. The material they wanted they would discover under their very noses in the age that began to unfold about 1830.

NOTES

1. Louis Maigron, *Le roman historique à l'époque romantique*, Paris, Hachette, 1898.

2. Henri Jacoubet, *Le Genre troubadour et les origines françaises du romantisme* Paris, Les Belles Lettres, 1929; Fernand Baldensperger, "Le Genre troubadour," in *Etudes d'histoire littéraire*, Paris, Hachette, 1907, vol. I.

3. Alice Killen, *Le Roman terrifiant*, Paris, Champion, 1923.

4. Georgette Bosset, *Fenimore Cooper et le roman d'aventure en France vers 1830*, Paris, Vrin, 1928.

5. William A. Watkins, "Portuguese literature in France," *Symposium*, IV (May, 1950), 70-83.

6. Henri Tronchon, *La Fortune intellectuelle de Herder en France*, Paris, Rieder, 1920.

7. Fernand Baldensperger, "La *Lénore* de Bürger," in *Études d'histoire littéraire*, Paris, Hachette, 1907, vol. I.

8. Fernand Baldensperger, *Goethe en France*, Paris, Hachette, 1904.

9. Edmond Eggli, *Schiller et le romantisme français*, Paris, Librairie Universitaire, 1927.

10. Marcel Breuillac, "Hoffmann en France," *RLC*, XIII, 1906, 427-57.

11. Paul Van Tiegham, *Ossian en France*, Paris, Rieder, 1917, 2 vols.

12. René Jasinski, *Les Années romantiques de Théophile Gautier*, Paris, Vuibert, 1929, p. 150.

13. Fernand Baldensperger, "Esquisse d'une histoire de Shakespeare en France," in *Études d'histoire littéraire*, Paris, Hachette, 1910, vol. II.

14. Henri Peyre, *Shelley et la France*, Cairo, Barbey, 1935.

15. Edmond Estève, *Byron et le romantisme français*, Paris, Furne, 1907.

16. Ernest Martinenche, *L'Espagne et le romantisme français*, Paris, Hachette, 1922; Paul Hazard, "Les Influences étrangères : le Midi," in *Le Romantisme et les lettres*, Paris, Aubier, 1929.

17. Chandler Beall, *La Fortune du Tasse en France*, Eugene, Oregon, University of Oregon Press, 1942.

18. Alceste Bisi, *L'Italie et le romantisme français*, Albrighi, Secati, 1914.

19. Dorothée Christeco, *La Fortune d'Alexandre Manzoni en France*, Paris, Editions Balzac, 1943; Nicolas Serban, *Leopardi et la France*, Paris, Champion, 1913.

20. *Goethe en France*, p. 3.

CHAPTER 4

THE NEW PUBLIC

SUCCESSFUL ROMANTICISM was to receive a great shock when, after *Hernani*, it discovered itself facing a public quite unlike any ever known, one that lived under conditions undreamed of by literary rebels. When the patrons disappeared in the rubble of the old regime, writers suddenly discovered that they must woo the buying public in order to make a living. But the purchaser of books had changed character since as recently as the Restoration. To make a decent living, a writer found himself forced to cater to the whims of large numbers of the newly educated who were scarcely literate enough to appreciate the old poetic values. The men who had struggled so hard for verse came to realize that the 19th century had become the age of the masses and that two new factors now had to be considered : the reading tastes of the multitude and the effects of the Industrial Revolution.

I

On the eve of the July Revolution, the romanticists found that they had won a Pyrrhic triumph. The classicists had been forced to admit defeat; but they could laugh at the fact that the victor had to satisfy a harsher taskmaster than any cultured aristocracy : the people, that strange segment of the population which the Revolution had thrust into prominence. The patrons who had sponsored the art of the past had vanished with the Ancien Régime. Even had they still existed, it is doubtful whether any would have risked many francs on so revolutionary an art. Thus, the writer, poet or prosateur, had to find a new source of income, and this could be earned only from the general public. But the young men stood to gain in one sense.

With so broad an audience, they could win fortunes without having to debase themselves like Molière or La Bruyère. The matter of intellectual prostitution to the masses had as yet not occurred to anybody, though it soon would become a topic for general discussion.

The author, therefore, had to aim at the broad base of society instead of appealing to the cultured few, to find a common denominator of art that would serve for the peasant, the bourgeoisie, and the strange new proletariat that swarmed in city slums. In terms of sales, he had to consider carefully the feelings of the middle class. This was the great day of its political and social dominance and, in a sense, it had replaced the nobility as the arbiter of a writer's fate. Consequently, only the rash dared attack the cherished bourgeois system of values : the sanctity of the home, the validity of the profit system, and a constitutional government directed by conservatives. In the cities, at least, the middle class dominated completely the heights of a Parnassus which it intended to police thoroughly.

Analysis of these groups clearly revealed to watchful authors that the literacy level of their audience had declined tremendously, principally because it had expanded so greatly. More people could read than ever, but they lacked the habit of literature. Subtleties of form escaped them entirely; content, not form, drew them to a given book, particularly if it were in prose. The more exciting the plot, the better they liked it, provided the story dealt with concepts within their realm of experience. These readers were practical, earth-bound, and they expected writers to confine themselves to the things of this life. The new audience, however, consisted not only of the middle class, but the new proletarians and the peasants. The literacy of the latter two groups had been the achievement of early 19th-century education. Although they did not form so important a part of the reading public as the bourgeoisie, they constituted an impressive and expanding section of the population. Any writer interested in monetary success had to consider the tastes of the totality since only those who found a denominator common to all could hope to appeal to the entire nation. And as the century aged, this became more and more mandatory for writers.

Not only had the romanticists thus to face a general lowering of literary capacity but, committed now to living off the largest possible sales, they also had to contend with the reading habits of the whole country. Paris might buy poetry, Paris might be considered intellectually acceptable to a writer, but unfortunately Paris had almost ceased to exist in the old literary sense of the word. To it had to be added Lyon, Marseille, Bordeaux, and many other cities and towns. True, contemporary salons struggled to maintain the traditions of the 17th and 18th centuries, but any alert writer knew that, in the last analysis, his fate depended on a new person, the average reader. Mme Récamier and the other grand ladies might fashion celebrities within the confines of their circles but they could not sell books. And, alas, Mme Récamier never would have acknowledged that the common man possessed any literary taste.

In more ways than one she was right. The average French citizen, particularly in the small towns and rural areas, had standards shocking to university graduates raised on the classics. By far the most popular reading material known to France dated from long ago. The almanac, especially the 17th-century *Almanach liégeois* supposedly written by Matthieu Laensberg, outsold all other books. And its nearest competitors were also almanacs.[1] In varying proportions these usually contained biographies of notables, a handful of dubious portraits, accounts of famous battles and voyages, a collection of educational maxims and proverbs that supposedly fitted all important conversational gambits, and uninhibited advice on hygiene, temperance, and the fear of God. In addition, the publishers provided country dwellers with a history of the principal national monuments, famous inventions, an account of the leading events of the last year, and an outline of the fine points of domestic animals. They presented some variety by interspersing among these a partial recital of some of Napoleon's campaigns, and for filler there were always the population statistics and lists of European kings. The more advanced publications also furnished crop advice and handy jokes for all occasions. Some, with literary pretentions, indiscriminately offered remedies for ailments both human and animal along with novels astounding for the amount of blood shed per chapter and the curious course of action taken by the plot. All in all, the almanacs were cleverly calculated to fit the literary needs of the poorly educated country dwellers, from parents to children.

To be sure, the almanacs never intended to spoil readers with unnecessary frills. Editors economically purchased all cuts dropped into the printers' lead pile with results that were sometimes startling, since publishers cared little whether captions and pictures matched. Thus, the *Almanach magique et anecdotique* of M. Hinzelin carried a portrait of the celebrated M. Ledru-Rollin just arising from the hands of his barber, his smile disdainful and his glance impudent, with the following legend : " I suddenly perceived that my wife had a wooden leg."[2]

Since religion formed a large part of rural life, publishers showed a predilection for stories like the *Trépassement de la sainte vierge* and the *Paraboles du Père Bonaventure*, spiced with *Le Juste Châtiment de Dieu envers les enfants qui sont désobéissants à leurs père et mère, et la peine qu'ils souffrent dans les enfers, avec plusieurs exemples*. With a straight face, peddlers sold the country folk various collections of holy songs or the lives of saints, like the *Cantique de saint Eustache*, martyr, whose life story was set to the music of *Où êtes-vous, Birène, mon amour?*

Inevitably, of course, there were conscious burlesques to please the more frolicsome. These must have been slipped to bachelors enjoying a fling at the local fair. For them, the editors had prepared gems like the *Catéchisme des amants, par demandes et réponses, où sont enseignés les principales maximes de l'amour et le devoir d'un véritable amant* (1838), or perchance, a *Catéchisme à l'usage des grandes filles qui veulent être mariées*. In addition there were burlesque sermons, or funeral orations like the *Éloge funèbre de Michel Morin, bedeau de l'église de Beauséjour : mort de son âne ; son testament*.

The literary diet of the non-urban citizen included the usual variety of cynical writings on the behavior of women, their malice, imperfections, and incredible wiles. But, at the same time, the peasant could indulge in an old favorite, the *Grand Grimoire, ou l'art de commander aux esprits célestes, aériens, terrestres, infernaux, avec le vrai secret de faire parler les morts, de gagner toutes les fois qu'on met aux loteries, de découvrir les trésors cachés*. Some books contained horrifying stories reminiscent of the terror novels, even printed in red. Satanism shared the pages with searches for the philosopher's stone or recipes for discovering hidden treasure. For the more superstitious there were dream books, aids to divining the future, or hints to answering such important questions as :

L'enfant auquel je pense est-il le fils de celui qu'il appelle son père?
Mon amant me sera-t-il fidèle?
Vivrai-je dans le célibat?

Almanacs made a few casual gestures at education by providing models of business letters, or phrases proper for a fiancé to address to his beloved. Some seem unusual for rural France, particularly the specimen in which a young man expressed to his mistress an unbounded joy at the happiness she had given him. Various treatises initiated the backward into the mysteries of the law, the use of the decimal system, how to play cards, dice, dominoes, or chess. These were interspersed with witty sayings and anecdotes for all occasions. Even the children were remembered with *abécédaires moraux*, or instruction in the rudiments of Latin.

Most popular of all, with editions running into millions of copies, were prose tales for the idle hours of those unfortunate enough to live outside of Paris. Many retold the fabulous adventures of Gargantua or Till Ulenspiegel; still more recounted the vicissitudes of Collet, the bandit, or the famous Diavolo, brigand of the Apennines. Occasionally English translations like *Osmond* or the *Bataille de la Boyne* titillated readers, but, in general, the French felt content with such masterpieces as *Le Château de lord Toris, ou les Malheurs d'une jeune orpheline*, *Chroniques d'un cimetière*, *Le Diable en province* or *Atal et Musacop, histoire péruvienne*. A small number of romances of chivalry could be added to the above, but few items could compete with the variations of *Les Quatre Fils Aymon*, *Robert le Diable* or *Richard sans peur*.

Among the modern novelists, Ducray-Duminil took first place, although Mmes Cottin, Daubenton, and d'Aulnoy gave him considerable competition. The former could boast that his works were more widely read than even those of Walter Scott. Certain titles like the *Petits Orphelins du hameau*, *Coelina*, the child of mystery, or *Paul ou la Ferme abandonnée* furnished almost standard fare for the country folk. Their success could be equalled only by that of *Gil Blas*, *Paul et Virginie*, or a collection of fairy tales.

Most of France knew this kind of literature, thanks to the colporteurs, who had been selling the same items to the provinces for centuries. Their trade dated back to the first presses, and their number had increased constantly with the volume of printed books. The Revolution favored their work, but the Emperor had made their situation precarious by holding the colporteur responsible for what he sold. A decree of February 5, 1810, reduced their stock to catechisms, religious tracts, and song books and even these were closely scrutinized by the censor for pro-Bourbon sentiments. The Restoration modified the decree slightly, though it maintained the harsh Napoleonic penalties, and new censors worked indefatigably to hunt out pro-Bonapartist or liberal allusions.

Shortly after the success of *Hernani*, Louis-Philippe gave the colporteurs a boon by requiring of them only municipal authorization. The trade expanded at precisely the moment the romanticists assumed control of French literature. The number of colporteurs grew to 3,500, but now they were arranged in brigades under a foreman. Their services could easily be utilized by the new school to carry their books to every corner of France. But, first of all, the romanticists had to give the readers simple, exciting literature that demanded little knowledge of literary finesse. These people were for the most part graduates of primary schools, and far too busy with the problems of life to worry about the unities or the glories of crossed rhymes.

II

Deprived of the pleasures of avant-garde literature by their distance from Paris, by lack of money or education, the people seemed amazingly unaffected by their plight. For those who could read but slightly, their diet of letters continued as it had for centuries. True, colporteurs occasionally hawked a Paris edition, but this was rare. Advertising had as yet not discovered how to make the country folk conscious of what they were missing. Therefore, the colporteurs trudged into towns loaded with the merchandise that always sold well, almanacs, crude prose renditions of epics, manuals on practical subjects, and popular novels. So welcome were their wares to the people that Alphonse du Valconseil, a die-hard conservative, complained bitterly, that the novel now constituted almost the sole reading of women, children, and lazy men. All the more discouraging was the fact that this same kind of prose was penetrating to the most isolated villages in France in the form of the almanac.[3]

Even in the provincial towns, the same low literary competency confronted the writer. The educational level fell so far below that of the capital that authors could expect to run into a kind of cultural lag. Tradition counted more than in Paris, for change meant an unsettling of the long-accepted habit around which daily life and cultural values had been shaped. Tastes altered slowly, almost imperceptibly. What was good enough for the father suited the son.[4]

For these citizens, the lending library symbolized culture. Since the Restoration had popularized their position as depositaries of accepted literature, a study of the holdings of these lending libraries reveals the situation facing the romanticists in the first years of the July Monarchy. In 1832 the shop of François Caillard in Narbonne carried the usual selection available in a small city. He stocked all the French classics, mostly from habit, since the records show that the movement of these books, at 1 franc fifty per month apiece, did not add appreciably to his income. Whereas there were few examples from the ancient literatures, translations of modern foreign novelists took up considerable space : 33 of Scott's works, nine of Cooper. Most of the writers represented were the same whose works the colporteurs peddled : Pigault-Lebrun, Ducray-Duminil, Lamothe-Langon, Mme de Souza, and the ever-present Mmes de Genlis and Cottin.

It is important to note that the taste of the provincial cities, as in the country, ran to prose. M. Caillard's collection contained almost no poetry and few plays. At least half the stock consisted of novels dating from the late 18th and early 19th centuries, mostly of the kind disparagingly known as *romans pour femme de chambre*. Romances of adventure, historical novels, and imitations of the English Gothic novels earned M. Caillard's bread and butter in a very satisfactory fashion.[5]

Much the same statements can be made of Lyon or Marseille. Prior to 1830, melodrama filled the Lyon theaters with women, though tragedy was not entirely forgotten. The local citizens cautiously listened to an acrimonious debate between classicist and romanticist, schools which they were hard put to define. Lyon shunned excess; it preferred novels of action and a vaporous kind of sentimentality just like its sister city Marseille, which never did accept the romantic revolution.[6]

III

The urgency of cozening the public impressed the romanticists all the more because France was undergoing a crisis in bookselling at the moment they were theoretically carrying off the literary palm. The July Revolution had swept Barba and Ladvocat into bankruptcy. The richest and most stable publishers were so shaken by the upheaval that a government never noted for generosity made 10,000,000 francs available to bolster tottering companies. On the basis of salable stock on the shelves, dealers could draw against this credit to avoid complete ruin.[7]

The depression in publishing was, in fact, older than romanticism. The Revolution had seemed to promise printers release from the restrictions of the hated *privilège* but bookselling fell into a deplorable state between 1789 and 1795. Few books appeared, and only one publisher, Pierre Didot, had the courage to continue. From 1795 to 1813 the trade recovered slowly from the repressive measures of the republican government. At the latter date, Jean-Jacques Lefèvre revolutionized business by sending his clerk, Hautcœur, into the departments to peddle books. Following his example, others began to cover France with the first literary travelling salesmen, a maneuver that considerably increased the volume of sales. Publishers belatedly discovered that it did not suffice to print books, but that they had to be sold. Gaudissart was in the process of creation, albeit slowly. The colporteur, however, still reigned supreme throughout most of the country for, even in 1828, publishers still clung sufficiently to the old ways to make travelling salesmen a rarity. The few that wandered over the provinces did so haphazardly, riding horseback into the main towns, preceded by circulars or prospectuses. As yet publishers refused the aid of advertising, even when newspapers would consider accepting it.

This situation was not materially helped by the attitude of Napoleon. Under the Empire, the number of publishing houses was strictly limited through the use of licenses. The Emperor, not one to miss an opportunity to control public opinion, carefully watched the printing of new books. In this he was aided by a drop in purchasing power and a simultaneous rise in the cost of living. As Werdet writes, the result was that, except for a few law and scientific books, and a number of best sellers, there was little turn over in the book trade, few printings, and almost no re-prints.[8]

Only under the Restoration did the publishing houses revive groggily, when they timidly presented lists composed mostly of editions of the 18th-century classics, actually a protest against the authoritarian tendencies of the Bourbons. When some easing of the paper shortage materially aided this form of rebellion, publishers began to choose political sides, with Dentu and Petit sponsoring the royalists, Ladvocat, Chaumerot, and Corréard representing at first the Bonapartists, then later the liberals. Delaunay and Pelissier remained aloof, preferring to devote themselves to the cult of the dividend.[9] With all the zeal of men in search of profits, publishers matched book for book. They recognized the potential of the great hinterland, with the result that more and more salesmen daily left Paris to carry culture to the hinterland. Where there had only been two or three booksellers in 1813, in 1825 the number had so grown that Toulouse alone could boast of seventeen.[10]

Thus, around 1830, everything conspired to make the romanticists aware of the average reader whom they had to reach. They suddenly found themselves in the age of the bourgeois triumphant. The relative positions of writer and public had changed so radically that a professional author sought to please an audience much larger than ever faced any of his predecessors, one with a markedly lower literacy rate. Woe to him who expected to profit from his pen and yet dared sneer at the purchaser. The mass of the population could be stirred to buy provided the romanticists realized that, in addition to Paris, it faced the men of the provinces, opinionated, cautious, and distrustful of revolution.

NOTES

1. Nisard, *Histoire des livres populaires*, Paris, Amyot, 1854, I, 24.
2. *Ibid.*, I, 79. The subsequent information on popular literature is also drawn from Nisard.
3. *Revue analytique et critique des romans contemporains*, Paris, Gaume, 1845, I, xxxiv-xxxv.

4. P. Barrière, " Notes sur le romantisme en Périgord, " *RHL*, XLII (1937), 33-62; 181-213.

5. Cf. P. Jourda, " Un Cabinet de lecture en province en 1832, " *RHL*, XLIV (1937).

6. Pierre Grosclaude, " Lyon et le mouvement romantique, " *RHL*, XLII (1935), 33-62, 181-213; A. Brun, " Le Romantisme et les Marseillais, " *Annales de la Faculté des Lettres d'Aix*, XXI (1938-39).

7. Edmond Werdet, *De la librairie française*, Paris, Dentu, 1860, VIII, 114-15.

8. *Ibid.*, p. 83.

9. *Ibid.*, pp. 99-100.

10. *Ibid.*, p. 109.

CHAPTER 5

THE AGE OF PROSE

THERE WAS NO QUESTION that the romanticist had entered an uncomfortably strange new world. Not only had he mounted a wobbly throne, but he was faced with two additional facts, both of which would contribute materially to changing his outlook on life: poetry, once the dominant genre, fell a poor second to prose in general sales; and romanticism suddenly found itself face to face with the social effects of the Industrial Revolution.

I

Early in the century, as the base of education began to broaden, curious results could be noted. Statistics are lacking for the first years of the age, although the *Journal de la librairie française*[1] announced that from the first day of nivôse an IX to frimaire an X, 1185 volumes had been published, 121 novels, 384 works of poetry. However, by November 6, 1806, the *Spectateur français* raised a cry that was to become the sad refrain of all the literary purists of the first half of the century :

> ... tant d'archives de mauvais goût, et souvent de mauvaises mœurs; ... tant de recueils d'insipides aventures ou de conceptions bizarres ! Quelle énorme quantité de nos romans et des romans anglais ou allemands, que, non contents de nos abondantes et stériles richesses en ce genre, nous transportons chaque jour dans notre langue.[2]

By 1818, the change in values had begun to disturb conservatives. The editor of the *Annuaire historique universel*, M. Lesur, announced huffily that poets and poetry enjoyed little credit. Everybody complained bitterly about the decline of public taste, yet everybody could well share the blame for the decline.[3] Simultaneously the editor blamed the romanticists both for the large number of novels then appearing and for the bad taste of the melodrama though he admitted that 1818 had not been any more sterile than the preceding years. In fact, it had produced as many poems as novels. And this awful situation he credited completely to the plethora of lending libraries, without which the flood of new novels would not have found any readers.[4]

Three years later, the editor's worst fears were realized. Though he catalogued some 400 books on " poétique et poésie," he reluctantly had to add the sorrowful sum of 230 novels, without including translations from foreign tongues. By 1823 poetry had jumped a bit, perhaps because of the growing interest in romanticism, while the novel dropped to 210, a more fitting state of affairs. But the spirit of prose had gained ground, as Lesur, editor of the *Annuaire*, admitted. The good old days had passed. Not quite yet, for in 1824, he smirked that poetry had soared to 601 items, whereas the lowly novel registered only a paltry 320.[5] The next year, 1825, seemed to support the upsurge of interest in poetry, some 620 books of verse compared to only 330 novels, but the editor uttered a lugubrious warning : " Il faut l'avouer : les poëtes ont perdu de leur vogue et la poésie de son empire. Il faut qu'elle trouve, comme la science, à s'appliquer aux arts utiles, aux besoins de la vie; il faut qu'elle nous touche le cœur, qu'elle nous élève l'âme," qu'elle nous entretienne de nos intérêts ou de nos destinées à venir."[6] This was the day of the great debate and the last great moment for poetry, but the note of doom rang even in the prophet's voice. Unwittingly he was writing the verdict of the practical-minded bourgeoisie.

By 1827 the day of poetry seemed over. The two genres came closer together in numbers, though poetry still proudly held the lead : 494 items as opposed to 225 for the novel. After that date, poetry slid into a silent decline.[7] In 1831, the classically-minded editor commented bitterly that only two branches of literature flourished in Paris : the theater and the novel. As for the latter, it flourished to a degree no man could explain and no society could stand.[8]

In a desperate attempt to wean the public from the novel, publishers partial to verse had recourse to their friends the artists, particularly the wood engravers. Cuts were lavished to give poems eye-appeal, as the brothers Johannot and Devéria valiantly did their best. Poems of all kinds boasted artistic, sometimes macabre, frontispieces or vignettes, but the poets, published in editions of 500, were fortunate to sell half that number, even with the illustrations. Novels went much better, especially since the more democratic genre was printed on cheap paper and aimed at the lending libraries, the grisettes, and the ordinary housewife.[9]

By 1833, Lesur admitted the sad truth : prose far outreached verse. All items of poetry, and he included " tout ce qui présente enfin, au bout de lignes inégales, des mots à peu près de la même consonnance," came to 275 while the novel reached 355.[10]

To make matters far worse, Charles Louandre of the *Revue des Deux Mondes*, reported in his " statistique littéraire " that from 1830 on, though the number of poetry items might be high, this figure had to be controlled by a more depressing fact : the average edition for each volume of verse had dropped to 300, while that of the novel reached astronomic figures.[11]   *Coelina ou l'Enfant du mystère* of Ducray-Duminil had alone been published in an edition of some 100,000 copies. Practically any author of a Gothic novel could patronize the poets when it came to discussing sales. In far too many cases, the number of volumes of poetry published did not tell the story of the copies left gathering dust on dealers' shelves. Decidedly, the age of poetry had passed ingloriously at about the same time the romanticists had won the right to use a liberated verse form. Ironically the new school was fighting for a lost cause without knowing it.

Many of the romanticists at first remained unaware of the reversal in popular taste. Curiously, third-raters, their heads lower in the clouds of poetry, were first to grasp this, but even those who noticed it did not fully realize the grave state of affairs. They had no access to statistics, and perhaps cared little for the bewildering figures that led to nowhere. A few sensed that a great change had occurred but voiced their reaction softly. M. Pigoreau, a bookseller forced by the plethora of novels to issue a catalogue of the latest romances, glumly stated in 1823 : " Il faut des romans populaires, si j'ose m'exprimer ainsi, puisque le peuple veut lire des romans... De là tous ces romans d'un jour; toutes ces productions insipides."[12]

From 1830 on the novel enjoyed such a vogue that France itself seemed to constitute the writer's audience. Stendhal understood this, though he sneered that all French women read novels according

to their degree of education. Consequently there were novels for
chamber maids and novels for salons. Those for chamber maids,
available at M. Pigoreau's store, told of ravishingly handsome young
heroes who rescued fair damsels at the very moment their plight
threatened to become interestingly desperate.[13] These novels purveyed
such gripping excitement that it was a rare woman in the provinces
who could restrict herself to fewer than five or six a month, while
many read fifteen or twenty. But, to reach the mark of celebrity,
as Stendhal sarcastically remarked, the book had to carry engravings
by Tony Johannot and receive high praise from the leading newspapers.[14] The plots might be absurd but the novels sold well, provided
they made the provincials cry. The ladies of Paris, on the contrary,
demanded more realistic incidents, though they, too, expected to sob
at their ease.

II

The romanticists may not have grasped the importance of the shift
to prose, but only the blindest could miss the effects of the nation's
industrialization. The young poets lived too far up Parnassus to see
the factories abuilding, to hear the asthmatic snorts of the engines,
or to follow the statistical analyses of the national economic regeneration. But they could, and did, see the people; they could, and did,
encounter the results of mechanization as it affected the lives of the
people.

Given the gradual transformation of France, the country became
imperceptibly aware of the social disturbances that accompanied the
machine and, by 1825, the problem of industrial misery was obvious.
From 1814 to 1830, salaries dropped consistently, while working hours
and the cost of living mounted. Nevertheless, although the average
salary of the urban worker stayed at between 492 and 527 francs during
the Restoration, the population trend was to the cities, with labor
piling up in slums under miserable conditions. Industrialists began
using women and child labor to maintain their machines at the fastest
rate as cheaply as possible.[15]

Slowly the horror of the predicament piled up. In 1829 a large
loaf of bread cost 17 1/2 sous, yet the worker received only 15 for an
11 hour day. A considerable housing crisis resulting from the increasing

numbers of workers produced slums of the worst kind. Families of 5 or 6 people, sometimes two such families, were jammed into a single small, damp, badly lit room. Under such conditions, the life expectancy of the worker dropped sharply. A contemporary, Achille Pénot, calculated that whereas in 1812 a Mulhouse worker might expect to reach the ripe age of 25, in 1827 he could count his blessings after 21. Whereas the child of a manufacturer could reasonably hope to live to 28, that of his employee could only expect an existence of 1 1/2 years. Heaped one upon the other in stinking rooms, with no sanitation, beaten into chronic fatigue by excessive hours of labor, no worker welcomed the arrival of children, knowing full well what lay in store for them. Most saw them die with indifference, sometimes with glee.[16]

When workers could not provide for their families, they fell back on charities, a fad of the 19th century which the humanitarian romanticists encouraged. In the north, for instance, where many inhabited caves, 163,000 of 224,000 workers registered at benevolent organizations. But so great was their need that charity could not fill it. As a result, the men inured themselves to their lot by heavy drinking. In 1828 only a third could afford meat; the rest ate potatoes, corn, and oats. But they all drank. The number of beggars in the capital reached an all-time high. Meanwhile the women resorted to prostitution or abandoned themselves to the promiscuity which their crowded lodgings encouraged, with a resultant sharp rise in illegitimacy. At Paris, in 1817, 10,000 of 23,000 births were illegitimate, and of these 7800 children were abandoned. Mulhouse expected one out of five to be born out of wedlock and, between 1814 and 1828, Lyon reported the number of such cases as having doubled. In France generally, illegitimacy jumped about 50 per cent between 1815 and 1830. The plight of the worker had become one of the nation's most perplexing problems :

Sans instruction, sans prévoyance, abrutis par la débauche, énervés par les travaux des manufactures, entassés dans des caves obscures ou dans des greniers où ils sont exposés à toutes les rigueurs des saisons, les ouvriers parviennent à l'âge sans avoir fait aucune épargne, et hors d'état de suffire complètement à l'existence de leur famille, qui est presque toujours très nombreuse... Beaucoup sont en proie à des infirmités héréditaires.[17]

Conceivably the workers might have united to argue for amelioration of their lot but, during the Restoration, they still formed a small part of the population, without public support. Moreover, the Bourbons frowned on any idea of collective bargaining and decreed that workers carry identifying booklets that required an employer's attestation of probity and political purity. In 1824 the restrictions originally enforced by Napoleon were made even more stringent. The police carefully spied on all associations; and local ordinances, as at Lyon in 1822, specified police attendance at all labor meetings, and restricted treasuries to 300 francs lest the workers use them as a war chest for strikes.

During the Restoration few dared complain against such measures. For most employers, the people remained a miserable mass to be exploited. The workers registered hardly a protest, content, apparently, to submit to their fate. A small minority reacted against the new machines, but police action quickly dampened their ardor. Protests were sporadic and to no avail. Any worker attempting to strike found himself facing the Civil Code's harsh prescription on sedition and treason. He could certainly count on several months of prison, even though the magistrate might recognize the necessity of his rebellion. Sometimes the rules of a particular factory forbade even temporary associations of workers, under pain of dismissal. But, above all, there existed during the Restoration no feeling of a class, none of the mysticism of ensemble that was to crop up after 1830. The Industrial Revolution had not as yet sufficiently divided the people of France into employer and employee, two antagonistic classes working at cross purposes. Whereas the manufacturer was solidly placed in society, the worker had no voice in legislation. This resulted, perhaps, from the fact that he had no organ of expression, no newspapers or literature to state his case. He remained an orphan of society, suspect and outlawed.

1830-1831 saw hard days for the people when the July Monarchy began inauspiciously with a deep depression. Overproduction had so affected industry and the workers that, in 1832, only one-third of the French people ate meat.[18] Actually, between 1823 and 1848, France would know only ten years of prosperity, but fifteen of black crisis. The working day, which had not changed much since the Restoration, approximated 14 hours, depending on the industry. In factories utilizing the recently introduced mechanical spinners, the day lasted 14 or 15 hours during all seasons, regardless of the worker's sex or age. And since most of the help lived about 2 1/2 miles from the factory, travelling time should be added to the total. Work began at 5 A.M. and ended about 8 in the evening, sometimes at 9.[19]

Even then, the pay scarcely sufficed to keep the workers alive. Rates had hardly changed since the early days of the Bourbons despite the rising cost of living. The median salary for industrial workers at the beginning of the July Revolution was about 2 francs per day for a man, one for a woman, 45 centimes for a child of 8 to 12, and 75 centimes for a child 13 to 16. In general, a bachelor could save a small pittance, but a woman could not exist. Most families of two could expect a painfully gained annual wage of 477 francs without the aid of children, though in some regions, Alsace, for instance, the average dropped much lower.[20]

The influx of labor from the country made bad conditions worse. Though housing had become a serious consideration and France quickly saw the first industrially created slums cower in the shadow of new factories, the same sort of environment existed in the factories, themselves narrow, dark, dirty, and unsanitary. But nobody cared. Because of these surroundings the workers generally suffered from angina, rheumatism, or tuberculosis, and their life expectancy slumped spectacularly to age 21. But recruits for the machines still marched in from the country, driven cityward by the crisis in agriculture. Women sickened quickly, bore puny offspring who, if they survived, in turn went to work at the age of six or seven. Always indoors, the children of the proletariat suffered from spinal defects and rickets. Bad treatment by employers in no way helped them; blows, and in some cases, whips, were used to produce greater efforts.[21] In time of epidemics, as during the cholera plague of 1832, disease swept through the crowded quarters like a scythe, decimating the miserable inhabitants of overcrowded areas.

Given their daily pittance and the fact that most had large families, the workers faced an almost insoluble economic dilemma. Many fell into debt in their struggle to keep alive, and had to seek relief from charity. In 1835, one out of twelve persons in Paris was indigent, a burden too great for the 6,275 benevolent societies attempting to cope with the situation. Each year until the revolution of 1848, some 250 new institutions sprang into the gap.[22] A whole rash of writers like Bigot de la Morogue, with his *De la misère des ouvriers* (1832), tried to solve the problem of pauperism, but no solution appeared to work and meanwhile the workers died like flies amidst their own filth. In 1833 alone hospitals admitted some 425,000 indigents, while the charity centers aided 695,000 more. That year France shamefully confessed to 1,120,000 paupers. The situation became so bad that in 1840 the Académie des Sciences, always behind the times, offered a prize for the best essay on " en quoi consiste la misère; par quels signes elle se manifeste en divers pays; quelles sont ses causes."[23]

The growing misery may not be ascribed completely to the expansion of large industry, but the latter certainly contributed in great measure. Wherever considerable numbers of workers appeared, signs of the new poverty inevitably followed. In the textile centers, first to achieve industrial concentration, around the mines, the chemical industry, lurked the specter of famine and its gaunt sisters, hunger, alcoholism, and prostitution, evident to the most casual passerby.

III

When the manufacturer finally accepted the machine unreservedly, the worker was placed in a position where he began to feel himself outlawed from society. For the factory owner industrialization meant fewer workers and greater production, hence greater profit. The laborer inevitably sensed that he was being shunted into a position of dependence on the inanimate. Gone was the artisan's satisfaction at a job well done. For no apparent reason, he had been demoted to the ignominious level of servant to a monster that progressively seemed to require less help. The introduction of the machine cut all contact between the artisan and the material prepared, and the worker felt himself dispossessed spiritually and physically when technological advances made his services unnecessary.

The first reaction of the disinherited was to strike back with unthinking hatred at the equipment they served. On March 3, 1831, two thousand workers in Saint-Etienne marched on the Rives factory to demolish the equipment. In May, at Bordeaux, sawyers broke down doors to smash the power saws. At Paris, in September of that same year, fifteen hundred hands demonstrated in traditional style against the manufacturers of the rue de Cadran who had optimistically bought in Lyon a machine for cutting shawls. On the 7th of that month the workers gathered in the streets to shout, " Plus de mécaniques," but fled when the government called out the cavalry. Despite all protests and violence, the situation worsened. By 1841, Adolphe Boyer could write cynically :

Maintenant, avec la division du travail, les procédés nouveaux et les machines, la plupart des états tendent à devenir purement mécaniques et les ouvriers de toutes les professions seront bientôt rejetés dans la classe des hommes propres à tout faire... Bientôt, on n'aura plus besoin des travailleurs que pour tourner des manivelles, porter les fardeaux, et faire les courses; il est vrai qu'ils auront l'instruction primaire, c'est-à-dire que leur intelligence sera assez développée pour comprendre que la société les rejette comme des parias.[24]

When uncoordinated violence failed, the workers resorted to a more powerful form of resistance : they banded together for mutual protection, at least in the large cities. At the same time, they discovered the value of the strike as a means of preventing exploitation by their feudally-minded masters. In Lyon, about 35,000 silk weavers in the Croix-Rousse sector reacted violently when the introduction of machines lowered their salaries from 4 francs to 1 franc 50 per day. In 1831 the weavers attempted to reason with their employers, but the manufacturers refused to honor an agreement made by their own representatives on the grounds that the demands were preposterous. The workers promptly went into the streets, not for any specific purpose, but because death seemed preferable to the bleakness of their lives. The inevitable followed; troops smashed the revolt in bloody revenge, and the manufacturers could breathe easily for a time.

But the revolt set off a chain reaction. Because of the treatment of the Lyon rioters, other workers began to organize to meet modern conditions. Hitherto they had associated themselves in *compagnonnages* or *mutualités* (friendly societies). The former dated from the Middle Ages, and still maintained their strict rules of membership, mystic recognition signs, and hostility toward all outsiders. Prior to 1830, the various *compagnons* had jealously guarded their individuality, often indulging in bloody struggles with rivals. The mutualist societies tried to overcome this handicap, but they had the tradition of centuries to combat. More modern than the *compagnonnages*, they strove for general self-protection, but neither type of association could solve the problems of industrialization. As a result, other ideas began to win over the workers and, by 1831, mutualism was replaced by the *sociétés de résistance*, organizations designed to control the conditions of employment. These assumed various names but, unlike the *mutua-lités*, had no benefit features. They stressed, rather, the need for collective contracts, wage scales, and shorter hours in cleaner factories. Given the times, they had to be secret, but were free of the religious and ceremonial character of the *compagnonnages*.

With the workers close to mutiny, political organizations in opposition to the government rushed to attract the dissatisfied. The *Société des Amis du Peuple* and the *Société des Droits de l'Homme et du Citoyen* immediately began proselyting. In the latter case, the association broke into " sections," each devoted to a different trade : *La Montagne* and *Lebas* for tailors, *Cinq et Six juin*, *Mucius Scoevola*, for shoemakers, etc. To win the support of the workers, republican organizations flooded France with brochures and broadsides, all supposedly within the reach of the thinnest purse. In the space of 3 months, some six million pieces of propaganda left Paris for the country in the form of books, pamphlets, or newspapers.[25]

The government quickly took stringent measures to block any incipient revolt. The proletariat represented a new force, but there was always the Napoleonic precedent for handling dissidents. In December, 1831, the count d'Argout recommended to prefects the use of the anti-sedition measures, articles 414 and 415 of the Code, to curb manifestations of workers claiming salary increases. In 1834 the Orléans government felt so uneasy about the growing proletarian population that it revised Empire and Restoration legislation. A law forbade associations of even 20 persons, if they belonged to a larger group, and was intended to disband societies like the *Devoir Mutuel* of the Lyon weavers, which had sponsored the strikes of 1831 and 1834. The ordinance killed most mutual societies but not before the Lyon workers had shed considerable blood.

No matter what the government did, it was another case of King Canute. The law dragged an increasing number of workers into court for subversive activities, fined some, sent others to jail. Still the workers persisted in organizing as the urban population expanded from 15 per cent of the total population in 1830, to about 25 per cent in 1846. Slums swelled to the bursting point, the depressions made workers more restless and, as the Orléans Monarchy headed toward the reckoning of 1848, the less fortunate bitterly meditated Casimir Périer's advice that patience and resignation were the only remedies to their plight.[26]

Given the state of France, the romanticists, no matter how obtuse, could not fail to notice the turmoil. In fact, such a realization of the facts of contemporary life lay implicit in their espousal of the cause of local color and history. Even the purest of them recognized the signs of a change, not only in literature, but in society. The Industrial Revolution, still unidentified, was to provide many of the new themes which the young school had long sought : the people, particularly the urban workers, poverty, slums, prostitution, alcoholism, and the crime resultant from destitution. As time wore on, a large number of romanticists would identify themselves with the workers' claims to social justice, thus accomplishing a political revolution within the ranks of their literary movement. Heirs to the humanitarianism of the 18th century, imbued with a Messianic urge to lead the people to social salvation, most could only accept the logic of their opinions and recognize the people as those for whom, and about whom, literature was henceforth to be written.

NOTES

1. Treuttel et Würz, Strasbourg, 1800, 1801.

2. " Sur les romans, " Vol. IV. An article signed A., actually by M. de Féletz.

3. C.-L. Lesur, Paris, Desplaces, 1819, p. 597.

4. *Ibid.*, p. 600.

5. C.-L. Lesur, *Annuaire historique universelle*, Paris, Thoisnier-Desplaces, 1825.

6. *Ibid.*, 1826, p. 863.

7. *Ibid.*, 1828, p. 285.

8. *Ibid.*, 1832, p. 333.

9. Henri Bouchot, *Le Livre*, Paris, Picard, 1886, pp. 228-30.

10. *Ibid.*, p. 274.

11. *RDM*, 1847.

12. *Petite bibliographie biographico-romancière*, Paris, Pigoreau, 1823.

13. Stendhal, *Correspondance inédite*, Paris, Calmann-Lévy, nd, II, 174, lettre CXCI, à M. le Comte... Aquila, 13-18 octobre 1832.

14. *Ibid.*

15. S. Charléty, *La Restauration*, Paris, Hachette, 1921, pp. 316-17.

16. Edouard Dolléans, *Histoire du mouvement ouvrier*, Paris, Colin, 1947, I, 20-21.

17. *Ibid.*, p. 21.

18. Jean Montreuil, *Le Mouvement ouvrier en France*, Paris, Aubier, 1946, p. 59.

19. Edouard Dolléans, *Histoire du mouvement ouvrier*, Paris, Colin, 1947, I, 17-18.

20. *Ibid.*, 16-20.

21. Montreuil, *op. cit.*, pp. 54-55.

22. Charléty, *op. cit.*, p. 215.

23. Eugène Buret, *De la misère des classes laborieuses en Angleterre et en France*, Paris, Paulin, 1840, 2 vols.

24. Dolléans, *op. cit.*, I, 14.

25. *Ibid.*, I, 79-80.

26. *Ibid.*, I, 69.

CHAPTER 6

ADVENT OF THE NEWSPAPER

ROMANTICISM WAS THUS faced with two audiences : a city group educated in the tradition of the Ancien Régime, with a sound knowledge of the finer points of art; and a much larger segment of the population that lacked any appreciation of the freed Alexandrine, or even the simplest variations on a prose theme. Of the two, the first could grant reputation in the capital but the second, more silent, yet economically more important, could give a comfortable bank account. Furthermore, the public had apparently rejected the poetry of the romanticists along with that of the classicists. Decidedly the era clamored for prose, easy prose that told a simple, exciting tale to while away a dull evening, and which concerned itself with the realities of the present. To complicate this picture, the modern newspaper burst upon the scene, considerably changing the direction of the literature to come. It would provide romanticism with a means for reaching the masses at the same time that it acquainted them and the whole nation with the condition of the proletariat.

I

Shortly after the romanticists had successfully captured the theater, the same inventions that had made possible the appearance of a cheap, mass literature, also produced the first large-run daily newspapers, with a subsequent major influence on romanticism. By 1830 speedier presses had come from England and America : printers had solved the problem of inking type with rollers instead of tampons; inventors found means to produce larger sheets of paper; new inks were compounded and factories promised sufficient supplies for the greedy publishing houses. In short, the technology of printing was ready to permit the appearance of the greatest of mass media.

Prior to the Revolution, the newspaper had scarcely existed; its history was recent, its tradition weak. In the 17th century Théophraste Renaudot had founded the *Gazette* (May 30, 1631), the first French newspaper. This small bi-weekly, with announcements spread over the bottom of the page, enjoyed undisputed privilege until the Revolution, pampered and spoiled from the time Mazarin first smiled on it. Few others joined the *Gazette's* haphazard attempts to spread the news, either from lack of favor or lack of enterprise. For a time the *Gazette Burlesque* set the news to verse, then Doneau de Vizé's *Mercure Galant* began to record irregularly aristocratic marriages, deaths, births, and tales of love. Not until the end of the 18th century did the first daily paper appear, when the *Journal de Paris* (January 1, 1777) decided to relay gossip, carefully avoiding the more dangerous grounds of politics and court news.

Actually, France could muster only three newspapers prior to 1789. To these might be added Linguet's *Annales politiques et littéraires* and two monthlies. A few others such as the *Journal Ecclésiastique* of the abbé Baruel were printed for the benefit of specialized groups. Rigid censorship restricted the number of such periodicals, though many humorous or scandalous publications circulated around the nation. Liberty of the press did not exist nor was the reading public extensive enough to support a large newspaper. Still less were the scope and the potentialities of the medium understood. Most journals leaned to literature or gossip, with little concern for the unhealthy subject of politics.

With the Revolution, however, France went wild over newspapers. It became almost the inalienable right of any citizen with money or credit to publish complaints on anything he disliked. From practically none at all, the number of papers jumped to over 500 in 1789, each advancing a special point of view. Every club, and there was a staggering number of them, wanted an organ of publicity. And as the number of journals grew, they devised more ingenious ways to attract the attention of the comparatively few who could pay to read the news. When prices dropped, some die-hards even pasted their product on walls, determined to be heard even at their own expense. Between 1789 and 1800 some 800 papers were born and died, curious ephemera that bore brave and hopeful names. Many favored the title " Patriot " or insisted on being somebody's

" Friend." One outdid all rivals by grandiosely calling itself *L'Ami du genre humain*. Most were specialized, as the *Journal de la Compagnie des Arquebusiers royaux de la ville de Paris sur la révolution actuelle*, but there was also a *Journal des Incroyables, ou les Hommes à parole d'honneur*. The " Defenders " ran their vogue, many degenerating into such products of the lunatic fringe as *Finissez donc, cher père*, or *Pendez-moi! mais écoutez-moi!* All these sheets died an early and unmourned death either from financial malnutrition or the sudden, disastrous pressure of the powers that were. The Commune vigorously suppressed papers suspected of royalist leanings, a policy which the Directory extended to its own list of enemies.

Censorship became a fine art under Napoleon. The Consuls, that is, Bonaparte, decreed on January 17, 1800, that France had too long enjoyed irresponsible reporting. As almost a first act, the government reduced the number of political papers to 13, and later Napoleon subjected these to despotic controls. From his point of view, the press was to be used as a weapon, with the *Moniteur* as an official instrument for launching trial balloons or publishing grandiose accounts of his latest triumph.

Yet, curiously, it was under the great dictator that the first important newspapers appeared, the *Journal des Débats*, for instance, which quickly earned a magisterial reputation in the field of ideas. Since politics were tabu, the *Débats* centered its attention on literature and one of its critics, Geoffroy, attained a dubious kind of immortality by inventing the feuilleton, incidentally raising circulation to the then incredible figure of 32,000. In this the publishers made a major error. So many customers gave them a profit of over 200,000 francs, a fact that aroused the greed of Napoleon's friend, Fouché, who suddenly gained control of the newspaper, and changed its name to the *Journal de l'Empire*. Only the feuilleton kept its liberty, apparently harmless in the eyes of the Emperor, but Geoffroy showed rare judgment by dying only a few days before the fall of his master.

During the Restoration the press was at first permitted a greater measure of freedom, but the Bourbons soon found need to impose a censorship as severe as that of the Empire. In 1824, only 13 papers appeared in Paris, 7 pro-government, 6 opposed, and all together they could claim only 55,600 subscribers. Almost every year, from 1817 on, the Bourbons found an excuse to reduce freedom of the press,

until, finally, the *loi de tendance* of 1822 gave the government power
to suspend any paper that published articles in a spirit hostile to the
government. In 1827, the fantastically named *loi de justice et d'amour*
placed all publications at the mercy of the monarchy while taxing them
unmercifully.

So long had the French press been gagged that, when Louis-Philippe
came to power, it forced him to guarantee a measure of liberty.
Thus, with more and better paper and presses available, and with
a huge, eager, but poorly educated public waiting to be reached,
French journalism was ready to enter its golden age. To celebrate
this, Joly introduced the first cylindrical press for newspapers in
1834.

It fell to Emile de Girardin to import from England the revolutionary
concept of the penny press. During the Restoration most people could
not afford to subscribe to a journal at the current rate of 80 francs
per year. Publishers mailed each edition to the subscribers, and
few copies were hawked on the streets. With the high costs, soaring
taxes, poor primary education and the ever-present censorship, journals
could aim only at a wealthy élite, coincidentally the group which espoused the cause of the traditional literary values. For this clientele they
prepared cautious articles on foreign policy, or offered lengthy criticisms
of the latest neo-classical masterpiece. The literary critic occupied
an honored and powerful position, with a great deal of space at his
disposition. Until 1828 nobody thought of opening the pages of a
newspaper to advertisements. To be sure, some were used, but only
as fillers. Hence the readers paid all the costs of the paper at what
was then almost a prohibitive price.[1]

Girardin, however, decided to put advertising to work. In 1830
he launched a *Journal des connaissances utiles*, priced at half the usual
rate for other papers, and prepared for a far broader, if less well-
educated, audience. It was the first of a series, all to be financed from
the profits from publicity. When he could claim 130,000 readers after
two years, other publishers enthusiastically copied his ideas, with the
result that the number of papers sold in France jumped 50 per cent
by 1832. Girardin methodically continued to build an empire; by
1835 he had founded a chain of highly profitable ventures based on
mass appeal : *la Mode, le Voleur* and *le Panthéon littéraire*, in addition
to a *Bibliothèque économique et périodique des meilleurs romans* and a

Bibliothèque des professions et des ménages. The latter sold at one sou for 16 pages.

In 1836, two years after the introduction of the cylindrical press, a circulation war began. Girardin launched the *Presse* on July 1, the very day the rival *Siècle* appeared. Both based their economic life on Girardin's theory of financing through profits from advertising, a hypothesis which seemed proved when the *Presse* reached a sale of 10,000 at the end of six months; the *Siècle*, 40,000 at the end of two years. And the curve of success continued to rise during the whole century.

Some of the oldsters resented Girardin's creations, believing them Frankensteins. As early as 1825, Stendhal had raised a cry that was to make its fortune : " L'industrialisme, un peu cousin du charlatanisme, paie des journaux..."[2] A. Pommier *(Les Colères)* was so disturbed by the strange phenomenon of advertising that he reached dubious heights of lyricism in angry complaint :

> L'annonce a son génie et sa langue; un glossaire
> Pour comprendre ce style est vraiment nécessaire.
> Sagou, tapioka, racahout, frigidine,
> Sylvestrine, oleine, odontine, amandine,
> Chocolat blanc, gazeux, et gland doux en café,
> Capahu, palamont, allahtain, nofé...
> Et tant d'autres, criant au lecteur plein d'effroi :
> Prenez-moi ! mettez-moi ! mangez-moi ! buvez-moi !

But Girardin defended the notion of a mass literature with the zeal of a convert, simultaneously teaching the romanticists the correct way to understand their times : " Force il y a de mettre la science à pied quand les sociétés se carrent dans la boue; quand le peuple est dit souverain, il est décent que le souverain sache lire. Avec six sous on va lui donner une éducation. C'est bien le moins."[3] Then Girardin spelled out a message which showed that he had neither missed nor underestimated the impact of the Industrial Revolution : " Nous avons essayé de prouver comment la littérature à six sous était la conséquence immédiate et comique des machines à vapeur et des torrents chargés de produire dix mille épingles à la minute."[4]

Newspapers at first shared Girardin's optimism, mostly because they thought they possessed a huge reservoir of paying customers, but the *Siècle*, the *Presse*, and the *Constitutionnel*, along with their imitators, soon tapped the potential available at the moment. Although each year brought more education to France, hence more readers, at any given time illiteracy and monetary considerations restricted the number of subscribers. Therefore the newspapers began to cast about for means of raiding the circulation lists of their rivals. If advertisers were to pay publication costs, they had to be shown that news of their products reached the greatest number of customers possible. To satisfy them, papers abdicated their claim to authority over people's minds in a wild attempt to attract additional readers; they had to amuse, to pander, and to lure. Interested solely in profits, publishers hopefully enlarged formats to carry more copy, and page four became an all-important consideration, dedicated almost exclusively to advertising.

At first papers made extravagant promises about news coverage. L'*Époque* offered ten papers in one : political, army and navy, religion, public works, municipal and administrative, public instruction, science and medicine, commerce and agriculture and, of course, a feuilleton. For its part, the *Soleil* could muster only six-in-one. And so it went, with a mad scramble for popular attention. The public ruled as master of the press, and newspapers abandoned their former glory as they tended to become more like modern tabloids.

Girardin soon discovered that politics, though fascinating to a small number, could not long hold reader interest. Nor could plain sensationalism. Only the novel seemed capable of monopolizing public attention for any length of time. Therefore, in a marriage of convenience, the press turned to the roman-feuilleton for aid in boosting sales. Strange as it seems, literature also benefited from the unusual alliance, though with subsequent curious consequences. Since books sold badly because of their high prices, the feuilleton represented a monetary boon for both author and newspaper. The writer found a new market for his talent, for which he was happy to offer his services. Readers applauded the merger by frantically buying that paper which carried the day's best-seller.

In view of the public reaction, the papers did their best to attract writers of reputation. Certain specialists in the genre like Dumas, Sue, and Frédéric Soulié became the first of a new kind of literary lion. One by one most of the big names succumbed to temptation as papers like the *Presse* paid 300 francs for the slightest feuilleton. Dumas, père, bargained with Véron and Girardin for a contract guaranteeing 64,000 francs a year, then wrote 100,000 lines a year for the *Siècle* at 1 franc 50 per line. Other writers pursued the franc just as avidly. The *Presse* attracted George Sand, Mme d'Agoult, Delphine Gay, even Gérard de Nerval. Balzac prepared several of his novels with an eye to serialization. Gautier wrote *Le Roi Candaule*, Lamartine, the *Histoire des Girondins*, then splashed his private life over the front page in the *Confidences*. Rival editors fought for the services of men with large followings and paid well for the privilege. Most sought after of all was Eugène Sue. In 1842 the *Débats* published the *Mystères de Paris*, then the *Constitutionnel* paid 100,000 francs for the *Juif errant*. Such marked success earned the compliment of endless imitation. When writers found that the old romance could easily be adapted to the episodic form now required by the newspaper, the old genre found so great a renewal of favor that Balzac, himself the most enterprising of industrial writers, remarked in the beginning of *Béatrix* that writers no longer created works of art, but products.

However, the readers cared little for critical diatribes. Some stories met such great success that circulation changed crazily according to the magnetic power of the feuilleton. *Le Capitaine Paul*, a short novel by Alexandre Dumas, brought the *Siècle* 100,000 subscribers in three weeks. In fact, many readers who disagreed with the political views of a newspaper nevertheless continued to buy it for the current story. When Eugène Sue joined the *Constitutionnel*, circulation jumped from 3000 to 40,000. The first week of the feuilleton told the tale; if a success, the business manager could count on selling from 50,000 to 80,000 copies a day—or he could lose that many readers.[5]

With such smashing success, the romance could no longer be ignored by professional writers. It had suddenly jumped into the lead as the most profitable and potent genre in contemporary literature, a fact that was to lure young writers from the glories of poetry to the more substantial rewards of prose. Because of this, and other factors, too, the course of French romanticism would alter so radically in the period 1830 to 1848 that it seemed to reject many of the principles held earlier in its development.

NOTES

1. Emile Mermet, *La Presse, l'affichage et le colportage*, Paris, Marpon et Flammarion, 1881.

2. *D'un nouveau complot contre les industriels*, Paris, Sautelet.

3. " La Littérature à six sous, " *Revue de Paris*, VIII, NS, (août 1834), 131.

4. *Ibid.*, p. 203.

5. Nora Atkinson, *Eugène Sue et le roman-feuilleton*, Paris, Nizet et Bastard, 1929.

PART TWO

THE DEVELOPMENT OF ROMANTICISM

CHAPTER 7

FIRST REACTIONS

ONCE THE FIRST ELATION over the victory of *Hernani* had subsided, the romanticists came to earth with a thud. A dawning consciousness of reality made them inspect their surroundings warily, and they were confused, shocked, and somewhat unhappy at the kingdom they surveyed. They hoped momentarily to reserve the right to reject what they saw, even though such action might entail serious consequences. As professional writers they now had to choose between a very small, but highly literate group of Parisians, or the huge mass of the mediocrely educated. In the first instance they could indulge in the poetry they so dearly loved; in the second, the vogue for the romance, the attitude of publishers and, later, the advent of the newspaper, clearly indicated that the successful writer could live comfortably from the profits of his prose. As the price of this, his writing would contain fewer graceful periods and no subtle conceits, but only the prose that told of common things, that either discussed contemporary problems or allowed the reader to escape from these same perplexities.

The dilemma was to split the romantic school. Most of the older generation agreed to accept the age and to work with it, though this meant a change of direction in their art. Imbued with humanitarianism and the Messianic urge, the elders yearned to be leaders, wrote prose and descended into the political arena in defense of their theories on the good life in a machine age. They welcomed the changing times, albeit timidly. Some, to be sure, persisted in remaining poets, but only rarely, like Lamartine or Hugo, could they hope to make money. The younger generation, the boys who had made the balconies brilliant at *Hernani*, considered it disgraceful of their heroes to forsake the Muse. Under the leadership of Pétrus Borel and Théophile Gautier, they refused to acknowledge the triumph of the middle class, preferring to starve in Bohemia rather than pocket the material rewards of a

degenerate era of moneymaking, Alas, they, too, would be forced
to live with profit and loss despite their violent proclamation of the
sanctity of the theory of art for art's sake.

I

The theory, in fact, they owed to their immediate predecessors.
As Sainte-Beuve pointed out in " Espoir et vœu du mouvement littéraire
et poétique après la révolution de 1830," a nostalgic essay on the
work of the first generation of literary revolutionists, the theory of art
for art's sake lay implicit in the romantic revolution.[1] The phrase, in
fact, had first been used by Benjamin Constant, of all people, when
he immortalized it in his *Journal intime* after a conversation with
one of Schelling's disciples, Crabbe Robinson.[2] By demanding absolute
liberty of expression for the artist, the Cénacle liberated literature
from servitude to causes, thus permitting a clear development of the
pure-art theory.   But although the first generation timidly attested
the need for complete artistic freedom, most poets remained cir-
cumspect in their personal revolt. Hugo himself, later one of the
foremost proponents of utilitarian art, had given his followers a clear
statement of art for art's sake in the preface of the *Orientales*. " Si
donc aujourd'hui quelqu'un lui demande à quoi bon ces *Orientales*...
il répondra qu'il n'en sait rien, que c'est une idée qui lui a pris; et
qui lui a pris d'une façon assez ridicule." This was written in January,
1829, when Hugo, as the leader of a minority group, could still feel
free to bully the bourgeoisie. The poet, he insisted, must follow
his fancy : this could be the only law of art. As yet ignorant of the
problems that would confront France after *Hernani*, he defiantly
maintained that : " quel que soit le tumulte de la place publique,
que l'art persiste, que l'art s'enquête, que l'art reste fidèle à lui-même,
tenax propositi." At the same time, in the *Consolations* (XVII, 1830),
Sainte-Beuve was writing to Leroux

> — Oui, le plaisir s'envole,
> La passion nous ment; la gloire est une idole,
> Non pas l'Art : l'Art sublime, éternel et divin,
> Luit comme la Vertu; le reste seul est vain.

Sainte-Beuve held momentarily to the faith, then wavered. The
occasion for the change of heart came when on January 3, 1834,

Armand Carrel wrote bitingly in the *National* against the possibility of a literature based on the theory of art for art's sake. Sainte-Beuve congratulated Carrel in a short note the day after the appearance of the article : " Je suis complètement de votre avis... En ce qui concerne l'École de *l'Art pour l'Art* vous avez dit également bien des choses qui me semblent justes, sauf deux ou trois petites réserves ou du moins explications."[3]

Even Lamartine, watching with Olympian aloofness the frenzied activity of the cénacle, felt the attractiveness of a poet's doctrine. Abandoning the caution which budding political ambitions necessitated, Lamartine published in the preface of the *Harmonies* (May, 1830) a declaration of disdain for literary illiterates incapable of appreciating the majesty of art. His verse was aimed, he stated, at readers who lived in the solitude of their soul, to weep, to wait, or to pray. For him poetry had no other object than to fix fleeting impressions or to echo the poet's hopes and fears. But this creed lasted only until the urge to run for office made him reverse direction with the shameless ease of a master politician.

For once Lamartine seemed to agree with Pierre Leroux. At the end of 1831 the latter published an *Adresse* in which he challenged writers to use the social possibilities of literature. Under Leroux's guidance, the new *Globe* hoped to point the way to a utilitarian art. And though the *Globe* and Leroux actually had little influence on romanticism, the members of the first cénacle all seemed to be heading in the same direction. " Je ne sais pourquoi j'écris... Je sens en moi le besoin de dire à la société les idées que j'ai en moi et qui veulent sortir," Vigny confided to his *Journal* in 1835. A year earlier, Lamartine had published *Des destinées de la poésie* in repudiation of the *Harmonies* and as a dedication of his services as a poet :

> La poésie sera la raison chantée; voilà sa destinée pour longtemps; elle sera philosophique, religieuse, politique, sociale, comme les époques que le genre humain va traverser... Dans cette œuvre, la poésie a sa place... C'est elle qui plane sur la société et qui la juge, et qui, montrant à l'homme la vulgarité de son œuvre, l'appelle sans cesse en avant...

He repeated essentially the same ideas in the preface of *Jocelyn :* " Qu'est-ce qu'un homme qui, à la fin de sa vie, n'aurait fait que cadencer ses rêves poétiques." By that time Hugo had already committed himself to utilitarianism with *Claude Gueux* and *Le Dernier Jour d'un condamné.*

Prose, and, surprisingly, poetry, began to feel conscious of a purpose. The oldsters soon accepted as a challenge the possibility of guiding the cultural development of the masses or of influencing the political and social outlook of most of the nation. Filled with a sense of the position of letters in life, they were driven by a Messianic compulsion to lead France to perfection. The " utilitarians " felt impelled to show their fellow men how to harness the productivity of the new age, how to redistribute in socially desirable fashion the wealth born of the machine, and how to cure the ills of industrialization. They metamorphosed from advocates of melancholy into apostles of order and spiritual unity who wrote to exalt and teach an entire citizenry. The old themes gave way to an unlimited faith in the future and a passion for progress. Writers had never had any difficulty convincing themselves they were geniuses, but now they also proclaimed their divine right to propose solutions for all the woes of the nation. The word " mission " became an indispensable part of an author's vocabulary. Each man prepared his own textbook, and he confidently expected society to adopt it exclusively. Lamartine preached the benefits of a life close to the soil, slow and patient progress; Lamennais preferred a militant Catholicism, Gustave Drouineau, neo-Christianity; for others, Saint-Simonism relieved all ills. And so it went, with the public offered a plethora of panaceas, all guaranteed to cure painlessly. The older generation abandoned the path of art for art's sake and came down from its lofty position to walk in the streets.

II

Not so the young men who inherited the legacy of the Cénacle. At least ten years junior to the first generation, they clung in unregenerate fashion to the code which Hugo had proclaimed in the preface of the *Orientales :* " Il avait fait cela, parce qu'il avait fait cela." For an ancestor they could claim the gentle Emile Deschamps and take consolation in his *Études françaises*, in which all poets were cautioned to shape their language and rhythms like sculptors. There could be no static aesthetics; poetry was a perpetual creation. After him they could quote, " Le *Odi profanum vulgus et arceo* d'Horace, tout impertinent qu'il paraisse, devrait être l'épigraphe de chaque œuvre poétique."

Like the men of 1826, the proponents of art for art's sake found a rallying point in what they disliked rather than in what they proposed. They swore eternal faith to an exclusive cult of art that rejected the conventions and utilitarian outlook of the bourgeoisie, and they opposed the unity of scorn to a nation of shopkeepers and worshippers of double-entry bookkeeping. Proprietors, concierges, Louis-Philippe, the machine, progress and prose, they lumped them together as aesthetically undesirable. For them, art was a religion, the absolute of absolutes, its mysteries unveiled only after arduous dedication, and forever to be protected from profane eyes. Verse was their god, and they all echoed Gautier's fierce cry : " Des vers, et puis des vers et encore des vers. Il faut laisser la prose aux boutiques du boulevard."[4]

Such an attitude was not calculated to endear the younger romanticists either to publishers or to most contemporary readers. With most editions of verse down to 300 copies and the majority of these destined to gather dust on stock-room shelves, the poet could not really afford to be difficult. But he was. Pétrus Borel, for instance, published in the *Rhapsodies* (1832) an incandescent tirade against proponents of a circumscribed art, in which he wildly proclaimed an inalienable right to unbridled liberty, at the same time that he belabored materialistic minds.

But it was left to Théophile Gautier to state the case for all purists. France did not please him, with its smoking factories, contented manufacturers, and over-worked laborers. Hurt that the poetic product of weary hours should be rejected by crass publishers, he slashed back at those he considered his enemies : the middle class, all successful writers, a reading public with low taste, the newspapers and, above all, the ever-detestable prose.

In the preface to *Mlle de Maupin*, Gautier recorded the hates of all those lesser writers who yearned for a place in the sun of glory, yet never expected to bask in its rays. Gautier detested the way in which the railroad desecrated the face of nature, all for the sake of speed. He begged Louis-Philippe to suppress newspapers and their atrocious advertisements, promising in reward a dithyramb in free verse and crossed rhymes. He snickered at the very mention of the word utility, a meaningless concept. The dull proletariat seemed

fit only as feed for the machines or to cannonade in the streets, starve-
lings with no aesthetic sense. The new schools of economics peddled
a ridiculous jargon of windy promises : pious middle-class morality
that nauseated him with its shrill screeching for a life without pleasure.
As he complained in *La Charte de 1830*, poets were unjustly belittled
by purveyors of romance and utilitarian pathos.[5] The world, with
its Louis-Philippe, its Ballanche and its stock market, had turned
against the ideals of art for art's sake and deserved to wallow in the
muck surrounding its factories.

Sainte-Beuve deplored the change just as bitterly, though more
quietly. He resented, too, the fact that the great Hugo kept piling
up verse at home, but refused to publish for fear of becoming too
famous as a poet, a title which by then had begun to change into
a term of reproach. To budding poets he regretfully acknowledged
that he could help little in aiding them to publish, even in the *Revue
des Deux Mondes*, since Buloz shared the contemporary aversion for
verse.[6] This frustration, he admitted in a discouraged letter to Ulric
Guttinguer : " Je persiste à croire que tout ce qui est poète délicat
doit fuir ce Louis XIV-ci qui n'est que personnification manufacturière,
financière, industrielle (la mieux entendue) de cette société moderne
si dédaigneuse du vrai délicat."[7]

But the full blast of Sainte-Beuve's resentment did not appear until
1839 when, righteously indignant at the recent trends, he blasted
" industrial " literature as the shoddy product of the monetary-minded.
Not until the Restoration, he noted, had men wanted fame plus
fortune, a change which subsequently led to the desecration of the
old values. Sainte-Beuve reminded his readers that artistic purity
was no longer possible in an era in which a writer was judged according
to his income. Literature had become infected with bad taste when
authors began to consider their work as propaganda; it had abandoned
the witty learning of the Restoration in favor of morbid eccentricity,
unbridled egotism, and vapid pretension.

In a sense, Sainte-Beuve was writing an epitaph for the youthful
sponsors of art for art's sake, those hapless victims of the age whose
hope for fame was blighted by the chilling reception of a disinterested
public. But their elders also shared in this defeat, though they probably
never realized it. The first generation of romanticists had always
prided itself on the revolutionary dynamism of its art. Hugo himself

reminded readers of the *Contemplations* that he had capped the dictionary with a red bonnet and stirred up a tempest in the inkwell. To
be sure, Lamartine, Hugo, Vigny, Musset, and all their colleagues
had created a revolution in French poetry, but it would be more
correct to say that they started one, but never finished it.

Their efforts, and they cannot be belittled, were directed at loosening
the neo-classic stranglehold on poetry. At the same time they gave
verse a suppleness it had long lacked and posed the principles of
experimentation that would completely change the whole conception
of poetry. But this they did with hesitant timidity, as customary
in the early stages of a revolt. Much later, when they realized the
magnitude and far-reaching consequences of their acts, they would
proclaim long and loudly how they had renovated the face of art.
They believed themselves, and they made others believe them; but
to take their claims seriously is to misunderstand their contribution.
Actually, they deserted their revolution about the time it was really
getting under way.

This fact does not, of course, strip the Cénacle of any glory. What
they did for French verse set the stage for all later poetic movements,
even those supposedly in revolt against them. At a time when neo-
classicism could offer only a tired and over-age aesthetics, the first
generation of romanticists gave the Muses a new look. They asked
all the old questions again, but suggested answers different from those
sanctified in the textbooks. Up to the demise of the *Muse française*
aspiring writers had piously followed the neo-classic recipes, but
thereafter they proved with increasing daring that verse could be
intensely passionate and alive, imaginative and musical. Poetry
acquired a vigor and appeal long absent. Whereas classicism had
created its forms *a priori* according to established structures and
without any particular concern for lyrical qualities, the theorists of
romanticism had dared tamper with the holy of holies, the invariable
Alexandrine. Men like Emile Deschamps in the *Études françaises*,
Sainte-Beuve in the *Tableau*, had suggested a complete theory of style.
" Le vers, selon l'idée que nous en avons, ne se fabrique pas de pièces
plus ou moins étroitement adaptées entre elles, mais il s'engendre
au sein du génie par une création intime et obscure. Inséparable de
la pensée, il naît et croît avec elle; elle est comme l'esprit vital qui
le façonne par le dedans et l'organise."[8]

The basic change in poetry came about 1824 when the romanticists shifted its dominant characteristic to an emphasis on musicality. Thereafter, verse moved from the classical assimilation of poetry to painting, impeccable in design but colorless, to a modification of the precepts current during the 16th century. The essential problem of early 19th-century writers became that of abolishing the monotonous melody of the Alexandrine by avoiding the pitiless break of the old caesura and the cymbal clash of the final rhyme. In addition, they faced the task of renewing the vocabulary of poetry by making possible the use of all words, thus avoiding the complications of periphrasis. Under the neo-classical system a poet uttered plaintive cries, invoked the gods, beseeched kings, turned with horror from a sight that jangled his quivering nerves, but nevertheless paused breathlessly in the midst of a line, to begin again on a calmer tone, always respectful of caesura and rhyme. The classicists submitted to the ordeal of a kind of verbal gymnastics that failed to appeal to the 19th century.[9] The romanticists conceived of beauty on another plane, approached by different means and without the aid of the grammarians.

A large part of the romantic revolt was aimed precisely at these grammarians. On the advice of the latter, the classicists had arbitrarily divided the vowels and consonants into agreeable and disagreeable sounds. It was strictly forbidden to employ those considered harsh unless they were needed for a special effect. This attitude persisted until the romanticists questioned the phonetic values originally assigned and decided to associate sounds which a previous age had judged cacophonic. Imitative harmony as a conscious literary procedure disappeared, to be replaced by assonance and alliteration. Becq de Fouquières, theorist of romantic verse, even succeeded in completely reducing the new poetry to this system, but it was one in which assonance and alliteration lost constant ideational values and were utilized primarily to produce vague feelings, a state of mind, even the evocation of a landscape.

In their desire to attain lyricism, the romanticists destroyed the old caesura, when they replaced the earlier type of the Alexandrine with a *trimètre* or a *ternaire romantique*. By such means they avoided the accentuation of the sixth syllable, which had marked the older form and almost completely shackled poetry. All kinds of innovations were introduced, from creating three unequal segments to surrounding the median syllable with two strong *coupes*, one before and one after the hemistich. According to the strictest rules of classical versification the caesura marked the point where the voice reached its maximum force, then dropped progressively to the end of the line. The hemistich, therefore, possessed a constant musical value directly opposed to that of the rhyme. The romanticists fought this restriction on principle, since that it hampered their efforts toward the musicality and suppleness they desired.

Once having destroyed the caesura, the romanticists then turned to another problem. Rhyme for the 18th-century poet had meant a concluding intonation, and the final syllable had possessed a traditional modulation. Since this, too, blocked the possibility of a more supple line, the new school decided to practice *enjambement*. Furthermore, the romanticists shunned the past century's affection for endings in *er*, *é*, *ant*, or *able*, all considered flat. For them rhyme signified a harmony, not an artifice : it had musical value and they also expected it to possess color and picturesque qualities, in other words, to be rich.

In their search for a new music, the romanticists did not fail to consider the lines of various lengths which they had inherited. As a result the octosyllabic returned to favor, displacing the previously popular decasyllabic. Curiously, whenever the decasyllabic was employed, it was used according to the old construction of 5 + 5. With this exception, the romanticists revived and honored most of the shorter forms, which they employed with considerable virtuosity. In general the young rebels abandoned the elegy, the eclogue, the satire, the *épître*, and the didactic form, but they changed even those genres which they did accept from the classicists by judiciously mixing them to produce the lilting quality they so ardently sought. The heterometric system of versification appeared more frequently than the isometric, since combinations of strophes of different lengths permitted almost an infinite variety of rhythms and tones.

Within the strophe, the romanticists accomplished another great revolution. In addition to the techniques of displacing the caesura, using *enjambement* and heterometric forms, they changed rhythm by piling up sequences of proper names. Allegory practically disappeared, relieving the poet of the burden of the personification of Vice, Virtue, Evil, and Justice. No more did Father Time drag his scythe bumpily along the Alexandrine, and " poetic " words were

replaced by the *terme propre*. Spades became shovels. Romanticism
tried simultaneously to materialize and to sensualize poetic style. The
ordinary words of daily living, the common things of existence, now
fell within the province of the writer. This injected more color into
verse and ultimately led to the creation of some very exotic vocabularies.
As Gautier wrote : " J'ai attifé un peu ma phrase... j'ai cousu des
paillettes à sa robe de toile... En deux traits de plume, je m'en vais
lui faire une jupe d'adjectifs, un corset de périphrases et des panaches
de métaphores."[10]

Actually, despite their boasts, the great men of the first generation
were not nearly so venturesome and radical as they claimed. Pierre
Moreau's work on the *Classicisme des romantiques* demonstrates how
timidly the romanticists diverged from the art of their forebears.
Lamartine remained fairly indifferent to the vaunted reform of the
Alexandrine; Musset, at first a leading rebel, soon became bored with
the revolution; Vigny spent a great part of his life modifying the
opinions of his youth. Even in the matter of rhyme the first generation
experimented timidly, however much they fussed over *rime riche* or
plate. The famous *vers brisé* served to translate poetically the nature and
swing of simple conversations, but it was used for little else. The
romanticists talked loudly of reform though they actually did little
more than indicate possibilities.[11]

III

The very fact that the first romanticists became involved with the
consequences of the Industrial Revolution helped influence their
decision to abandon the prosodic revolution so proudly begun. During
the twilight of the Restoration they had carefully investigated the
possibilities of verse and had reached some radical conclusions concerning its structure. Unfortunately, at the moment they had convinced
the nation of their right to experiment, other factors intruded to alter
the development of their ideas. They consciously chose to become
involved in their age and consequently had to adjust their initial
position. As self-proclaimed, but self-supporting, Messiahs they needed
to reach the new public, and to do so effectively, they were almost
forced to accept prose. Even when they continued to write poetry
they could not, under the circumstances, experiment too radically

for fear of losing an easily baffled audience. Given the choice between further innovation and the more substantial rewards of prose or a political life, the elders did not even hesitate. They quietly resigned from the revolution.

To be sure, the revolt continued. Sainte-Beuve always kept alive a flickering hope for the possibility of a rejuvenated poetry, and in his later years Hugo practiced many of the changes he had previously preached. But it remained for the relatively unknown followers of art for art's sake to fulfill the promise of the preface of *Cromwell* and to endow the Parnassians and the Symbolists with the means to create a modern poetry. Philothée O'Neddy pointed out in a fragment of an unpublished work, *Une Fièvre de l'époque,* that in 1830 some six thousand young men stood ready to serve as neophytes in the new religion of art.[12] As fervent as converts, they burned to carry out the plans outlined in Hugo's *Orientales,* to remake art from top to bottom, and to loose on society the creativeness of their inflamed imaginations. This they resolved to do in the consciousness that they alone defended a cause they considered sacred and they were quite willing, at first, to accept as a price for their " mission " the possibility that society might reject them, just as they were determined to repudiate the dubious advantages of 19th-century civilization.

But the society of 1830 offered a climate hostile to such dreams, dominated as it was by the triumphant followers of Louis-Philippe. The reading public now consisted of a vast, amorphous middle class that was interested primarily in the pragmatic or the escapist. No matter how neat the phrase, how clever the rhyme scheme, the people for whom these niceties were destined all seemed to have faded into a Golden Age of the past. Gautier announced this disappointing discovery to the hosts of would be poet-laureates :

Autrefois il y avait un parterre composé de connaisseurs, d'hommes instruits, qui avaient fait leurs humanités, qui pesaient une pièce vers par vers, qui dissertaient sur la nuance et la portée d'un mot...; ces gens-là sentaient la valeur d'une définition ingénieuse, d'une maxime bien frappée, d'une expression poétique; ils en savaient plus long sur le français que bien des académiciens d'aujourd'hui. Pour un pareil public, des gens de lettres et des poètes pouvaient écrire, ils étaient sûrs d'être compris.[13]

Now the average reader had metamorphosed into an ogre. Instead of the suave, distinguished aristocrat, there appeared a business man who sought in literature the defense and illustration of his way of life. He stood for the penny saved, the bird in hand, administrative efficiency, and the sanctity of the conservative way of life. The French version of Poor Richard had a horror of sudden, unexplained change; the middle of the road agreed with him, and what had suited his grandfather was almost certain to please him. His mind followed prose more easily than anything but double-entry bookkeeping. Now that France had a constitutional monarch, this was the best of all possible worlds and woe to him who tried to change it.

The young poets soon discovered that their wares had no sales value to men of such mind. Public lack of appreciation, a scarcity of sales, and even open hostility on the part of the newspapers soon convinced the fledglings that society had no place for them. At the very start of his career, a feeling of frustration settled on the Jeune-France when he found to his dismay that the word " culture " was open to many interpretations, none of which included him. " Oh, que c'est malheureux que le poète soit homme !" Xavier Forneret wailed.[14] The so-called " poète maudit " came into existence, as a new version of the Byronic hero, isolated from the common run of society and distinguished from his fellow man by a feeling of otherness. He neither judged like others, nor seemed to feel the same sensations. More important, he did not see the world as they did, and he came to consider himself as living in another universe, grander, more mysterious and more desirable than a mere heaven filled only with angels. He knew that the bourgeois considered him dangerous to established order and he huddled together for mutual protection with the other literary outlaws of his age.

This sense of being outcast would generate in the young men a whole pattern of attitudes, chief among which was a publicly-avowed hatred for the middle-class, which they blamed for all their difficulties. To them, the bourgeoisie had woven a monstrous plot to prevent youth from earning its share of the world's plaudits. Therefore, they swore an undying enmity for Louis-Philippe, and Philothée O'Neddy acted according to pattern when he snapped in *Feu et flamme* (1833) : " Je méprise de toute la hauteur de mon âme l'ordre social et surtout l'ordre politique qui en est l'excrément." This was the proper sentiment for a *bousingo* in good standing, as Charles Lassailly agreed :

Quand partout débordait la plate bourgeoisie
Ainsi qu'un monstrueux crapaud,
Crevant d'aise à ramper dans l'écume moisie
Dont il se gorge, le ribaud...[15]

Alphonse Rabbe disdained " ce peuple imbécile," but the inimitable Pétrus Borel delivered the insult deadly where he expected it would most hurt the enemy. In the preface to *Champavert* he provocatively introduced a short essay on the topic : " Marchand et voleur est synonyme."

Anything that could sting the middle class served as ammunition. Hence Pétrus illogically paraded the reddest of Republicanism before a conservative public he expected to purchase his *Rhapsodies*, while O'Neddy shouted " malédiction sur la mère-patrie." In the *Roueries de Trialph*, Lassailly's hero explained his politics to the heroine in a decidedly unconventional manner. " Un matin que je rencontrerai la signora Société dans les rues de Paris, je veux en passant, lui jeter au nez cette prédiction qu'elle mourra l'année prochaine, s'il éclôt par hasard en France trois faquins de bouffons comme moi."

Here, for the first time, the avant-garde of literature moved to the left politically in reaction against the arbiters of current taste. It henceforth became the fashion for poets to be in " advance " of their times, to espouse deliberately political doctrines objectionable to the majority of their fellow citizens. It was one way of expressing contempt for the common man. Each rebel would fall from the exaltation of finishing first verses into the black despair that followed the shock of rejection, then react wildly by seeking to correct by violent means a social situation in which his work had no value.

Not all the young romanticists, of course, flaunted an exasperating radicalism, but almost all revolted religiously. Though their youth made some of them indifferent to politics, this same lack of years led them to a vehement attack on Christianity. Not many seasons had passed since their first Communion; all could still remember clearly the responses of their catechism. Therefore, in their fury at the conservative, they struck at what they considered his most cherished belief, repeating, as did O'Neddy, that :

Depuis longtemps j'ai dit un éternel adieu
A l'absolvo du prêtre, aux hymnes du saint lieu.

For the Christ of the bourgeois they substituted Lucifer. Satan

attracted them not only because he had been properly introduced
by Byron, but because he symbolized the greatest revolt the mind
of man could imagine.

In their bitterness they confused hate for the creature with hate for
the Creation, and this feeling they expressed in terms remembered
from their religious education. Borel had attended the seminaries
of Saint-Roch and Sainte-Elizabeth; Esquiros had been a pupil of
the Abbé Colonna at Saint-Nicolas; Lassailly had enjoyed a reputation
as a pious child. Such a background titillated their senses, gave more
force to their rebellion, and even made their violence more blasphemous.

> Malice de l'enfer !... A nous la guillotine !...
> A nous qui n'adorons rien que la trinité
> De l'amour, de la gloire et de la liberté !...
> Ciel et terre !... Est-ce que les âmes de poète
> N'auront pas quelque jour leur revanche complète ![16]

Almost to a man they cultivated a frenzied mock Satanism that
heaped scorn on the national religion. Esquiros wrote anti-clerical
novels; Lassailly supposedly never went to bed without offering choice
bits of blasphemy to the god of the bourgeoisie. This kind of defiance
apparently gave greater satisfaction because it was couched in the
language of the adversary, and they came with great pride to consider
themselves kin to the fallen archangel, fellow pariahs, " maudits," " dam-
nés." For some, like Jean Polonius, the revolt led to a kind of Titanism
in which the poet dreamed of helping Satan storm the heavens.[17]

The acceptance of damnation led them to associate their condition
with all the great rebels of mythology, a comforting, if somewhat
egotistical, position. From this they passed to one where they pictured
their heroes in the image of Satan, or the Titans, or of themselves.
Lassailly's unbelievable Trialph was affectionately called Satanas by
his mistress, an identification quite in keeping with the hero's vicious
habits. But Jules Lefèvre-Deumier apparently outdistanced them
all in the Martyrs d'Arezzo, which seems the first attempt in the
novel to identify human and demoniac psychology. While drawing
a portrait of Lucifer, the painter Aretino feels himself invaded by
his subject to the point where, despite himself, his mind passed through
all the degrees of Satan's revolt, to arrive with the archangel at the
verge of the fall he was about to paint. Esquiros tried to match this,
but could only succeed in boasting :

J'ai...
Forcé dans la nuit à me parler un peu
Ce serpent qui promit de faire l'homme Dieu.

The rebellion, religious, political, and economic, the hatred for the
middle class, led to the introduction into literature of a new brand
of humor as another way of teasing the bourgeoisie. Characters
calculated to infuriate the more moderate citizen crowded the pages
of the young writers. From the terror novel they borrowed ragged
tramps, hideous monsters and weird rites; from the vogue for the
medieval came supernatural creatures, scenes of black magic or dark
violence, as in Gautier's *Albertus*. To them they added spendthrifts,
adulterers, men-about-town, all treated sympathetically in direct
hostility to the established moral values. Borel uttered strange pro-
phecies in *Madame Putiphar*, even announcing the coming of the
Avenging Angel under the guise of a deep red lobster with no blood
in its veins. In *Champavert*, he antagonized readers with provocative
epigraphs, chapter titles in English, Latin, Spanish, or Provençal.
Andréas Vesalius, the hero, murders his wife's lover not only to
satisfy a desire for revenge, but also to discover the laws of locomotion
and the circulation of the blood, a fact he generously reveals to his
wife shortly before his scalpel dissects her, too. Borel's friends delighted
in convincing their neighbors that they held wild orgies, drank flaming
punch from the skulls of dead mistresses, or summoned the devil
from the depths of hell. Certainly the staid *Figaro* of 1831 gave this
impression in a series of satires on the Jeune-France, and men like
O'Neddy were only too glad to perpetuate the myth in works like
Pandaemonium (1833). In *Madame Putiphar*, Borel favored bloody
scenes in which virtue always suffered at the hands of leering rascals,
but Trialph seems to top all these psychological misfits. To one of
his mistresses, he declared his affection in unorthodox terms : " Je
vous aime autant que la République." So original was Trialph that
when he decided to rid himself of a bothersome girl, he nonchalantly
tickled the bottoms of her feet until she expired with a choked giggle.
The acid Jules Janin scolded writers for pandering to the current
peculiar taste for macabre sensations but, even so, his own *L'Ane
Mort et la femme guillotinée* was jammed with executions, burials, and
scenes in the morgue.

The young men enjoyed their morbid jokes but they also worked hard. Since art had become for them an absolute which replaced religion and country in their system of values, they also lavished on their work the hot emotion involved in their frenzied hates and pseudo-Satanism. It seemed all they had in a materialistic world, and they paid deep reverence to their god as each made obeisance in his own way. The old conception of poetry gave way to a new prosody, implicit in the way they handled their verse, explicit in their proudly trumpeted declarations of faith :

> L'Art vrai sur tous les flots toujours vogue en aval.
> Il est jaloux, tyran, et n'a point de rival...
> Si vous choisissez l'Art, repoussez loin le monde :
> A l'Art tous nos pensers, point de commerce immonde;
> Car il se vêt de lin, et ses pieds argentés,
> Quand on les traîne en ville, en reviennent crottés.[18]

Any justification needed for this new religion they could easily find in the masters of the great generation, but in one way the pupils differed radically from their teachers. A hint of this can be discerned in the titles of their works. Amidst the *Pandaemoniums*, the *Incantations*, and the *Succubes*, are found the *Onyx* of Charles Coran (1840), the *Auréoles* of Siméon Chaumeir (1841), Arthur Ponroy's *Formes et couleurs* (1842), to say nothing of Banville's *Stalactites*. A new kind of plastic romanticism was being born that led straight to the Parnassians. With the fashioning of verse now compared to the carving of stones, or the shaping of statues, as well as the painting of pictures and the creation of melodies, the poets were on the verge of the theory of the transposition of the arts.

To a large extent the young men continued along the way indicated by Hugo and Lamartine but, in some important respects, they struck out on their own. For one thing, as their choice of titles indicated, they had come to consider poetry as a resistant medium in which each verse was to be cut as finely and carefully as a gem. Consequently, they shifted away from the organic theory of art so common to their elders by admitting the difficulties of creation. Hugo, like Lamartine, had insisted on trying to convince readers that the genius differed from the craftsman. Since the genius carried within him a divine spark, his work showed the hand of God. When an idea came to mind, he committed it to paper, and from the original inspiration the work sprang full blown. Thus, all the parts of a novel, the chapters and the paragraphs, followed one after another in proper order from the moment pen met paper; the lines of a poem flowed as preordained from the poet's " soul." Hugo had even proclaimed in the preface of *Notre-Dame de Paris* that " une fois la chose faite, ne vous ravisez pas, n'y retouchez plus." To do so might cast doubt on the artist's talent.

Such an attitude appealed to the Cénacle, but the youngsters, less gifted than their elders and more in love with their art, preferred to lavish time and lovingkindness on their lines. Unlike Lamartine, they did not feel the need to convince anybody that their work was divinely inspired. Thus, in some ways, Gautier's *Art poétique* is less a forecast than the literary testament of the young *bousingos* with whom Théophile had lived in the days of the first Bohemia.

Since the Jeune-France prided himself on his verse, he delighted in the experiments which his conception of art tended to encourage. For one thing, he followed Sainte-Beuve in resuscitating the sonnet; the longer poetic forms, in fact, the young men tended to disregard. The Comte de Gramont, as Gautier pointed out in *Les Progrès de la poésie française* composed a large number of sonnets for which Théophile had the greatest respect. Furthermore, Gramont had experimented in a new form called *rhythmes*, and had even succeeded in reproducing the difficult *sextines*, in which the rhymes of the first stanza change place in the following stanzas, intertwined, and always repeated. The young Henri Blaze de Bury had written " Le Souper chez le commandeur " for the *Revue des Deux Mondes* (1833), a bizarre work in which he tried to marry prose to poetry in a pseudo-Shakespearian alliance. Pierre Dupont, later a close friend of Baudelaire, invented a kind of chanson that owes nothing to Béranger, and which hides its delicacy under apparent rusticity. In *Pandaemonium*, O'Neddy played with verse forms just as Hugo had done in the *Odes* and *Ballades*. He combined the " free " Alexandrine with lines of 8 syllables; he alternated strophes of 5 lines of 8-syllable verse with strophes of 6 lines, 5 Alexandrines, the 6th of 8 syllables. Later Leconte de Lisle would show a marked preference for the same 5 line stanza which O'Neddy sometimes practiced. Philothée not only delighted in such novelties, he also utilized a precision of imagery which seems to be of later date.

Even the hated prose attained new prestige when the *poème en prose* attracted many of the experimenters. In *Feu et flamme* O'Neddy had claimed that the aesthetics of the Jeune-France called for a deep hatred of the bourgeoisie, the code and prose. But apparently the addition of the word *poème* magically altered the language of M. Jourdain for, as early as 1828, Louis Bertrand had informed David d'Angers that he was trying to create a new genre in prose.[19] Baudelaire would later take the idea from him, though there the borrowing stopped.

To be sure, poetic prose had existed prior to the romantic age, and occasionally it is pointed out that bits like Lucile de Chateaubriand's *Invocation à la lune* approximate this genre.[20] Nonetheless, Bertrand made a distinct contribution by making the prose poem a form and not an effusion, and this in the face of the disapproval of men like Vigny, who stated flatly in his *Journal* (1834) that there was no such thing as a prose poem. *Gaspard de la Nuit* is artistically constructed according to a plan, with each evocation adding to the impression of an organic whole. This same hope of marrying prose and poetry was also motivating others for, almost at the same time that *Gaspard* appeared, another Burgundian, Xavier Forneret, published a similar collection, *Vapeurs, ni prose ni vers*. Two years later (1840), Forneret again completed a volume of prose poems, *Pièce des pièces, temps perdu*, a curious work printed only on one side of the page, prepared typographically and technically with the greatest care.

But perhaps the most ambitious of them all was Maurice de Guérin's *Centaure*. Written during 1835-1836, it offers a dialogue in which only one voice is heard : " Accord du sens, dans sa plus profonde logique, avec les images et les mots, leurs signes sonores, accord de la syntaxe et de son rythme propre avec l'émotion et ses tremblements."[21] Using tonic rhythms, Guérin cadenced his prose almost arithmetically, played with alliteration, and occasionally even introduced a discreet bit of rhyme. The repetition of a kind of refrain, or rather the clever manipulation of assonance, created the atmosphere desired. Guérin even utilized the " blanc " in his phrases to vary the rhythm of the prose, proceeding after each with a substitution of ideas, constantly progressing harmoniously toward a given end. As Bernard d'Harcourt has shown, a typographical rearrangement of the prose in lines of varying lengths as suggested by the " blancs," indicates the amazing skill and sensitivity used in the construction of Guérin's verse.[22] Here a younger romanticist had pushed the limits of art far beyond those indicated by his predecessors.

But the Petit Cénacle excelled in theory as well as in technique. Like so many of the ideas exploited in the thirties, the theory of correspondences, a kind of French transcendentalism, had been voiced a decade earlier. In his *Cours d'esthétique*, Jouffroy had offered a principle on which they might build : " L'invisible est le vrai pouvoir esthétique." What counts for the writer is not apparent reality, but that which it expresses. For him the entire universe hid a living force and power perceptible only to the most sensitive. Thus, the role of the conscious artist was to interpret the symbols surrounding man and to seek the true meaning of objects. Sainte-Beuve momentarily perceived it. In *Joseph Delorme* he touched on transcendentalist theory when he glorified the poet who has " reçu en naissant la clef des symboles et l'intelligence des figures." But he never explored the road for himself. Others, like Jules Lefèvre-Deumier, reacted more positively to the possibilities of such ideas. His *Explication des songes* admitted the necessity of a poetic approach to metaphysics : " Je m'étais fait, dans ma jeunesse une théorie des âmes aussi neuve que bizarre, et qui ne laissait pas d'être ingénieuse et poétique. Je me figurais que l'âme n'était point en nous; qu'elle était extérieure, une sorte de fil électrique qui nous suspendait à la main du Tout-Puissant et nous communiquait ses volontés."[23]

Certainly, the *bousingo* thought a great deal of the supernatural when he was not busy shocking the bourgeoisie. In the *Parricide* (1823) Lefèvre's Edgar, like many of his contemporaries, felt himself exiled to earth from his proper sphere. Thus the young men simultaneously revolted against the god of the middle class, and sought the peace and security of a vision of the " au-delà," reserved for their own eyes, and hidden from materialistic shopkeepers. It was an exciting thought, no less so because it did not logically match their other attitudes. After all, theirs was not a rational world but one of vision and faith in the sanctity of their task.

Hence their concern with dreams, and the sybilline nature of some of their later work. This, of course, had originated with such recent ancestors as Nodier. *Smarra* had indicated the way for the new disciples, and they could feel free to dabble in surreality, to explore the possibilities of ghosts, were-wolves, or nightmares, long before Baudelaire. Nerval in the *Chimères*, Nodier, or Guérin, had sensed the possibility of groping through the mists of reality via dreams.

In the case of Guérin's *Centaure*, the dream itself formed the basis of the work. Macarée offers the key to the symbols that throng the work : Life is a game played on two stages : actuality, and the reflected vision of something which, to the poet is grander and more important. Guérin sees " visions en ombres vagues et fuyantes," " formes ondoyantes et lumineuses," which he hopes to capture for the reader. To some writers this aspect of their work became so important that they tried to transcend reality by the use of drugs, in the hope that narcotics might offer a key to the beyond.

But despite all the effort, despite all the theorizing, the young romanticists fought a losing battle, a fact which they came to appreciate slowly and tragically. And the moment they realized their plight a new *mal du siècle* was born, one that would plague Maldoror. Little by little, they discovered that talent alone did not suffice for the task they had set; they suspected that the genius they attributed to themselves did not really exist. Somehow life had not been changed by their revolt, nor had they stormed the heights of Heaven. In effect they realized that their revolution had failed pitifully as one by one they came to the same bitter frame of mind as Xavier Forneret : " Oh ! que c'est malheureux que le poète soit homme !" The question of their genius became a torment, almost a punishment for their defiance of God, as Jules Lefèvre noted when he complained of his " feu dévorant." In *Gaspard de la nuit* Aloysius Bertrand likened poetry to an almond tree, with its perfumed flowers and its bitter fruit. For thirty years Gaspard sought the end of the rainbow that would yield a magic formula for great poetry, but in the end he could only conclude, " Le néant ne vivifie le néant." That which the young men held priceless had turned to brass. For them there remained only the bleakness of despair when their proud hopes disintegrated in self-condemnation. " Mon malheur passe de beaucoup ce que j'imaginais," cried Rabbe.[24] More pathetically, Borel summed up in *Madame Putiphar* a life of failure for all the might-have-beens who had dared dream of changing the course of literary history in the wake of Lamartine and Hugo :

> Une douleur renaît pour une évanouie;
> Quand un chagrin s'éteint c'est qu'un autre est éclos;
> La vie est une ronce aux pleurs épanouie.

They felt so frustrated that Rabbe prepared the *Philosophie du désespoir* for them as a justification of suicide.   And suicide seemed their last right, for all else had been taken from them.   It was only decent that society grant them the privilege of recognizing their own inadequacy, of allowing the individual to greet " le dernier combattant, le cavalier sonore," whenever he thought fit.   In a sense it also constituted a last defiance of society, a pathetic flight into the " beyond " they had so bravely sought.   And well they might escape, for their group had reached the curious stage where Gautier, once the darling of Bohemia, could mock his former friends.   In the *Jeunes-France*, Daniel Jovard, the *bousingo*, became the caricature of a gallant attempt. This marked the end of the line, but not before a group of writers who would impress history little had nonetheless set the pattern for greater men, for Lautréamont, or, more importantly, for Baudelaire.

NOTES

1. *Premiers Lundis*, I, 394-406.
2. G. Matoré, " Art et artistes, " *Revue des Sciences Humaines*, avril-septembre 1951, p. 125.
3. *Correspondance générale*, Paris, Stock, 1935, I, 417.
4. Jules Marsan, " La Réaction bourgeoise, " in *La Bataille romantique*, Paris, Hachette, *2me* série, n.d.
5. January 16, 1837.
6. *Correspondance générale*, Paris, Stock, 1936, II, à Céphas Rossignol, 22 janvier 1839.
7. *Ibid.*, 18 mai 1838.
8. Jules Marsan, *La Bataille romantique*, Hachette, 1912, séries I, 179.
9. G. Lote, " Le Vers romantique, " *RCC*, XXXII, 1re série, p. 189.
10. G. Lote, " Le Vers romantique, " *RCC*, XXIII, 1re série, 219.
11. G. Lote, " Le Vers romantique, " *RCC*, XXXI, pp. 88, 93.
12. Ernest Havet, *Notice sur Philothée O'Neddy*, Paris, Charpentier, 1877, p. 26.
13. G. Lote, " Le Vers romantique, " *RCC*, XXXII, 1re série, pp. 45-46.
14. Francis Dumont, " Xavier Forneret, " in *Les Petits Romantiques français*, Paris, Cahiers du Sud, 1949, p. 139.
15. *Poésie sur la mort du fils de Bonaparte*, Paris, Renduel, 1832.
16. O'Neddy, *Feu et Flamme*.
17. Armand Hoog, " Révolte métaphysique des petits romantiques, " in Francis Dumont, *Les Petits Romantiques français*, Paris, Cahiers du Sud, 1949, p. 25.
18. Pétrus Borel, *Rhapsodies*, Paris, La Force Française, 1922, pp. 227-8.
19. Jules Marsan, *Bohème romantique*, Paris, Cahiers Libres, 1929, p. 17.

20. René Lalou, *De Sainte-Beuve à Baudelaire*, Paris, Crês, 1927; Vista Clayton, *The prose poem in French literature of the 18th century*, New York, Institute of French Studies, 1936.

21. Bernard d'Harcourt, *Maurice de Guérin et le poème en prose*, Paris, Presses Universitaires, 1932, p. 221.

22. *Ibid.*, p. 354 ff.

23. Hoog, *loc. cit.*, p. 21.

24. *Album d'un pessimiste*, Paris, Presses Françaises, p. 123.

CHAPTER 8

A PEOPLE'S LITERATURE: THE SPONSORS

THE FEELING OF futility which haunted the young poets deepened even more when they became aware of a new phenomenon, the rise of a competing literature aimed at the people. Ironically, most of it was written in verse and had been sponsored by those of the Cénacle who had deserted experimental art for utilitarianism. The beloved poetry of the purists was twice debased and, worse still, the new industrial age seemed destined to destroy all beauty.

As the new technical factors introduced by the Industrial Revolution coincided about 1830 with the rise in literacy, France saw the birth of a literature written by the people for themselves. Similar works had, of course, existed in some measure since the Middle Ages, but most of them had been oral and restricted to small regions. No true people's literature on a national basis could exist until technology permitted cheap, quantity publication, the general educational level rose, and the workers gained a sense of class unity. And these three prerequisites were not fulfilled until the beginning of the July Monarchy, when the people became a recognizable political and economic entity. By then the workers had become sufficiently educated to participate in the intellectual movements then developing in France. Simultaneously economists and reformers of all manner began to address countless pamphlets to the people. It was the age of the followers of Saint-Simon and Fourier, and despite the fact that most leaflets did not reach their destination, they caused deep ferment. The workers began to consider themselves as apart, with special problems of their own. A feeling of difference, even hostility toward the middle classes, lay beneath the surface of an apparent tranquillity.

The first sign of their reaction to the industrial age came in a flurry of newspapers which preached the gospel of class unity. These enjoyed a few lusty shouts in demand of the rights of the proletariat, then sank into oblivion. Not until about 1840 did there appear any workers' papers of consequence. A second development came through the *goguette*, the poor man's singing society. These, too, had long existed, but now the various groups sang songs to fit contemporary conditions and, more important, yearned to immortalize in print what they had created. Those romanticists who accepted the new age, the " utilitarians," smiled benignly on this movement; and each hastened to establish himself as the patron of one or more fledgling authors. It became a style, a mark of literary status, to aid worker-writers.

At first the protégés responded by imitating their gods, copying their techniques and themes. Since most of the greats of the early July Monarchy were poets, the workers at first accepted the great tradition of the primacy of verse, though later they transferred allegiance to prose. Roughly, this literature may be assigned to four categories : 1) a very small literature in dialect; 2) poetry and prose, for the most part extremely religious in feeling, which portrayed simple rural pleasures and the joys of resignation; 3) an urban poetry imitative of the contemporary masters which described the life of the worker; and 4) a primarily urban literature that became more and more socialistic in tone as 1848 approached.

This new kind of writing, sponsored by the romanticists, in turn affected them curiously. Aware of the emergence of another social class, they began to note carefully its changes of moods, its desires and hopes. Each would adjust his particular kind of writing to take into account the aspiration of the new class, thus creating a second revolution.

I

Immediately after the July Revolution, the strict censorship maintained by the Bourbons lifted momentarily. During that moment of grace, a few groups of workers took advantage of the respite to found newspapers. In Paris, most of these proved ephemeral, with runs of scarcely a week or more; but in September, 1830, the workers' press began a long career when on the 19th the *Journal des Ouvriers* appeared, on the 26th, *L'Artisan*, and, four days later, *Le Peuple, journal général des ouvriers, rédigé par eux-mêmes*. In the belief that the Orléans Monarchy heralded a great social transformation, they immediately concerned themselves with political questions. Mostly the papers registered a hatred for the machines that were then appearing; only the *Artisan* dared praise the monsters on the grounds that they would relieve daily drudgery in the factory. Little was said of the right to unite; in fact, most of the demands seemed moderate and restrained. In Lyon the same phenomenon occurred, though papers there seemed to last longer. *L'Echo des travailleurs, La Glaneuse, Le Précurseur, L'Echo de la fabrique, La Tribune prolétaire*, and others duplicated the efforts of their Parisian colleagues. For a time all enjoyed the rare privilege of freedom.

But only momentarily. At first too busy to notice the new spirit of the workers, the Orléans government suddenly awoke to what it considered a menace to the ruling class and its startled reaction was to invoke censorship again. The time of the proletarian newspapers had obviously not yet come. In addition to legal obstacles, editors sadly discovered that the public was still too small and costs too high to ensure success.

Not until much later, about 1840, when advancing technology made printing cheaper, and when some measure of education had seeped generally through the working class, did the first important workers' dailies appear. It is impossible to consider them all, but the *Atelier* and the *Ruche populaire* offer a clear view of this branch of the contemporary press. They shared their public with *le Travail*, published at Lyon from June to September, 1841, *la Fraternité*, which appeared from January, 1845, to February, 1848, and a host of shorter-lived projects.

The *Atelier*, destined for ten years of stormy life (1840-1850), represents the political side of the journalistic picture. From the day of its founding it carried a shaky chip on its shoulder : " Jusqu'à ce jour les classes ouvrières ont été défendues par des gens qui leur étaient étrangers. En conséquence, on a pu dire qu'ils ne soutenaient notre cause qu'afin de faire de nous un instrument politique destiné à être brisé aussitôt qu'il cesserait d'être utile à leur fortune." From then on it promised to defend the worker with all its angry might.

For a long time the *Atelier* ignored literature as the plaything of the useless rich, but the time came when it reluctantly recognized that at least a few workers were publishing. These men the *Atelier* regarded with deep suspicion, its criticism lavishly pro or con depending

on the amount of political consciousness it could read into a work.
It broke a long silence on the subject of literature when in May, 1842,
it deigned to recognize Poncy's *Marines*, though it found the verse
spoiled by imitation of the romanticists. Begrudgingly the editors
admitted Poncy's talent, but took him to task for prostituting art
by misusing it for personal effusions. According to them, a worker
should write only in the defense of the oppressed.

Actually the *Atelier* cared for literature only when a particular item
contained the political bias of which it approved. Thus it loudly
applauded a gem entitled " A propos des marchands fraudeurs," and
rained compliments on " 70,000 pauvres."[1] For the most part, the
paper snapped angrily at such useless frills as books. Poets? Except
for Béranger, the editors were hard put to recall any of consequence.
The theater seemed worse, but the novel drew from these experts
in calumny a veritable symphony of insults : " Nous avons peu de
choses à dire des romans, si ce n'est que tout ce que la dépravation
du dernier siècle a produit de bêtement ordurier et de corrupteur,
nos romanciers l'ont dépassé." Even the people's darling, the reportedly
humanitarian Eugène Sue, drew editorial snorts. Nothing, not even
the poor man's singing club, the *goguette*, earned a pleased smile.
The latter was castigated for inspiring only dull and insipid songs
without any clear-cut political direction.[2] This, obviously, the *Atelier*
hoped it could supply.

The *Ruche populaire*, another *journal des ouvriers rédigé et publié
par eux-mêmes*, took the opposite point of view. No love was lost
between the two, since the *Atelier* treated its colleague as weak-kneed,
while the *Ruche* retaliated by calling its rival barbaric. The *Ruche
populaire* came into being when a hundred workers united to found
the *Parti socialiste des travailleurs*, convinced that the interests of their
class were not being represented by the bourgeois press. Hands
awkward with a pen hoped to attain more skill with practice, and
the *Ruche* could thus become a school where one taught many. Though
the paper admitted no political affiliation, Vinçard, the editor, beat
the call to his fellow workers with " Appel " :

> Alerte, alerte, alerte, enfants
> De la grande patrie,
> Soldats de l'industrie,
> Garde à vous, à vos rangs !

Unlike the *Atelier*, the *Ruche populaire* favored any and all literary attempts by its subscribers. Each issue carried samples from the work of the various proletarian writers, particularly the poets. Thus, certain names reappear constantly : Michel Roly, *menuisier;* F.-C. Sailer, *typographe;* Francis Tourte, *commis en nouveautés;* Savinien Lapointe, *cordonnier;* P. Caplain, *peintre en porcelaine;* and Vinçard. These were joined by a host of lesser lights : J. M. Dufour, *cultivateur;* Mlle Cécile Dufour, *ouvrière en modes;* Robert, *tapissier;* or Robert, *fabricant de parapluies.*

Most of the poems managed to rework all the platitudes expressed since the birth of poetry. Auguste Rougbier, *typographe*, sang of the " Jeune Malade " : " Oh ! ce jour-là le ciel était bien sombre," while Carle Daniel wrote " Aux Mânes de Madame Veuve Agasse." Many poets re-discovered the wonders of nature, in masterpieces like " L'Abeille," " La Rose et la Violette," " Les Branches et les Racines," or " Le Rossignol et le Serin."

Little by little, however, these worker-poets deserted the arid fields of clichés to cultivate their own sources. From them came a new note, a long complaint on the terrible situation of their kind. Francis Tourte asked simply : " Pourquoi, Seigneur, pourquoi, n'ai-je donc que des larmes ?" but Vinçard pointedly entitled one of his class-conscious poems : " Le Prolétaire." From 1840 on, the worker-writers became increasingly critical of their lot in such works as " Travail et Misère " (Francis Tourte), or " Un Prolétaire aux riches " (Eugène Bouteiller).

When the paper first started, it pledged allegiance to the great gods of romanticism, to Béranger, Lamartine, and Hugo. The last two, particularly, held a special place in the hearts of the editors of the *Ruche populaire;* but, like jealous mistresses, the publishers carefully watched their idols, unwilling to forgive any deviation from perfection. Thus, Cécile Dufour wrote " A M. de Lamartine " to scold the author of *Jocelyn* for the line which claimed that

La seule loi du peuple est la mort au plus digne.[3]

When she reminded the ambitious politician that he was a model for all the workers, a chastened Lamartine apologized on October 26, 1840. He explained glibly that the young lady had misinterpreted him and he stood nobly on his record with the pious reminder that his entire political career spelled but one thing : " l'amour du Peuple et les institutions utilement populaires."

Hugo fared no better, despite his position as an established leader. His acceptance speech to the Academy irritated Vinçard with its inconsistencies.[4] Hugo had repeated the generally accepted cliché that, " le poète a charge d'âmes," but had unfortunately added, " qu'il a les populaces en dédain." Vinçard rushed to answer the insult with the inevitable public letter. Hugo reacted like Lamartine; he, too, explained in a masterpiece of double talk that he loved the people, that " people " did not mean " populace." But his argument did not carry; the self-appointed Messiah lost face with those he expected to follow his commandments.

The subject of the popular newspapers could, of course, be discussed at great length, but the fact remains that few of them admitted the esoteric matter of literature to their precious columns. In this regard the *Ruche populaire* stands almost alone. At a time when the notion of class struggle was just beginning to spread, it maintained a sense of proportion unknown to the *Atelier*, and it furnished a vast number of worker-writers with a medium for publication, all in the interest of a common cause.

II

Happily for the neophytes, the literary opportunities which technology and a recently acquired literacy had given them were not confined to the newspapers. There were always the *goguettes*. This institution had probably existed since the Middle Ages, but after the Restoration it became important as a breeding ground for the new literature. The singing society was to produce the first crop of popular heroes for the workers, all followers of Béranger. These were the men who prepared lilting songs for their own kind, a Pierre Tournemine, a Jean Marchand, or an Emile Debraux. About 1818, writers like them had timidly tried to make the public hear the wishes and hopes of the underprivileged when Dauphine, Perchelet, Francis, Blondel, Charles Lepage, Hippolyte Roussel, or the frères Favard chanted patriotic songs, many to the glory of the Emperor. But, until 1830, members of the *goguettes* followed current opinion on all matters, without any noticeable deviation from the norm. All went well under the Bourbons, and the people remained tranquil.

After 1830 the *goguette* experienced a tremendous expansion; singing societies sprouted all over France in the warmth of expanded political freedom. Song writers composed in hitherto undreamed of numbers and their compositions were then printed in impressive editions and sold in the workers' section. By 1845, the singing society had become so popular that in Paris alone there existed some 480 authorized clubs, each of which claimed about 20 members. And these 9600 singers produced the astounding annual total of some 15,200 songs. So numerous were the clients that enterprising publishers printed special newspapers for this audience. *Momus, Chanson, La Chanson illustrée, L'Echo lyrique, Le Divan, l'Étoile* and *La Muse gauloise* kept interested amateurs acquainted with developments in the leading singing societies.[5]

During the Orléans Monarchy the *goguettes* were classified according to the manner in which singers were accompanied. The comparatively rare *grande goguette* boasted a piano; the *petite goguette* had to be satisfied with a guitar. In addition there also existed the *goguette ballardeuse*, which specialized in caustic political songs and hence met secretly to avoid police raids. Some even followed a ritual, but all enjoyed the pleasure of such high-sounding and whimsical names as : *Amis de la vigne, les Bergers de Syracuse, Ordre lyrique des Templiers, les Rats*, or the *Enfants de l'étonnoir*. All worshipped Béranger, but other, less awesome, figures enjoyed the compliment of imitation : Louis Festeau, Elisa Fleury, Eugène Petit, Gustave Leroy, and Lachambeaudie.

Meetings followed a general pattern. They were usually held periodically in the rear of a modest cabaret, at the door of which stood a member delegated to greet guests and usher strangers to seats. On the walls were pasted the rules of the group. These, as Gérard de Nerval copied them down,[6] forbade all songs attacking religion or the government; persons under the influence of liquor could not be admitted; and anybody who persisted in a disturbance after two warnings would be asked to leave. Other signs requested respect for ladies, or carried such innocuous opinions as *Gloire à Béranger* or *Honneur aux Polonais !* Mindful of the heavy hand of the authorities, most of the *goguettes* wryly advised customers that : " Il est interdit de parler politique, mais on peut fumer." Anybody could offer to sing his own compositions and at the end of each selection the president regulated the duration of the bravos—if any. "Nous applaudissons encore une fois, bien fort, au grand plaisir d'avoir entendu notre camarade qui s'est fait l'interprète d'un tel pour les paroles et d'un tel pour la musique." If the artist happened to be a woman, the president called for heavier applause with true Gallic courtesy.

Since the police eyed the *goguettes* carefully, the political opposition had little chance to exploit the propaganda possibilities of these groups. Nevertheless, more and more unauthorized societies appeared as the Orléans Monarchy careened toward 1848. First indications were timid expressions of hope for a fuller life but, little by little, these changed to hardier demands for better working conditions. In a way, the *goguette* of the age of Louis-Philippe began to resemble such societies as the *Amis de la Gloire*, which had met unbeknownst to the Bourbons to praise Napoleon after a hearty supper of *gibelote de lapin* in some modest cabaret.

Almost inevitably, some of the *goguettes* began to change character noticeably about 1840; singing societies like *l'Enfer* met surreptitiously in secluded cabarets to sing politico-social songs and to complain of their lot under the factory system. Each member, or *démon*, arrived faithfully for the *Grande Chaudrière*, the appointed hour of meeting, at some secluded spot where he could listen to songs which the government considered seditious. Unfortunately the police managed to banish most of the membership to the local bastille, though such punishment never did stop the new trend.

III

Naturally, as some writers succeeded in attaining a modicum of reputation and in collecting an impressive heap of manuscripts, they meditated on the immortality of publication. Out of this drive would come a literature that could only have been born when romanticism and the Industrial Revolution made an alliance. Always before these authors flickered the shadow of Béranger, a hero whom they expected to emulate. But the magazines showed such contempt for their work that on July 5, 1842, one N. Martin sent Bonnaire, the editor of the *Revue de Paris*, a poem entitled *Humble requête* :

Par Apollon, Monsier B...,
Pour nous soyez plus débonnaire,
Ouvrez votre cœur aux chansons
Et votre *Revue* aux pinsons,...[7]

Since the periodicals failed to respond, other means of publication had to be sought. Occasionally, as with Agricol Perdiguier, fellow workers pooled resources to pay printing costs. In 1834, thirty-three Paris *compagnons* subsidized a selection of his songs, the pamphlet to be distributed free along the *tour de France*. Again, in 1836, twice that number united for the same purpose, bringing national fame and the attention of George Sand to *Avignonnais-la-Vertu*, carpenter.

The romanticists, that is, the " utilitarians," did not overlook the proletarian poets as they surveyed the age in which they lived. In their eagerness to shape the contemporary mind they seized on these neophytes as prospective apostles of their particular creeds and it became a point of pride for them to sponsor a worker's verse, particularly since the writer could then bask in the glory of a disciple. Each of the well-known romanticists took turns " discovering " talent and in escorting it proudly to the nearest printer. Thus, Hugo graciously welcomed Savinien Lapointe, Lamennais and Vigny entertained Poncy. Even the women, the muses of romanticism, found favorites. Marceline Desbordes-Valmore sponsored Théodore Lebreton, while Mme Amable Tastu favored Marie Carpentier and Louise Crombach. Béranger, the great god of the *goguette*, could name to his credit Lapointe, Chintreuil, Hégésippe Moreau, Magu, Eugène Pottier and Jasmin, plus an uncounted number of others who wrote to him for advice and consolation. Lamartine enjoyed a place second only to that of Béranger, with a whole string of satellites. Jean Reboul, a baker in Nîmes, Reine Garde, a dressmaker of Aix-en-Provence, Antoinette Quarré, from Dijon, and Hégésippe Moreau, all owed allegiance to the tall, handsome romantic. Eugène Sue came late to the scramble, but he managed to share with Béranger the honor of " discovering " Lapointe. Dumas and Baudelaire joined in the game; the former acted as patron for Jean Reboul, while the latter accepted Pierre Dupont as a pupil. Even such a purist as Gérard de Nerval became affected by the rage though he refrained from becoming a " sponsor." He did, however, collect some " Notes de doctrine sociale," from which he planned to write on such subjects as

8

political and property rights.[8] Not that the masters always approved
of what their pupils did. Because of haphazard education and uncertain techniques, the efforts of the protégés often seemed formless
and timid, pale imitations of the current vogue. But a large collection
of disciples confirmed the sponsors' opinion of themselves, and they
liked the heady intoxication of incense wafted from below.

Of all the great romanticists, it was probably George Sand who
best understood the phenomenon that occurred when the workers
crowded to Parnassus. Béranger may have had the adoration of the
goguette, but he gave counsel sparingly. Not so with Milady of Nohant.
She ungrudgingly bestowed her time and experience on any who
asked. Not only did she aid Agricol Perdiguier, père Magu and his
son-in-law, Jérôme-Pierre Gilland, but she lavished on Charles Poncy
and his family her large stock of love for the underprivileged. In
addition she wrote four articles in the *Revue Indépendante* on " les
poètes populaires," signed Gustave Bounib, and published the chatty
" Dialogues familiers sur la poésie des prolétaires."

In essence, she was answering the question which the publication
of the first worker-writers had posed. Immediately after 1830 critics
began to ask : Is it possible to have a proletarian literature ? Are
workers capable of creating it themselves ? Liberals answered the
first in the affirmative but George Sand was among the few to agree
to the second. Already a convert to Ballanche's doctrine of *palingénésie
sociale*, she determinedly set to work to realize the dream of a literature
created by the workers themselves, in her mind the logical continuation
of romanticism. With a kind of ferocious maternalism she espoused
the cause of the proletariat, sometimes to its discomfort, and soon
became the venerated protector of a whole circle of neophytes.

Though she lavished her advice on a large brood of beginners,
she hovered most about Poncy who, according to her, could become
the greatest poet of all France. From the moment he came to her
attention, she seized on him avidly, anxious to shape nascent talent,
to make firm, and to purify a hesitant taste. Above all, she hoped
to warn him against all that could seduce a poet. Through each of
his poems she hunted for " tainted " influences, the dandyism of the
later Musset, an unforgivable " hugotisme " that marred his proletarian
purity, or the vague religiosity of Lamartine. From her came the
most astounding of all possible advice : " Voulez-vous être un vrai

poète? soyez un saint!" Poncy must love his wife and no other, at the peril of losing his talent! On all sides she scented a conspiracy to raise him from his class, a move she contemplated with horror.[9] Yet, while keeping a tight rein, she acted as his literary agent and sent samples of his poems to influential people with a letter enjoining them to read carefully.

Throughout her correspondence with Poncy, she outlined a complete regimen for the worker-author but, more important, she also managed to theorize on the nature and function of this paragon's work. The poet of the people had lessons in virtue to give to the " corrupt " classes, but only if he remained austere and pure. To be great, Poncy must read Pierre Leroux; *she* had, " moi qui suis femme et romancier." And Poncy had ever to be careful. He could not send complimentary copies of his publications to certain famous authors, not to Musset, " il crachera sur votre volume," nor to Lerminier, that arch enemy who waited like an evil spider for naïve proletarian poets to appear.

With unconquerable optimism, George Sand persisted in trying to spread the gospel of the workers' literature. In the *Revue Indépendante*, November, 1841, she praised the work of women like Elise Moreau, Louise Crombach, Antoinette Quarré, and Marie Charpentier as well as that of her favorites. As often as possible she tried to attract attention to their productions through the medium of prefaces when, in February, 1844, she wrote an introduction to Poncy's *Chantier* that described the miracle of the new poetry. Again and again she hammered at the thesis that only Paris refused to recognize writers who had become the object of a proud cult in the provinces. And this state of affairs she blamed completely on the conservative press.[10] Meanwhile she whipped Poncy on to produce the *Chanson de chaque métier*, a volume of simple lyrics that honored the trades of the barely literate. In this way, she hoped, the rich could be taught to respect the poor and the poor to respect themselves. Her last great effort came in a preface for Gilland's *Conteurs ouvriers* (1849). A few years later, in 1852, she surveyed the reaction against the workers who had poured into the streets in 1848 and grimly assessed the results of the effort she had invested in trying to found a workers' literature : " La littérature prolétaire, il est vrai, est à cette heure enterrée."[11]

IV

Lamartine ran George Sand a close second as mentor to the proletarian poets. By 1830 the mantle of the Messiah hung heavy on his shoulders and political ambition gnawed at his heart. He eyed the people speculatively and came to a conclusion which he complacently explained to M. de Latour : " songez que toute poésie politique doit être poésie populaire, elle doit se servir du mot propre et de grosses et fortes images saisies par toutes les rudes imaginations auxquelles elles s'adressent."[12] Lamartine thus took his first timid step toward the people, and from then till his death he was to consider himself the guardian of public morality, a poet of the people and a divinely appointed reformer.

But the interpretation of the word " people " separated Lamartine from most romanticists. Reared in a feudal atmosphere, he persisted in considering the peasants the backbone of France. The new proletariat so mystified him that he never did reach a sympathetic understanding of its problems and aspirations. It always seemed an undisciplined rabble which continually threatened the national security because it stupidly refused to accept the peasant's passive contentment with his lot.

For a while he tried hard to like the new class. In 1832, on his return from England, where the Chartist movement was flourishing, Lamartine felt conscious enough of the worker's power to propose as topic for the prize essay contest of the Academy of Macon : " Déterminer les principales causes qui rendent les populations manufacturières généralement moins heureuses et moins morales que les populations agricoles." But even then he picked sides. The restlessness of pugnacious factory hands frightened him. Perhaps he remembered his own warning to Aimé-Martin : " Ne les remuez pas. Vous y trouveriez ce qui est de toute éternité : Aveuglement, nonsens, jalousie cruelle de toute supériorité sociale, lâcheté et cruauté."[13]

After his first voyage to the East, Lamartine finally realized his ambition to enter politics and this new career softened his public attitude toward the worker. In 1835 he appeared quite gracious when he wrote in an appendix to the *Voyage en Orient* of " les prolétaires ... classe qui, aujourd'hui, livrée à elle-même par la suppression de ses patrons et par l'individualisme, est dans une condition pire qu'elle n'a jamais été, a reconquis des droits stériles sans avoir le nécessaire, et remuera la société jusqu'à ce que le " socialisme " ait succédé à l'odieux individualisme." But it must be remembered that Lamartine meant socialism to be " une sorte d'assurance mutuelle à des conditions équitables entre la société possédante et la société non possédante."

With this aura of political liberalism, Lamartine moved toward a literature for the people in *Jocelyn*, a book he piously hoped to see in the pocket of every shoemaker. Here he turned to his first love, country life, and fidelity conceived in feudal terms. The proletariat lurked in the background, but only as a secondary character, smiling and contended with its lot.

However disdainful he might feel about popular literature, as a politician it behooved Lamartine to encourage the new writers, who might be useful in influencing public opinion. But he hoped to have them subscribe to his doctrine of passive submission. From time to time he sent a word of congratulation to a worker-writer, or spoke to one of the many labor groups then sprouting all over France. In the same vein, Lamartine nobly encouraged in a new preface for *Jocelyn* (September 27, 1840) the workers who spent their few moments of leisure at the hard task of creating poetry.

With them in mind, on July 6, 1843, he wrote " Des publications populaires," full of directions and advice for neophytes. For their benefit he pointed out the virtues of history as a corrective to the " immoral " theory of success. It was the people, not governments, that had to be changed. And Lamartine bemoaned the literary fare set before the masses : sinister sagas of crime, cheap novels for housemaids, atrocious almanac verse. As an alternative he suggested a paper the subscription to which would cost only 5 days work. Written from no particular political point of view, it would, he believed, operate a moral revolution in France.

This constant insistence on the slow regeneration of the worker, with few words on the improvement of his economic status, made observers like George Sand suspect the poet's motives. But Lamartine persisted in propounding his pet theories, as when he addressed the Athénée of Marseille in August, 1847. Since he apparently wholeheartedly espoused their cause, the workers listened eagerly. They all recalled that not long ago he had helped Antoinette Quarré, a

Dijon dressmaker, to publish her *Poésies* (July, 1843). Yet Lamartine squirmed at the thought that the orphan he had so nobly protected might turn into a Frankenstein at any moment. The writers he faced, once so willing to parrot the ideas of the romanticists, were stirring strangely, even letting murmurs of dissatisfaction creep into their verse.

Violent acclamations started an impromptu celebration which Lamartine accepted as gracefully as possible. A long line of workers escorted the deputy to his hotel, where a delegation awkwardly handed him a bunch of flowers. Lamartine answered a halting speech, then shook hands enthusiastically with the delegates. The ceremonies over, he retreated within the hotel, accompanied by Autran, a local poet. When the door had closed, Lamartine flung the flowers angrily against the wall and snarled, " Voilà, pourtant, à quel prix s'achète la popularité."[14]

He preferred writers more complacent in their attitude, like Reine Garde, the seamstress from Aix-en-Provence who had ground out an education by working through the textbooks of the daughters of the family for which she worked. The reading of *Jocelyn* had stirred her to imitate Lamartine in poems which received considerable local approval, and, one day, when her hero stopped in Marseille on his way to Smyrna, Reine quietly left Aix to visit him, carrying bits of poetry as a votive offering. Though he noted the monotony of her verse, the great man approved her scorn for the spirit of revolt found in men like Malfilâtre, Gilbert, or Hégésippe Moreau. Lamartine made his encouragement positive; later he was to publish her work in the *Conseiller du peuple* and to defend her against the attacks of Cuvillier-Fleury of the *Débats* and Gustave Planche of the *Revue des Deux Mondes*.

But this was still before 1848, and Lamartine then limited himself to vocal support. He carefully maintained the attitude of patron, especially since he depended on the common man for political support. The *Girondins*, in 1847, carried his usual message, but Lamartine showed a touch of cynicism when, in March, 1848, he warned Molé : " Ne lisez pas cela [les *Girondins*] ... c'est écrit pour le peuple. Il va jouer le grand rôle, il faut l'y disposer, lui donner l'aversion des supplices pour que la prochaine révolution soit pure des excès de la première. Il est de mon devoir de préparer le peuple, de me préparer moi-même; car je serai l'homme d'une société nouvelle." To Royer-Collard he spoke even more emphatically, " Je suis le Messie !"[15]

The Revolution of 1848 sadly disillusioned the neophyte leader. From a pinnacle of popularity, where he could sway crowds with the magic of his voice, Lamartine's popularity sagged to the point where he deliberately invited death at the hands of rioters. He finally retired from active politics, though he persisted in his mission. This time he would work through the medium of books for the people. But not for the workers; he had had his fill of them.

With *Geneviève* (1850), Lamartine really laid a foundation for his version of a literature for the masses, but for peasants and agricultural workers, or gentle dressmakers like Reine Garde. The preface of this homely short novel gathered together many of the ideas scattered through Lamartine's correspondence and works. Recounting the episode of Reine Garde's visit, Lamartine used the story to lecture on the need for an art designed exclusively for the people, prepared by " un génie populaire, un Homère ouvrier, un Milton laboureur, un Tasse soldat, un Dante industriel..." In ten years, he promised, there would exist even a science for the people, a journalism for the people, a philosophy, poetry, and novels for the people.

This missionary work Lamartine willingly assumed, certain he could measure up to the formidable requirements necessary for the task. He proposed simple, natural prose stories taken from the hearths of the families themselves, cheap, and written in the language of the people. Simultaneously he expected to found a newspaper to instruct subscribers in art, literature and politics. But despite all this good will, the precise direction of Lamartine's thought was betrayed in *Geneviève* by Marthe, Jocelyn's faithful country servant. In times of stress, Marthe sounded much like Reine Garde : " Mon Dieu ! faites-moi la grâce de trouver la servitude douce et de l'accepter sans murmure, comme la condition que vous nous avez imposée à tous en nous envoyant dans ce monde."

Successively Lamartine wrote the *Tailleur de pierres de Saint-Point*, *Graziella*, *Antoniella*, and *Lectures pour tous*. To these he added a long series of biographies of great men, with the moral plainly marked. And only one of his later works, the *Vie de Jacquard, mécanicien*, deals with the proletariat, though not very gently. Interspersed among these were newspapers and series such as *Le Conseiller du peuple*, *Les Foyers du peuple*, *Portraits et biographies*, and *Civilisateurs et conquérants*. In each issue of the *Conseiller* appeared an *almanach politique* for the worker, while the *Civilisateur* modestly claimed to be the Plutarch of the masses.

Meanwhile the poet still smarted at the repudiation of 1848. On January 14, 1859 he boasted publicly in an open letter to the *Union*, of having fought socialism to the death. Turning on worker-writers he jeered at the untalented mediocrity of a proletarian literature that expected to change the course of art. Four years later he warned that a nation with seven million workers in its active population needed a large, powerful, and obedient army to counterbalance " cette foule du Mont-Avenin."[16] And all this pent-up scorn exploded in the *Cours familier de littérature* on the occasion of the appearance of Hugo's *Les Misérables :*

> Le titre du livre de Victor Hugo est faux, parce que ce ne sont pas les Misérables mais les Coupables et les Paresseux car presque personne n'y est innocent et personne n'y travaille, dans cette société de voleurs, de débauchés, de fainéants, de filles de joie et de vagabonds. C'est le poème des vices trop punis peut-être, et des châtiments les mieux mérités... Ce livre d'accusation contre la société s'intitulerait plus justement l'Epopée de la canaille...

In his rejection of the urban worker, Lamartine made a serious error. Instead of enjoying the position of a 19th-century Messiah, he found himself dropping into the wake of contemporary events. As the proletariat rose to political importance, the books Lamartine ground out in his years of penury became increasingly removed from reality, never reaching the active, vocal group that created the social fact. Furthermore, in limiting himself to a literature for peasant and provincial, Lamartine deserted poetry for simple prose. He failed to renew himself artistically, even to maintain what artistry he had once possessed. Content—the propagation of his social beliefs in a series of pot boilers—stifled the poet in him. He completely lost touch with his era, and, after his death, that section of his work aged quickly and dropped into the limbo of the misconceived. Through an inability to assess his century, to retain his sense of art, Lamartine consigned a large part of his work to oblivion.

But Lamartine's change of heart failed to deter others. Even a poetic purist like Baudelaire joined the parade of those who indulged in the great game of sponsoring proletarian writers. In fact, the same interest in the new literature can be traced in most of the great romanticists, certainly those who had earned from their younger colleagues the terrible epithet of " utilitarians." But more on this subject would only lead to the tedious repetition of the same facts and a catalogue of forgotten names. For that reason the examples of George Sand and Lamartine may be considered as samples taken from a plethora of material. In a sense they represent the poles of opinion on a workers' literature and all their colleagues rallied around one or the other position. Few writers felt they could afford to overlook a phenomenon so closely associated with the spirit and fact of contemporary life.

NOTES

1. November, 1843, and December, 1843.

2. May, 1844; August, 1844.

3. September, 1840.

4. " De la populace, à propos du discours académique de M. Victor Hugo. "

5. A. Audiganne, " Du mouvement intellectuel parmi les populations ouvrières, " *RDM*, 1851, p. 909; cf. also L. Bryois, *La Goguette et les goguettiers, étude parisienne*, Paris, 1873.

6. *Petits Châteaux de Bohême*, Paris, Champion, 1926, p. 140; cf. also Georges Montorgueil, *Henri Murger, romancier de la Bohême*, Paris, Grasset, 1928, p. 21.

7. Sainte-Beuve, *Correspondance générale*, Paris, Stock, 1938, III, 174, note.

8. *Mercure de France*, 1045 (1er septembre 1950).

9. Samuel Rocheblave, " George Sand, lettres à Poncy, " *RDM*, August 1, 1909, p. 608.

10. George Sand, *Questions d'art et de littérature*, Paris, Calmann Lévy, 1878, p. 169.

11. Rocheblave, *op. cit.*, p. 926.

12. Quoted in René Doumic, " Lamartine en 1830 et le Voyage en Orient, " *RDM*, 1908, — letter of November 12, 1830.

13. Henri Guillemin, *Lamartine et la question sociale*, Genève, La Palatine, 1946, p. 207.

14. Guillemin, *op. cit.*, p. 217.

15. Henry Derieux, *Lamartine raconté par ceux qui l'ont vu*, Paris, Stock, Delamaine et Boutelleau, 1938, p. 190.

16. Guillemin, *op. cit.*, p. 206.

CHAPTER 9

A PEOPLE'S LITERATURE:
THE WRITERS

THE MATTER OF IMPOSING the worker-writer on the world turned
out to be more difficult than the romanticists first thought. France
was not frantically awaiting the literary phenomenon of the industrial
age, nor was it eager to accept just any writer, even on the recom-
mendation of the contemporary giants. The critics, especially, failed
to warm their chilly hearts at the new fires.

Sometimes it took the concerted efforts of a group to gain recognition
for the beginners and then often with dubious success. The Saint-
Simoniens, for instance, had early recognized the proletariat's
place in literature. In 1827, Allier had demanded a social art, a
position maintained in 1830 by Emile Barrault in a speech " Aux
Artistes." Hostile to the concept of pure art, the Saint-Simoniens
defended the utilitarian principle in the *Globe* (1831-32) while
simultaneously attacking the lyric themes of romanticism. As
the protector of the people the poet had to defend the rights of
the poorest and most numerous.[1] After 1830, the group began a
concerted drive to back its favorite authors, some of whose works
were later published by Boissy in the *Poésies saint-simoniennes et pha-
lanstériennes.*

The results of this patronage could have been better. A torrent
of inconsequential verse poured over France, all class conscious. Poems
to Fourier, *Aux Femmes* and *Aux Enfants*, succeeded proletarian
masterpieces on *La Phalanstérienne, Pour l'anniversaire de la naissance
du Père Enfantin* or *Le Vieux Prolétaire.* The level of production
was not likely to make Sainte-Beuve take notice. Driven by an im-
pulsion to fit their ideology to poetry, the Saint-Simoniens finally
managed to produce a workers' literature of sorts, but one in which
dogma stifled all poetry. But one thing the Saint-Simoniens did teach

the workers : to dare complain of their lot. Throughout a goodly
proportion of the poems ran a thread of discontent :

> L'esclave devient *serf*, le serf *salarié*,
> Il faudra bien un jour qu'il soit associé.

In 1841, Olinde Rodrigues more successfully presented the worker-
poets in an anthology.[2] His selections showed a catholicity of taste
that covered the gamut of recent productions, though most of the
material came from the *Ruche populaire*. Elisa Fleury, Caplain, Piron,
Poncy, Savinien Lapointe, Vinçard, all the old favorites found a niche
in his book.   In their works, this unregenerate utopian thought he
had found a way of spreading peace on earth through the miracle
of poetry. Thus, *La Poésie sociale*, from the inspirations of the great
to the popular songs of the people, could aid in the foundation of
Le Parti social. With this in mind, Rodrigues collected in a single
volume all the workers' poetry that seemed to fit his own ideas.

The selections may have helped the cause of Saint-Simonism,
but they did little for poetry. Throughout all of them threaded the
echoes of French literary tradition, with heavy emphasis on the work
of contemporaries.   Savinien Lapointe utilized the old troubadour
genre in *Le Vieux Château*, but in *L'Infanticide* came closer to his
age : the poem recounted the old story of a poor but beautiful girl
who succumbed to the wiles of a rich seducer, then killed the child
of their illicit love.   Later, in *La Rue*, he bemoaned the influence
of the daughters of Sodom over young adolescents. Like Victor Hugo,
he sentimentally foresaw the possibility of their regeneration in true love.

While the anthology offered a cross-section of imitations of the
best French poetry of the past two decades, a new sound was heard.
No longer did the worker-poet ape his patron, he began to chafe
at the restraints placed on him by the age of Louis-Philippe. Thus,
whereas Elisa Fleury staunchly advocated virtue, or Caplain counted
his blessings, and Michel Roly rhymed the tale of the nightingale
and the canary, Vinçard beat the drum of discontent in *Invocation*.

> Le peuple est encore dans les fers
> Oh ! craignez qu'en son âme,
> La flamme
> D'un feu vengeur
> Jusque dans son cœur
> Ne porte son foyer rongeur !

Even those who had earlier been satisfied to accept the life society imposed on them stirred uneasily. Roly complained of " le dur propriétaire "; Savinien Lapointe commented bitterly that " oui, le pauvre est de trop." Decidedly, the child of romanticism had shed its baby clothes and was about to live its own life.

But few were the men who fashioned anthologies of the worker-poets. For the most part, proletarian writers had to find their own publishers, and this with difficulty. For that reason the aid of the great romanticists was more than welcome. They could furnish recommendations that might conceivably pry open the doors of the publishers, a genus renowned for hardness of heart.

II

The work of the individual workers falls roughly into three categories. There were those who followed closely in the steps of the more famous romanticists, and who calmly accepted their lot; then the urban writers who, about 1840, began to dissociate themselves from the influence of the masters and to think strictly in terms of their own problems. This second group consists of the men and women who were the precursors of a later literature of class-conscious revolt. Finally, there also existed a small body of local, dialect writers with a very limited circulation. These last, however, are of little interest for present purposes since their use of patois tended to restrict their audience to the few acquainted with their language.

Of the other two groups, the largest to take adantage of its literary emancipation followed closely in the steps of the great romanticists. All of these particular worker-writers accepted the world in which they lived without a murmur and without much imagination. Most of their poems merely chanted the praises of God or consisted of conventional lyrics dedicated to the idols. Jean Reboul, a baker from Nîmes, for instance, had met Lamartine in 1828, at a time when the baker had not yet reached fame, but Reboul never forgot either his gracious welcome or the limpidity of his verse. This style Jean tried to copy, with sufficient success to make Dumas comment that the people had now found their own Lamartine.[3] When Reboul fully acknowledged his debt, a compliment no sponsor could overlook broadcasting, Lamartine answered with *Le Génie dans l'obscurité* in tones guaranteed to heap credit on both Reboul and himself. His protégé thereupon dedicated a series of poems to the great; beyond that he padded his volume with the usual poems : *A la Vierge, Au Christ* and *Mes Premiers Vers.*

Magu, *tisserand à Lizy-sur-Ourcq* (Seine-et-Marne), followed the same pattern. His favorites, too, were Lamartine, Byron, and Chateaubriand, with the curious addition of Voltaire, but it goes almost without saying that Béranger occupied first place in his heart. Magu apparently struck Paris as more important than Reboul, for in 1839 he earned the honor of a phrenological study as a preface to his *Poésies.* Like Reboul, Magu could boast very little schooling, a mere three winters' worth at Tancrou; yet he managed to become a part-time poet despite the affliction of cataracts, writing gently of the " douleurs d'artisan," or the " amère contemplation de l'état social." Most of his work appeared in a great scattering of provincial papers like the *Mémorial Dieppois,* the *Annonciateur du Cher,* and even the *Journal de Phrénologie.* The major part of his verse can be classified as *vers de circonstance,* yet, despite his repeated flattery of the established masters, Magu still kept sufficient sense of proportion to poke fun at the current tendency toward préciosité in *Un Romantique rencontre sa maîtresse.* Even so, Paris made a lion of him for a season, with hostesses vying to exhibit a real literate worker. Then, the excitement over, they passed on to the hero of the next hour.

On the other hand, Savinien Lapointe, son of a shoemaker and man of all work, spoke directly to his own kind.[4] Lapointe had little schooling. In fact, it took a sojourn as political prisoner in Sainte Pélagie to drive him to study. But at the beginning of his career he became the protégé of Béranger, Hugo, and Léon Gozlan, which augured well for his success. Vinçard published his works in the *Ruche populaire,* while Olinde Rodrigues " discovered " him for inclusion in his anthology. At first an imitator of the great, similar in almost all respects to dozens of other proletarian writers, Lapointe later distinguished himself by becoming a sharp critic of the Orléans monarchy, though he raised a lonely voice in the new wilderness :

> Ah ! sur ce globe étroit la multitude abonde;
> Oui, le pauvre est de trop !...

Needless to say, this first group contained a woman's auxiliary. One might even count Auguste Abadie *(Rose et Dahlias)* among them except for his sex. Abadie dedicated most of his work to young ladies, specializing in such poems as " Variations sur la beauté de la belle jambe." More properly, however, Reine Garde and Antoinette Quarré belong in this category. The story of the first is well known because of the preface to *Geneviève*, but Antoinette Quarré could also claim Lamartine as a patron, though not the honor of being immortalized in the introduction to one of his books. More than that, Antoinette could boast that Saint-Marc Girardin, high priest of the prose-minded and keeper of bourgeois values, had subscribed to her *Poésies*.

Antoinette Quarré's effusions earned approbation from the most conservative critics, at least for her subject matter. In fact her poetry tends to monotony because of its poverty of themes : religious topics, advice to young ladies and *vers de circonstance*. A firm believer in the sacred mission of the poet, this simple seamstress rarely became too personal, except in such cases as " Un Fils," when she expressed a hungry yearning for what had been denied her. Otherwise, her verse showed so little distinction that even Roger de Belloquet, the eloquent composer of a preface to the *Poésies*, had to admit she was dull. Roger seems no fool; his acquaintance with the subject caused him to make a statement which indicated the failure of another poetic revolution : " Je vois grandir en France des ouvriers poètes, plutôt qu'une poésie des ouvriers." Antoinette also made excursions into prose, most of which appeared in the virginal *Journal des Demoiselles*. As in poetry, so in prose : she departed not one step from the prescribed path with *Médavy-Bras-de-Fer* or *Emma et Marguerite*.

In this respect she could lay claim to a literary kinship to Louise Crombach. Louise, the more fecund of the two, literarily speaking, emphasized prose more than poetry, though she did occasionally attempt verse on the urging of Mme Amable Tastu. In the matter of prose, Louise Crombach and Antoinette Quarré represented a new side of the worker-writer. Most had chosen to work with the un-compromising matter of verse, but a few began to explore the unknown reaches of prose, possibly because poetry baffled them. Mlle Crombach recounted her tales in a pre-Horatio Alger tradition, as in *Le Petit Marchand*, the story of a young lad who was supposed to attend classes at the local school, but refused to go for fear of his fellow pupils. Taught to read at home, he became a peddler of thread, interested only in earning a living, until one night he heard the story of Pancreas, the thief, at the home of a peasant. From then on he dedicated himself to helping his neighbors. The rest of the story tells how the hero was caught stealing sausage in an inn, then igno-miniously blamed for a theft he did not commit. Subsequently com-mitted to reform school, he learned to read, write, and to become an expert in optical instruments. Later, as chief apprentice in an atelier, he even won a prize for his master, and was rewarded with the hand of the patron's daughter. Virtue conquered all!

This vein seemed rich to Mlle Crombach. In *Hélène et Laurence*, she told of a poor rich woman whom a maid saved from perdition by disclosing how to found a charitable society. Such zeal earned a place for her *Les Papillons et les Enfants* in a series entitled *Les Petits Livres de M. le Curé, Bibliothèque du Presbytère, de la Famille et des Écoles*. Chapters like " Dieu bénit les bons cœurs," or " L'ange gardien " must have endeared her to the ecclesiastical authorities, because in 1845 *Un Pauvre devant Dieu* received the archepiscopal blessing. This last recounted the adventures of a young boy who passed through unbelievable trials, even including incarceration in Siberia, until he belatedly realized that happiness lay in tending the garden of a kind-hearted patron.

Savinien Lapointe, like his feminine colleagues, tried his hand at prose with a selection of *Contes*, fairy tales for the young, but more important is Gilland's *Les Conteurs ouvriers, dédiés aux enfants des classes laborieuses avec une préface de George Sand*. Despite the enthusiasm of the lady of Nohant, not much can be said for the collection. *Le Fermier et le Curé, La Rose blanche, La Fille du braconnier*, all bear the mark of a writer who had dreamed larger dreams than he could realize, and who had dwelt too long in the shadow of Jean-Jacques Rousseau. Except that Gilland really tried to live his fantasies. In the great tradition of the romantic hero, he fell in love with a loose woman whom he hoped to save by marriage from a fate worse than death. He demanded, however, that she purify herself by adopting the child of a poor widowed conscript. The lady hesitated, then rejected Gilland because she had fallen in love with a less exacting worker. When later she fell ill and died, Gilland felt called upon to preach the gospel of morality. He considered his position as an intellectual leader of the untutored masses so important that he even refused to become a proprietor, for which principle he paid dearly in 1848 when the country turned against the Revolution. At that time he was labelled a " buveur de sang," a " débauché " and a man who regularly beat his wife.

Gilland, Reine Garde, Louise Crombach, all the others, represented the school that followed eagerly in the footsteps of respected sponsors, theirs not to challenge nor to change. But there also existed a contingent of men and women who thought as political and social Messiahs. Few could write well. For them education had been a luxury the age would not permit. Each letter of the alphabet meant hours stolen from the travail that gave bread to their families. Of them it could be said, as of Perdiguier, that they could " passablement lire, pas trop bien écrire, peu calculer."[5] Self-educated like Père Magu, the proletarian writers managed to exercise such great influence among their fellow workers, despite the hostility of the bourgeoisie, that in 1841 François Arago marvelled at the great intellectual revolution that was stirring the entire working class.[6]

These men began early to contradict the message preached by their more peaceful confrères, particularly the women writers. In 1832 Hégésippe Moreau, later to die in a charity ward, somberly remarked :

> J'ai bien maudit le jour qui m'a vu naître.[7]

Moreau had known bitter personal disillusionment, but even Pierre Corréard, despite an occasional lapse into poems like *A ma sœur le jour de ses noces* or *Le Premier Amour*, remembered as early as 1827 to speak coldly to God :

> Délivre-nous de tout mauvais génie,
> Délivre-nous des prêtres imposteurs;
> Pour extirper l'impure tyrannie,
> Arme ton bras de ses foudres vengeurs.[8]

Such mutterings were unusual prior to 1840, since the workers were still learning how to express their recently acquired sense of class unity. But after that date the proletarian writers increasingly voiced dissatisfaction with events and the men who shaped them. Christian Sailer, for example, openly prophesied a future bloody struggle in the *Lyre prolétaire*.[9] Anti-clerical and class-conscious, he firmly believed that poetry could be used to instruct the workers

9

how to protect their rights and his was only one of the many voices raised in growing resentment as the Orléans Monarchy tightened an irksome leash on labor.

Under the prodding of George Sand, Poncy repeated the same ideas. At her request he composed *La Chanson de chaque métier*, published after the February Revolution, but written before that date. " Je me suis attaché surtout à démontrer la solidarité qui existe entre tous les métiers." Then followed an impressive collection of lyrics for each trade, among them songs for organ grinders and grave diggers. Most remained well within the tradition earlier established, but the *Chanson du canut* repeats the theme of social injustice used by Chrétien de Troyes for the girl weavers of the Château de Pesme Aventure.

More and more such resentment piled up in proletarian writers and spilled over into written criticisms of their economic and social status. Furthermore, they had at last learned the lesson so painfully taught to the partisans of art for art's sake : in the new age, poetry had lost its prestige. As Hégésippe Moreau told his sister in the early days of the July Monarchy, unless poems were signed by Lamartine or Hugo, a journal would make the author pay the costs of printing them.[10]

Nonetheless, to the horror of reigning critics, the workers continued to pile up mountains of verse, little of it original. At the same time class-conscious reviewers unblushingly touted hesitant imitations of Hugo and Lamartine as the work of unrecognized genius. To some extent the romanticists themselves can be blamed for the situation since they praised their protegés so highly that critics already antagonistic to the masters looked biliously on the pupils. In the age of Louis-Philippe most critics felt a sense of the inviolable dignity of their class. Hence they regarded men like Poncy or Savinien Lapointe with contemptuous suspicion. The French Revolution still flamed wildly in their memory, and they had little desire for any enlargement of the theory of equality, particularly in literature. All was well with their world and they wished it to remain so. Proletarian writers who espoused the theory of the literary Messiah could lead to the annoying danger of social upset.

For the first ten years of the Constitutional Monarchy, the critics deliberately tried to ignore the new phenomenon. But when Olinde Rodrigues published his *Poésies sociales des ouvriers*, Cuvillier-Fleury of the *Débats* could no longer contain his righteous rage. Perhaps he sensed the advent of the socialist literature that would later rise from this source but, at any rate, he fired broadsides at these shadowy imitations of greater men or sneered at thoughtless claims for their genius. In this he was joined by a formidable team composed of Lerminier, Champfleury, and Charles Louandre.

Through the last three the *Revue des Deux Mondes* established itself solidly as an enemy of any literature spawned of the union of technological advance and a new literacy, no matter who sponsored it. Champfleury summed it up as " les puérilités de la littérature enseignante, cette monotone et illisible littérature,"[11] while Louandre grumbled peevishly in his " Statistique littéraire " of 1847 at the plethora of popular geniuses being discovered daily. Louandre sounded depressed by the roll call; the monotonous repetition of themes; the innumerable *vers de circonstance*, the insipid lines composed for the slightest village celebration, made him wonder about the future of art.

But of all the enemies of the new literature, the most terrible was Lerminier. He showed no mercy whatsoever for the awkward products of the new " talent." In fact, the contemporary rage for seizing pen and paper at the slightest provocation seemed to madden him.[12] Lerminier disagreed, too, with the theory that it was possible to create a literature specifically for one segment of the population without any reference to that written for the nation as a whole; all this seemed to smack ominously of a caste system. He reacted violently to the victory cries of writers like George Sand, who shrilled on every occasion that they had created a modern miracle. Genius, he felt, needed more than a peremptory announcement, and it seemed rash to announce the end of the bourgeoisie simply because some plumber had discovered that words rhymed. Lerminier found the people unprepared to seize the opportunity to write which the age provided. Poorly educated, lacking any feeling for poetry, they were trying to force oral tradition into the unyielding form of a more sophisticated genre. And this by imitating Hugo, Lamartine, and Béranger. Not that he opposed a workers' literature, Lerminier exclaimed piously, but it seemed difficult for a man to be worker and poet at the same time. And he propounded a vigorous defense of his class against the new group : " il n'y a plus à fonder une littérature prolétaire qu'une caste ouvrière dont l'organisation politique et les intérêts seraient hostiles à la bour-

geoisie. Ne comprendra-t-on jamais que le véritable génie de la démo-
cratie est d'unir et non pas de séparer ?"

NOTES

1. C. L. de Liefde, *Le Saint-Simonisme dans la poésie française entre 1825
et 1865*, Haarlem, Amicitia, 1927.

2. *Poésies sociales des ouvriers*, Paris, Paulin, 1841.

3. *Poésies*, par Jean Reboul de Nîmes, précédées d'une préface par M.
Alexandre Dumas, et d'une lettre à l'éditeur par M. Alphonse de Lamartine.
Paris, Gosselin, 1836.

4. *Essais poétiques*, Sarlat, Antoine Dauriac, 1829.

5. Jean Larnac, " Une Révolution dans les lettres il y a cent ans, " *Europe*,
XXVI, no. 26, Feb., 1948, p. 67.

6. *Ibid.*, p. 75.

7. *Poésies et contes*, Paris, Michaud, 1908.

8. *Chansons*, Lyon, Aymé, 1833.

9. Paris, Masgana, 1840.

10. *Poésies et contes*, Paris, Michaud, 1908, p. vi.

11. *De la littérature populaire en France*, Paris, Poulet-Malassis, 1861, p. 18.

12. " De la littérature des ouvriers, " *RDM*, décembre 1841, p. 957.

CHAPTER 10

DEVELOPMENT OF THE NOVEL

MORE IMPORTANT, artistically speaking, than the appearance of a people's literature was the fact that writers of the early 19th century tended increasingly to seek prose as the best medium of communicating their thoughts to the vast new audience which modern technology had provided. And as prose more and more replaced poetry in the public favor, it inevitably followed that some of those who had chosen to exploit its possibilities should be curious enough about their medium to wonder about the artistic principles governing the products that so delighted the public. A few of the more inquisitive, a minority of the practitioners of the long prose forms, to be sure, meditated on what they were doing, and out of their consideration came a series of shifts in the practices inherited from the past that formed the basis for a new art form : the modern novel.

I

The modern " novel," or the long prose form, seems to date from the 17th century. The term has been so loosely used by literary historians that the name has been given to practically any work of prose fiction with more than one hundred pages, but one thing is certain : the 17th century was very much aware of the genre which it utilized and of the limitations with which theorists had surrounded it. The age of classicism tried valiantly, though in vain, to prepare a " poetics " for the latest child of literature.

Actually, the " novels " which the 17th century created are more properly called romances, prose tales similar in form to the stories of Chrétien de Troyes. As the century advanced, increased practice of the romance tended to move it into the category of recipe literature.

The plot consisted of a series of equally important episodes strung together bead-fashion. Since the point of narration lay outside the story, writers intruded on their readers to indicate moral lessons or special meanings, and such a construction invited digressions or a story so lengthy that only the exhaustion of the author terminated it. Plot had no direction except to carry out the didactic aims of the writer and to prove that pure love conquers all. Story was woven through story to maintain an elementary kind of suspense, each populated by stylized characters tinged with allegory. The author manipulated these flat personalities according to the requirements of primary purpose, sometimes opposing them in obvious antithesis, or grouping them to indicate a play of ideas. In general they were propped against a historical background, though never intimately related to it, strangers to the reality with which they were associated since their creator wished only to gain credence for a super-imposed fiction. Lovers met, were separated, and met again, but in the meantime the hero had summoned every ounce of his considerable will power to avoid the wiles of charmers. Likewise, the heroine had stoutly preserved her virtue through incredible assaults. Both passed through unbelievable events, sometimes whole wars, all during the period of a year.[1] In no case did the average citizen appear in all the drabness of his existence, upset by the petty woes of life. On the contrary, the romance painted in fresco style, amplified and distorted for the pleasure of a small audience. Since the author deliberately appealed to a tiny elite, his technique included hiding real people under flat characters, sometimes introducing minor events well known to his readers. The characters might play salon games, but they always discussed matters considered important to the socially elect. Yet, for all that the author wished to amuse, he did it distantly. To dissociate himself from the vulgarity of prose, many a writer adopted anonymity or the device of the recovered manuscript. The 17th century produced some 1600 works which can be classed as romances and, of course, about 400 were unsigned.[2]

Despite its disdain for prose, the 17th century nonetheless spent considerable time delineating the limits of the romance. Huet pioneered in the discussion of theory by establishing in the *Traité de l'origine des romans* a definition that would remain standard until well into the 19th century. According to him, romances were " fictions d'aventures amoureuses," written in prose for the pleasure and edification of the readers. Love had to be the principal subject, and didacticism demanded that virtue conquer vice. But, above all, "les romans sont des fictions de choses qui ont pu être, et qui n'ont point été."

Actually, the theory of the 17th-century novel was to a large extent controlled by the fact that its purpose was primarily didactic, secondarily for entertainment. The other three main points of contemporary theorizing, *vraisemblance, bienséances,* and *plaire davantage,* would be influenced in all cases by the author's main purpose. For Lannel, Camus, and Mlle Scudéry, romances served as mirrors in which a reader might behold and correct himself.[3] *Le Grand Cyrus* and *Clélie,* were written as guides to correct social usage.

All writers subscribed to the thesis that virtue had to conquer vice, but this did not prevent them from trying to entertain the reader. As Camus pointed out in *Agathonphile,* a light touch helped to soothe the irritation of didacticism. The temptation seemed irresistible for authors to increase the amusement potential and retard the moral explanation until the last possible moment. Consequently, the relationship of amusement to moral purpose burdened the author with the difficult task of demonstrating the joys of virtue and the futility of vice. Strange uses of the theory resulted : Sorel maintained in *Francion* that a hatred of wrong compelled him to use the depiction of evil as a lure for readers; similarly, Furetière explained tongue-in-cheek that the *Roman bourgeois* portrayed sin because the story of men's errors would deter the impressionable. The morality supposedly outlined by this unusual procedure was the observance of fidelity in love, chastity, and reverence to God.

Furthermore the authors pretended to utilize historical backgrounds to enlarge the didactic scope of their work, but it was history just distant enough from the present to permit an author the convenience of inserting events which might have astounded a historian.

Les beaux Romans ne sont pas sans instruction... principalement depuis qu'on y mêle l'histoire, et ceux qui les écrivent, sçavans dans les mœurs des nations, imaginent des avantures qui s'y rapportent, et qui nous en instruisent.[4]

The key to the 17th-century novel lay in the interplay of the three theories of *vraisemblance, bienséances,* and *plaire davantage,* the first of which controlled the other two. As generally accepted, this doctrine

meant writing of what fell within the realm of imaginative possibility.[5]
Jean Antoine Charnes defined it loosely as " l'image de la vérité,"[6]
while Scudéry claimed that " le véritable art du mensonge est de
bien ressembler à la vérité."[7] Somaize, however, wrote more specifically :

> Il seroit besoin ici de faire un long discours pour expliquer ce que c'est que
> vraye-semblance; mais, pour te le dire en deux mots, c'est tout ce qui, bien
> qu'extraordinaire par sa nouveauté, tombe néantmoins assez dessous les sens
> pour persuader à l'esprit que cela peut arriver sans renverser l'ordre estably
> dans le cours des choses, ce qui despend souvent bien plus de l'arengement
> des actions que des actions mesmes.[7]

The word denoted a distant kind of realism, but in practice the didactic
intent of the novel tended to modify the contemporary notion of what
was probable. The most unlikely coincidence was deemed within
bounds if it could be considered of didactic value, and it was precisely
this urge to teach which made *vraisemblance* so important. As Scudéry
noted, improbability of characterization, plot, or description might
so alienate readers that it would defeat the author's purpose.[9] Stemming
from a desire to give credence to a story, *vraisemblance* served as a
guide to writers for establishing a rapport between author and reader.

The principle of *vraisemblance*, or the imaginably probable, however,
was restricted by the theory of the *bienséances*. In all likelihood a
product of the précieux movement, the latter doctrine acted as a
corrective to any possible violation of the accepted code of social
behavior which uncontrolled *vraisemblance* might suggest. Thus, La
Calprenède could boast in *Cassandre*, " au moins y trouvera-t-on peu
de choses qui puissent choquer, ny la vray-semblance ny la bien-
séance."[10] Didactically motivated writers hoped to maintain high
standards of social nicety, simultaneously indicating ideal behavior
and accepted norms.

This attitude tended to modify another conception of the 17th-
century author, *le beau idéal*. Segrais, for instance, advocated that
the *roman* concern itself primarily with " *beaux* sentiments."[11] Pure
qualified this with four recommendations : evil passions should be
eliminated; the ordinary faults of life were to be corrected; desire
was to be purified; and a book could contain only " ce que la belle
ame peut desirer ou penser de beau."[12] Scudéry, however, refused
to accept the theory to the point where *vraisemblance* might be

menaced.[13] Charnes agreed that " il suffit que les objets soient dépeint tels que l'on montre avoir eu l'intention de les dépeindre. On n'est pas obligé de les faire paraître beaux en tout. Il ne faut que les repré-senter par le beau, en éloigner les idées desagréables, & les faire voir conforme à la nature."[14] Yet all concurred on ideal justice : virtue had to triumph over vice, even if historical fact were altered to meet the requirements.

In turn, all these theories were adjusted to fit a principle no writer could afford to ignore : *plaire davantage.* In all probability first elaborated by la Tour Hotman in the preface to his *Histoire celtique* in 1634, it was more clearly defined by Scudéry : " Qu'on se donne la peine d'étudier le siècle qu'on a choisi... on puisse avec jugement les [customs] accommoder un peu à l'usage du siècle où l'on vit, afin de plaire davantage."[15] With one eye on the reader, an author corrected history or manipulated facts to increase interest, a technique controlled only by the requirements of the *bienséances* and *vraisem-blance.* Consequently writers tended to make situations more titillating, or to turn their works into *romans à clef*, a deviation not in violation of *vraisemblance.*[16]

Inevitably the theorizing left its mark on practice in more than the preceding situations. Characters were stereotyped, not necessarily aristocrats, though nobility of character seemed an important require-ment. Diversity of situation seemed a legitimate method of holding reader interest, even though it complicated plot to an incredible extent. As Huet pointed out, since the *roman* was less elevated than poetry, such meandering did not constitute a breach of rules.

In fact, digression itself seemed built into the 17th-century concep-tion of the romance. Theory required only one main action, to the successful conclusion of which all subordinate plots should contri-bute.[17] Episodes had to be related, but only by the fact that the same characters participated in them. Scudéry and Huet both insisted that digression be related to the main action,[18] but Charnes claimed that any episode, however distantly connected, might be introduced.[19] Far from frowning on this lack of unity, Camus claimed that such a tech-nique made the *roman* more interesting and time-consuming.[20] Di-gression was used to interrupt the main action and heighten suspense on the grounds that prolonged desire yields more pleasure than the pleasure itself. Similarly, such extraneous material was used to provide the background necessary for both characters and events. Thus, even in their lack of unity, the 17th-century theorists found reason for practices which contradicted the contemporary desire for precision and clarity.

II

Such was the 17th-century romance. Not everybody, of course, seemed to subscribe to its tenets, though close inspection shows that most such critics practiced what they did not preach. In the *Connaissance des Bons Livres, ou Examen de Plusieurs Autheurs*, Sorel doubted the validity of the didactic theory; everywhere he found a lack of regularity, false history, adventure piled on adventure solely to fill volumes of impressive length and number, each author robbing his predecessor's stock of stereotyped themes and characters.

By 1658, the heroic-historical theory of the romances had provoked the ridicule of the less naïve. Not only were Boileau and Molière to make violent attack on the exaggeration of their conventions, but Furetière, Segrais, and Scarron, as well as Sorel, would mock " les morceaux de ridicule papier où sont écrites leurs histoires."[21] For them ideality, that is, the preference for characters that never did exist, and propriety, the belief that characters should act strictly in accordance with the supposed etiquette of their station, clashed with the principle of *vraisemblance*. They sponsored a more realistic approach to characterization which finally triumphed about 1680. A better approximation of life as it is, described in less high-flown language, displaced the artificial monologues, the preciosity, and the stilted behavior of over-genteel aristocrats.

Furetière and Sorel led the attack on the 17th-century romance, the former being especially critical in the *Roman bourgeois*. Furetière deliberately utilized characters from the middle class, with a mode of life far different from that of the *précieuses;* Scarron agreed, adding that the ordinary detail of the commonplace had to be used in the story. Both men came to the aid of Pure in criticizing stock situations and characters, insipid heroes and heroines. Valincour railed at the abuse of digression, while Segrais called attention to the romance's lack of verisimilitude. For their part, Sorel and Furetière mocked the excess of pomp, the clumsiness of the box-car construction, the technique of beginning *in medias res* and the general lack of probability.[22]

But this criticism contained little that was positive; these men had nothing to offer in place of the recipe in vogue. Worse still, when they came to practice what they preached, the so-called realists differed little from the " idealists," no matter how scornfully they might ridicule them. When Furetière wrote the *Roman bourgeois*, he carefully stated that he was teaching by horrible example as a purge for the wicked.[23] The book even began in the approved manner with a coy intimation of the existence of a key, together with a promise not to indulge in useless descriptions, " sans pompe et sans appareil."

But from then on Furetière floundered. In the introduction, he defined a *roman* as " rien qu'une poésie en prose," then changed his purpose to that of telling " sincèrement et avec fidélité plusieurs historiettes ou galanteries arrivées entre des personnes qui ne seront ny heros ny heroïnes." In fact, by the time he had arrived at part II, he forgot his demands for unity in the works of others :

Si vous avez attendu, lecteur, que ce livre soit la suite du premier, et qu'il y ait une connexité nécessaire entr'eux, vous estes prix pour duppe. Détrompez-vous de bonne heure, et sçachez que cet enchaînement d'intrigues les uns avec les autres est bien séant à ces poëmes héroïques et fabuleux où l'on peut tailler et rogner à sa fantaisie... Ce sont de petites histoires et advantures arrivées en divers quartiers de la ville, qui n'ont rien de commun ensemble, et que je tasche de rapprocher les unes des autres autant qu'il m'est possible. Pour le soin de la liaison, je le laisse à celuy qui reliera le livre. Prenez donc cela pour des historiettes séparées, et ne demandez point que j'observe ny l'unité des temps ny des lieux.[24]

In fact, " ne l'appelez plus roman." His characters were handled cavalierly, one being shoved aside when the nonchalant author tired of him; " imaginez-vous qu'il soit ici tué," he soothed any indignant reader. One chapter led aimlessly to another until Furetière frankly admitted that his plot meandered hopelessly.

Sorel maintained a similar attitude; the *Histoire comique de Francion* showed the same strengths and weaknesses as the *Roman bourgeois*. In the preface of 1623, Sorel announced a didactic aim, though he gagged at the prospect, imagining himself a druggist who sugared pills to trap the wary. But the composition was rushed, uncorrected, and without any unity. The author even bragged that he had scribbled at least thirty-two pages a day. What pride he had in his work came from the fact that his characters acted like ordinary human beings and not stilted aristocrats. Since his contemporaries had criticized him harshly for this bit of realism, he repeated his intentions in the preface to the edition of 1626, " ayant entrepris de blasmer tous les vices des hommes, il a falu que j'aye descrit beaucoup de choses en leur naifveté."

Sorel and Furetière could well compliment themselves on introducing into the romance the kind of life lived by a larger segment of the population. Their work sounded the death knell of the précieux romance; the lofty language, the delicate conceits, and the overpowering concern with courtly love tended to disappear. Nevertheless the romance changed little in terms of form. Sorel and Furetière altered the meaning of *vraisemblance* and the conception of the *bienséances*, but both the intent and basic pattern of the romance remained essentially the same. The realist-bourgeois, the psychological, the sentimental, and the philosophic types were to adhere to the same kind of structure until the Revolution, the only shift of consequence being an increase of interest in the middle class.

Not even Mme de Lafayette departed to any extent from the traditional ways. The *Princesse de Clèves* holds basically to the same pattern as *Cassandre* or the *Roman comique*. To be sure, her book was the first in which the psychological interest overshadowed in importance the intrigues and adventures, this principally through the speeches of the characters rather than their actions.[25] But the story is filled with memories of past readings : old romances, memoirs, even a contemporary novel written by Mme de Villedieu, from whom she seems to have borrowed the basis for the *Princesse*. Actually, Mme de Lafayette believed she was writing a *roman historique* of the variety well-known to her age. As she later told Lescheraine, the book was not a *roman*, but " des mémoires." The court she painted was one that could not otherwise be described if it were to please her audience.

Like her predecessors, Madame sought to teach. The *Princesse* outlined a *morale laïque* suitable for an age in the process of losing its faith. To make her points clear, she had Mme de Chartres underline the moral instruction to be conveyed. Ideal justice is accepted, and virtue triumphs over vice when the princess rejects Nemours' suit and gets herself to a nunnery.

Madame de Lafayette concerned herself as much with the accepted theories as any of her predecessors. Writing " mémoires," she recognized the importance of *vraisemblance*, though she faltered in some respects. Madame de Clèves' confession to her husband roused Valincour to protest its probability in the *Lettres à Mme *** sur le sujet de la Princesse de Clèves* (1678), a criticism which Charnes tried to disarm with the observation that in general the book represented the ordinary course of life.[26] The author had indeed been forced to take liberties with the *bienséances* in order to strengthen the use of the verisimilar. Perhaps to *plaire davantage* she permitted a lover to violate the proprieties with an open declaration, or pictured the mental infidelity of a wife in a sordid affair with the treacherous Nemours. For the same reason, she idealized the court of Anne of Austria and Louis XIV contrary to historical fact, and carefully sheltered her heroine from any suggestion of physical passion by making her adhere to the précieux code. Even the most minor characters are shown in terms of the *beau idéal*.

Furthermore, the structure of the *Princesse de Clèves* is amazingly similar to that of the *Roman comique*. There are the same wandering interruptions : a digressive introduction full of portraits, with little connection to the main action; an extraneous explanation of the personal animosities of the court, others on the statue of the *reine dauphine*, Mme Valentinois' past, the life of Mme Tournon, the king's horoscope, Anne de Boulen, the tourney and the court changes after the death of the king, to mention only a few.

Even disregarding these extras, it is to be noted that no true conflict motivates the action of the main characters. Mme de Clèves' purity is never really assailed, even when she declares her love to Nemours. A virtue solidly established at the beginning never permits any doubt about her actions. An iron will, a fear of public reproof, and a powerful sense of *devoir* constitute social assets which make her a relative of Chimène. What plot there is comes from her reactions to a knowledge of her love, but never does she waver in her duty.

Actually, the shortness of the *Princesse*, its interpretation of *vraisemblance*, the fact that it was an *histoire suivie*, led Valincour to call it a *nouvelle*. Certainly, the multitude of its digressions, its box-car construction, explicit didacticism, and the intrusion of the author, mark it as differing from the novel. The *Princesse de Clèves* marks a change in the development of the French romance, but only a slight change. The novel was still to come.

III

The 18th century early lost interest in the work of authors like Scudéry and La Calprenède because of its rejection of a vapid preciosity. Similarly it discarded even those volumes which had originated a reaction against an overly sophisticated language. But the 17th century left in legacy a curiosity about the existence of the middle and lower classes. Furthermore, there still remained some of the spirit of the Spanish picaresque novel, though mostly in translations. Otherwise the traditional form of the French romance continued, except for minor shifts. The respectful ravishers disappeared, as did the corpses that miraculously revived, the lovers who met accidentally in a hidden wilderness after years of absence, men disguised as women, or women disguised as men, but the sharp taste for adventure persisted. *Annales*, *Histoires secrètes*, or *Témoins* fed contemporaries with vicarious thrills from the life of exciting heroes and heroines.

The *roman* blossomed in the first fifty years of the 18th century despite the fact that it was outlawed by classicism. Some 1600 were published prior to 1750, though the word itself almost disappeared from titles.[27] The 17th-century romance vanished except for a few reprints of *Cassandre* and *Ibrahim*, to be replaced by various *Amours de...*, *Aventures de...*, or *Histoire de....* About half were anonymous or pseudonymous, their authors too careful to allow the writing of prose to endanger their social position, and most were men, women still being in the great minority on Parnassus. Many used the first person to lend credence to their imaginings, while all claimed to offer historically accurate and documented facts.

The number of authors, small during the previous age, grew alarmingly during the 18th century, but few did more than stumble along the path the 17th century had blazed. Neither Vannel, Mlle Déritier, Madame de Murot, Madame de Villediece, nor Le Noble, however, altered the course of literary history to any great extent. What they did was to compress plot more than formerly had been done. Furthermore, they tended to disdain the crude devices of *deux ex machina* or the marvelous in favor of probability and a primitive kind of realism. This is perhaps all that can be said over the literary tombs of such forgotten people as Mme Petit-Dunoyer, Beaudot de Juilly, or Marguerite de Lussan.

Some of the better known writers, Sandras, for instance, contributed little to the development of the genre they practiced. His name dominates the history of the " novel " during the first part of the century, along with that of Hamilton, his most successful imitator. The *Mémoires de Grammont* are better written than anything Sandras produced, but neither man had a clear idea of what he was doing except that it amused people and brought some measure of profit. They hopped from one episode to another with gleeful abandon, wandered through intricate plots, finally to rescue themselves with the aid of history.

Even the men to whom posterity has been kinder spared little of the time spent on producing numerous volumes to consider the nature and limits of their writing. Lesage employed the same procedure in *Gil Blas* as that used in the *Caractères* or the *Lettres persanes*. A tenuous thread guided an incredible series of characters through multiple adventures, connected only by the author's determination to unmask the infinite varieties of human stupidity and rascality. " L'utilité mêlé avec l'agréable," Gil Blas told the reader. In the *Diable Boiteux* as well as in *Gil Blas*, Lesage aimed at painting contemporary manners and morals. Consequently, Guzman d'Alfarache and Gil Blas live the same kind of hazardous life, gaining a wealth of expensive experience from the chance adventures they tumble into, their misfortunes forming *romans à tiroir* for those too lazy to start at the beginning. His heroes stuff enough excitement into one existence to satisfy any six men and, as a result, composition suffers. Episode is tacked haphazardly onto episode, and hordes of secondary characters relate their adventures in minute detail, until even the author is fatigued. *Gil Blas* ends twice, but since the author cannot bear to leave unfinished business, Gil's hegira begins anew even though he seems to have retired.

Lesage skirted the *bienséances*, emphasized *vraisemblance* but, more important, sought principally to amuse. He did so well with his gallery that inevitably readers began to identify his personages. Even when Lesage indignantly denied having produced a *roman à clef*, the game continued because it had not occurred to contemporaries that such realism might be wasted on imaginary people. The shift toward the depiction of every-day life had been so successful that the 17th-century identification game now fitted naturally the scheme of the realist-bourgeois romance.

Prévost, too, experimented little with the adventure recipe. He had read all too closely the works of d'Urfé, La Calprenède, Mme de Villedieu, and Courtilz de Sandras. At breakneck speed he stuffed six or eight volumes full of adventures in the accepted manner; once he seized a pen he found difficulty in restraining an over-active imagination. To lend credence to this amazing complex of disguises, abductions, captivities in Algiers, and peripatetic characters, he fell back on scenes from history often unrelated to the main plot. Most of his works were in memoir form, " given " to the author by a son of Clèveland, the main character, or merely " printed " by Prévost " from the manuscript " of the Marquis de ***.

Here again, as with Lesage, appeared the compelling urge to teach through bad example. Prévost appreciated the theory of *plaire davantage*, as he noted in the preface of the *Doyen de Killerine*, but he insisted on showing how vice leads to downfall in a kind of reverse Horatio Algerism. The *bienséances* might suffer, the sacred principle of *vraisemblance* might seem flouted, but Prévost insisted only on making solid Christians of his readers. For this he needed the adventures, the unsettled personalities, the coincidences and unmotivated episodes of *Manon*. Consequently, in his case, the end justified using the same old means which the 17th-century romance had made standard.

A similar story could be repeated for the entire century in an uninspired catalogue of repetitions. Such an account would be unfair in that it would omit indicating the art with which certain writers handled the romance, the novelties and genius infused in their works. Yet neither Crébillon fils nor Marivaux can be called novelists. *La Vie de Marianne* contains delightful bits, but neither it nor the *Paysan parvenu* show much new in terms of structure. Whereas in *Pharsamond ou les folies romanesques* (1712) and the *Voiture embourbée* (1714) Marivaux had parodied La Calprenède and Mlle de Scudéry, he later progressed to imitation in the *Aventures de *** ou effets surprenants de la sympathie*. He never recovered from the experience. More simple than the works of Lesage, closer to ordinary life, his books all take shape around the traditional structure of the romance, without unity or a single motivating force for all the episodes. *Marianne* was finished only after the author's death and the last three parts form a separate story. Similarly, only the first five sections of the *Paysan parvenu* come from Marivaux, and even these contain long digressions such as the sharp criticism of Crébillon fils. The latter, sometimes called the " Marivaux des petites maisons Louis XV," fits better into a history of the short story with *Tanzai et Néadarné*, the *Amours de Zéo Kinisul*, and the *Sopha*. His " novels," the *Lettres de la Marquise de M. au comte de R.* and *Egarements du cœur et de l'esprit* are not only incoherent but the last one remained unfinished.

As André Le Breton has pointed out,[28] Voltaire has no place in a discussion of the novel, since his prose includes only *contes*, fantastic and fanciful tales like *Candide* or *Micromégas* which nobody, least of all the sardonic Voltaire, expected to seem realistic. Actually *Candide* and *Zadig*, among other things, were written to mock the novel. Voltaire the traditionalist seconded the sour dictum of Boileau on long prose writings, " production d'un esprit faible écrivant avec facilité des choses indignes d'être lues par des esprits sérieux."[29] Ironically enough, editors generally entitle his prose works *contes et romans*.

For Rousseau, the case is more complicated. Jean-Jacques imagined that he was re-writing the *Princesse de Clèves*, creating a new morality for a godless age. With all the passion of his tempestuous nature, he hoped to show that moral grandeur could be founded on controlled love. Furthermore, he never seems to have made up his mind about the novel, sometimes praising Richardson, as in the *Lettre sur les spectacles*, or scolding him in the *Confessions*. However, in the second preface to the *Nouvelle Héloïse*, he gave the reader a bit of advice. " Vous jugez ce que vous avez lu comme un roman. Ce n'en est point un... C'est une longue romance..." Actually, Rousseau kept stumbling over his own thesis. The *Nouvelle Héloïse* tried to say two things : part I satirized contemporary life and portrayed a grand passion; part II offered advice on happiness in marriage. At all times the " novel " was buried under the thesis, a fact which led to digressions on music or gardens. Episodes like Saint-Preux's stay in Paris are planned only to further the sermon. Nor do the personalities of the two chief characters fit the age; they live in an unreal world, talking at enormous length on all occasions and striving mightily to earn sainthood.

So little attention did the 18th century pay to the genre that even the *Encyclopédie* could add nothing to Huet's definition :

Roman, s.m. (Fictions d'esprit) récit fictif de diverses avantures merveilleuses ou vraisemblables de la vie humaine ; le plus beau roman du monde, Télémaque, est un vrai poëme à la mesure et à la rime près.

The Chevalier de Jaucourt, author of the section, admired the *Astrée* but scorned *Cyme* and *Clélie*. In fact, he advocated only those works which proved useful in teaching the social virtues, and clucked disapprovingly at the rage for complicated adventure which so absorbed readers that they ignored Plato and Aristotle.

His disparagement did little to deter the spread of the genre, since imitators and admirers of Rousseau sprang up in droves. Restif de La Bretonne printed interminable sermons on evil; Bernardin de Saint-Pierre tried to manipulate the traditional form in support of the thesis that happiness came from living virtuously according to " nature," producing magnificently painted backgrounds for ludicrous actions.

At no time during the course of the century did anybody greatly alter the old recipe. Even the ever-curious Diderot paid it little attention. " I had always regarded novels as rather frivolous productions; I have finally discovered that they are good for the ' vapors '; I shall indicate the prescription to Tronchin the first time I see him."[30] *Jacques le fataliste* in no way approaches the concept of the realistic novel. Rather it seems like a dialogue between parts of the mind or a " novelized essay on the novel."

At the end of the century, the Marquis de Sade, of all people, paused long enough to throw together a few " *Idées sur les romans*." But the Marquis only repeated 17th-century theory. He urged his colleagues to paint a picture of secular life, to seek models in " nature," and to avoid the urge to moralize. Above all else *vraisemblance* was the cardinal point of the writer's creed and, to this end, Sade advised carefully sketching the plot, though he conceded that an author need not be restrained by his plan. " On ne te demande point d'être vrai, mais seulement d'être vraisemblable." However, in one respect he differed from his predecessors : the dénouement had to come naturally from the circumstances of the plot, never contrived or, as he sneered, " je n'exige pas de toi comme les auteurs de l'Encyclopédie, qu'il soit *conforme au désir du lecteur*."[31]

NOTES

1. Arpad Steiner, " Les Idées esthétiques de Mlle de Scudéry, " *RR*, XVI (1925) p. 175, quotes from the preface of *Ibrahim* : " A l'instar de la tragédie dont l'action ne peut durer que 24 heures, les anciens ont fait (et moy après eux) que l'Histoire ne dure qu'une année et que le reste est par narration. "

2. Ralph C. Williams, *Bibliography of the 17th-century novel in France.* New York, Century Company, 1931.

3. Jean de Lannel, *Le Romant satyrique*, Paris, Toussainet du Bray, 1624, *Au Lecteur.*

4. Segrais, *Les Nouvelles Françoises*, La Haye, Paupie, 1741, I, 15-18.

5. Philip Wadsworth, *The novels of Gomberville*, New Haven, Yale University Press, 1942, p. 62.

6. *Conversations sur la critique de la Princesse de Clèves*, Paris, Barbin, 1679, pp. 147-48.

7. *Clélie*, Paris, Courbé, 1658, VIII, 1128-29.

8. *Le Dictionnaire des précieuses*, Paris, Jannet, 1856, II, 54-55.

9. " Préface à Ibrahim, " in *Idées et doctrines littéraires du XVIIe siècle*, Paris, Delagrave, 1922, pp. 53-54.

10. Paris, De Sommaville, 1644, III, *Au Lecteur.*

11. *Les Nouvelles françoises*, La Haye, Paupie, 1741, I, 142.

12. Michel de Pure, *La Prétieuse ou le Mystère des ruelles*, Paris, Droz, 1938, p. 147.

13. Arthur Tieje, *The theory of characterization in prose fiction prior to* 1740, Minneapolis, University of Minnesota, 1916, pp. 16-17.

14. Jean Antoine de Charnes, *Conversations sur la critique de la Princesse de Clèves*, Paris, Barbin, 1679, pp. 147-48.

15. *Clélie*, VIII, p. 1136.

16. Tieje, *op. cit.*, 24.

17. Huet, *Traité de l'origine des romans*, Paris, Desessarts, an VII, pp. 32-33; Scudéry, préface to *Ibrahim*, pp. 53-54.

18. *Ibid.*, 53-54; Huet, *op. cit.*, 32-33.

19. Charnes, *op. cit.*, pp. 184-5.

20. *Agathonphile*, Rouen, Vaultier, 1641, pp. 897, 905.

21. Boileau, *Les Héros du roman*, Boston, Ginn, 1902, p. 228.

22. Sorel, *Le Tombeau des romans*, Paris, Claude Morlot, 1626.

23. *Advertissement du Librairie : au lecteur*, Paris, Garnier, 1924.

24. *Roman bourgeois*, Paris, Garnier, 1924, p. 209.

25. H. Ashton, *Madame de Lafayette*, Cambridge, England, University Press, 1922, p. 155.

26. *Op. cit.*, p. 136.

27. Silas Paul Jones, *A list of French prose fiction, 1700-50*, New York, H. W. Wilson, 1939.

28. *Le Roman au dix-huitième siècle*, Paris, Société française, n. d.

29. *Ibid.*, pp. 210-11.

30. Quoted in J. Robert Loy, *Diderot's determined fatalist*, New York, King's Crown Press, 1950, p. 188.

31. Paris, Palimugre, n.d., pp. 48-49.

CHAPTER 11

THE NOVEL COMES OF AGE

THE REVOLUTION SETTLED many an old problem, but it did little for literature. From 1789 to the Directory, few " novels " appeared and, of these, none seems to have felt the shock of the great revolt.[1] The rare authors who produced long prose works are most charitably forgotten : Louvet du Couvray *(Amours du Chevalier de Faublas)*, Lavallée *(Le Nègre comme il y a peu de blancs)*, or the Comtesse d'Hautpoul *(Zilia)*. Even by 1800, Huet still seems the acknowledged authority on prose fiction. An edition of the *Traité* was published in the year VII, because, the editor remarked, the appearance of enormous numbers of *romans* made it fitting that contemporaries understand their origin.

Few did, and even fewer cared, except perhaps for Senancour, who pointed out in an essay on " Du style dans la plupart des romans " that a new name was needed to distinguish the *roman* from the *anecdotes amoureuses* that pleased many a literary palate.[2] Or Madame de Staël, who paid very active attention to the problem in the *Essai sur les fictions*. Though she wrote on fiction in both prose and poetry, she made a particular point of discussing the novel. Like Senancour, she noted sadly that the novelist was held in low esteem because of the general mediocrity of the genre in which he worked. And, she added, it was primarily a dedication to the portrayal of violent passion that had brought the " novel " into disrepute. Personally, she considered the romance an art form which could be used to raise public and private morality.

In this respect, Mme de Staël was very much of the 18th century. Her cure for the prevailing situation was a suggestion that subject matter be extended to include more socially acceptable themes such as concern for duty or the cult of parents and friendship. In some respects she seemed to be pointing the way for Balzac when she advised

neophytes to paint avarice, pride, ambition and vanity as they existed
in the social fabric. Not that an author should preach. The morality
of the book should rise from the development of the plot and the
reactions òf characters to situations. But Mme de Staël never did
stray far from the 18th century in her theorizing. For her, too, love
remained the principal theme, all else being secondary. But there
Corinne stopped. She still thought the " novel " could ape the drama,
and had not come to distinguish between the various kinds of *fictions*
except in an elementary way.

The early years of the 19th century produced a series of feminine
writers who paid scarcely any attention to what Mme de Staël had
said. Corinne had condemned uncontrolled imagination and the
dedication to love plots; but her colleagues grimly maintained the
tradition, flooding France with the sentimental fantasies that once
delighted a generation of upstairs maids. One after another, Mme de
Genlis, Mme de Charrière, the Baronne de Krudener, Mme de Souza,
Mme de Rémusat, Mme de Duras, Pauline de Meulan, and Sophie
Gay produced romances lush with sentimental intrigue. Most bore
titles that clearly indicated their stereotyped nature : *Adèle et Théodore*
(Genlis), *Eugène et Mathilde, Charles et Marie* (Souza), *Charles et
Claire* (Rémusat), or *Conseils de morale* (Meulan). All the books ended
on a tone of high morality, with the guilty punished and the pure
in heart amply rewarded, providing the reader with a replenished
stock of well-worn maxims and moral anecdotes. But a dull, grey
monotony hangs over their work. Love always ran an uneven course,
principally because the characters never stopped preaching long enough
to think. Furthermore, as André Le Breton has pointed out, the
good ladies borrowed indiscriminately, if not wisely, from each other.[3]
Their fundamental premise was always the same, and a number of
episodes reappeared with startling frequency. All paraphrased their
own lives with an eagerness to divulge innermost thoughts that is
disconcerting, to say the least. Indeed, up to the end of the Restoration,
no one seems to have deviated much from the formula so assiduously
followed by Marivaux and Prévost.

Until the romanticists first timidly dabbled in prose, the *roman*
had never been given the honor of serious study by a qualified practi-
tioner. Some proposed an enlargement of the traditional subject
matter, others recommended more respect for the principle of *vraisem-*

THE NOVEL COMES OF AGE

blance, unity of action, or a dénouement born of the logic of events. Subject matter attracted most of the attention given, but little notice was paid to the relationship of form and characterization to story. Writers were required only to amuse, though by the 19th century most of them had taken seriously their secondary role of moral mentor.

The *roman* had fallen into three main categories : the *roman d'intrigue sentimentale*, the *roman noir*, and the *roman gai*, all of which used differing techniques. Most lady writers tended to work within the restricting confines of the frustrated and pure love of English heroines. The *roman noir*, on the other hand, required a stronger stomach. Specters, bandits, renegade priests, moral monsters of all varieties peopled a world in which a lute-playing heiress was vigorously pursued through a dingy castle by tenacious rascals. The young lady generally enjoyed ill health and weak nerves. Sometimes a cloud covered her past, but this did not deter the hero, usually a devoted, if not very intelligent, young man in possession of all the duller virtues. In almost all cases, this unappetizing pair was saved from certain destruction at the hands of a wily traitor only through the busy intervention of divine Providence. On the other hand, the *roman gai* catered more to the bourgeoisie with an adaptation of the picaresque novel. Since this type emphasized the comic aspects of the characters, their importance shifted from the greatness of misfortune to the absurdity of situation. Variety of effect was produced by multiplying scenes and adventures.

In all three categories authors tended to treat the unity of action cavalierly. By the end of the Empire, convention had established a length of three, four or five volumes in-12° of 250-300 pages each. Since the normal total length ran to four volumes, writers were hard put to fill their quota. As a result they multiplied episode, digressed and padded, or used such techniques as the rapid dialogue borrowed from the melodrama. On the other hand, exposition or the explanation of past events practically disappeared because intrigue increasingly came to depend on an element of mystery.

II

Early romanticism brought no changes to the romance, though it did shuffle some of the ingredients. The romanticists scorned the products of the past, particularly any tinged with classicism, but they unwittingly accepted the old theories as they passed through English sources. 17th- and 18th-century theorizing on the nature and problems of prose fiction had crossed the channel to England where authors lengthily discussed and enlarged their original borrowings. England knew well the works of La Calprenède, Scudéry, and d'Urfé, as well as the foremost French romances of the 18th century. Sir George Mackenzie, Congreve, Fielding, Richardson, Clara Reeve, Mrs. Radcliffe, and Monk Lewis all theorized in terms of their own and French works until 18th-century England came to a firm understanding of what the romance attempted to do in contrast to the novel. As Clara Reeve explained in the *Progress of Romance* :

The Romance is an heroic fable, which treats of fabulous persons and things. The Novel is a picture of real life and manners, and of the times in which it is written. The Romance in lofty and elevated language, describes what never happened nor is likely to happen. The Novel gives a familiar relation of such things, as pass every day before our eyes, such as may happen to our friend, or to ourselves; and the perfection of it, is to represent every scene, in so easy and natural a manner, and to make them appear so probable, as to deceive us into a persuasion (at least while we are reading) that all is real, until we are affected by the joys or distresses, of the persons in the story, as if they were our own.[4]

Walter Scott accepted the distinction between novel and romance, though he consciously chose the latter as his medium. He held firmly to the plot structure popular in his day, the unplanned story of episodes strung pearl-fashion in the manner of *Gil Blas*.

I have generally written to the middle of one of these novels, without having the least idea of how it was to end, in short in the *hab nab at a venture* style of composition.

I sometimes think my fingers set up for themselves independent of my head; for twenty times I have begun a thing on a certain plan, and never in my life adhered to it... for half an hour together.[5]

Since Scott was fundamentally a story-teller interested in amusing his readers, he accepted the pattern of the popular romances of the day : a handsome hero, a chaste heroine, and a surfeit of adventures calculated to hinder their union. But, as the French read him, history formed the nucleus around which his work took shape. Plot and characters had value only insofar as they presented different aspects of the period under consideration. Each personage represented some phase of the moral and social conditions of a given class; and plot, once an end in itself, now became a means. Thus, with the emphasis on history came a corresponding stress on reality. This attitude toward the romance coincided with that which France had been developing. The notion of realism, or a concern with every-day life, historical and actual, was the gift of 18th-century writers. The combination of these two constituted a legacy which youthful romanticism was to inherit.

III

By the time budding romanticism had begun to recognize itself as a literary movement, the *roman* had become almost a national rage. The vogue for Walter Scott's work inspired an army of imitators, and wise publishers with their hand on the public pulse kept printing historical romances as fast as the presses could move. M. Pigoreau, book dealer and former professor of Greek, published in 1821 a *Petite Bibliographie biographico-romancière* which listed the new titles on his shelves. M. Pigoreau did not approve. " Il y a cinquante ans, on ne connaissait dans Paris qu'un seul Cabinet de lecture; aujourd'hui chaque rue a le sien; la province en est inondée."[6] Though the Church forbade such works, he warned, the trade had so flourished that forty-five novels had appeared in December, 1821 alone. Consequently, each month he had to issue a supplement to the original bibliography in a desperate attempt to keep up with the trade, a state of affairs which he ungallantly blamed on women, both as readers and authors. In all his masculine pride he advanced the highly interesting theory that whereas men tended toward " haute littérature," women, being less well-educated, preferred romances which " s'écrit sous la dictée de la nature."[7]   And he ended with a great sneer at the insipidity of these works.

Young poets eager for fame and already meeting increased sales resistance to poetry took thoughtful note of the vogue. The obvious advantages of the genre attracted them, though they approached it shamefacedly, as if jeopardizing their artistic status. Prose had as yet won only a bare measure of respectability, despite its myriad practitioners. Still, even the fear of losing face could not blind the young men to the fact that prose sold, and sales meant income and reputation. In their race with each other for glory and leadership, some of the romanticists were lured up the primrose path toward the romance.

Despite the brilliance of their respective styles, the young romanticists handled the romance awkwardly. Hugo labored long and brought forth *Bug-Jargal* and *Hans d'Islande*, poor examples of a mixture of Scott and the terror novel. The same tired old recipe was saddled with monsters in addition to the stereotypes dear to contemporary readers. Balzac began his career the same way, though he prudently hid a flickering talent under various pseudonyms. It was the day of *Coelina ou l'Enfant du mystère*, and Balzac knew it. Hence the number of pot boilers like *L'Héritière de Birague* which he foisted on the public, a detestable novel which even its author called a "cochonnerie littéraire."[8] Assassination followed assassination as specters surged from all the dark corners of the usual unlighted castle.

Even when Hugo undertook to compete with Scott in *Notre-Dame de Paris*, he adopted the master's techniques. But he added a mystique of literature favored by the romanticists, the organic theory of creation. Emerson has perhaps best stated the case for this conception of art in his essay on " The Poet."

> For it is not metres, but a metre-making argument that makes a poem—a thought so passionate and alive that like the spirit of a plant or an animal it has an architecture of its own, and adorns nature with a new thing. The thought and the form are equal in the order of time, but in the order of genesis the thought is prior to the form.

Hugo held so firmly to this attitude—or he wanted his readers to think so—that he vigorously upheld it in the preface to *Notre-Dame*. • He claimed not to understand how an author could retouch what he had finished.• A first draft had to stand as written, or the whole series of assumptions which propped up the romantic ego would collapse. •Writers, particularly romanticists, had genius; genius came from God; the romantic writers thus created under the guidance of God; therefore their writings were of divine origin and, as such, could not be improved.• Hence, for Hugo, " un roman... naît, d'une façon en quelque sorte nécessaire, avec tous ses chapitres... La greffe et la soudure prennent mal sur des œuvres de cette nature, qui doivent jaillir d'un seul jet et rester telles quelles. Une fois la chose faite, ne vous ravisez pas, n'y retouchez plus."

• Because of this attitude, Hugo lost all sense of unity and proportion in his work. • Notre-Dame contained sermons, digressions, and an erroneous conception of history. To make his thesis seem plausible, he manipulated a series of marionettes called Phœbus, Frollo and Esmeralda with the result that Notre-Dame remains a curious combination of the historical romance and the terror novel, with borrowings from the melodrama, strung together in traditional manner. It contained a complete repertory of all the literary clichés since 1789, but offered nothing except rich and sonorous prose to cover the psychological nakedness of the characters. Hugo continued the worst elements of the romance recipe because he gave so little thought to his prose, an effect that would also show up in Les Misérables. Much better planned than Notre-Dame, it nevertheless compounded its digressions and meanderings, with interpolated chapters that impede the plot.

Vigny also tried his hand at the romance, but not to prepare a treatise on medieval architecture. Rather he assumed the difficult task of defending the nobility. The preface to Cinq-Mars carried a warning that art must never be considered except in its relationship to ideal beauty; truth was a secondary consideration. Vigny frankly admitted that the roman served only as a medium through which he could moralize; and since he drew his plot from the 17th century, the historical romance à la Scott seemed best suited to his need.

In 1830, the critics, as well as the authors, were little aware of the possibilities of prose. The abbé de Féletz, for one, could only repeat Huet's definition in his own consideration of the longer prose forms.[9] Certainly Musset was confused, since he called the Confession d'un enfant du siècle a novel.[10] Nor could George Sand clarify his position for him since she had had difficulty discovering what she planned to do herself. As she reminisced in the preface to Indiana (1852): " J'ai écrit Indiana durant l'automne de 1831. C'est mon premier roman; je l'ai fait sans aucun plan, sans aucune théorie d'art ou de

philosophie dans l'esprit." Apparently she prided herself on this
lack of direction for she repeated the same story in the *Histoire de
ma vie : Indiana* had been produced in a single outpouring, under
the pressure of an emotion so powerful that she wrote almost automatically. George Sand planned to instruct the readers with all the
passion in her big heart, to show how human dignity and happiness
could exist in society without great modification of the social structure.
She wept bitter tears over her characters, but these same tears so
blinded her to the problems of the medium in which she worked
that in 1835 she wrote to the Comtesse d'Agoult : " Vous avez envie
d'écrire ? par dieu, écrivez ! Écrivez vite, avant d'avoir pensé beaucoup ;
quand vous aurez réfléchi à tout, vous n'aurez plus de goût à rien
en particulier et vous écrirez par habitude. Écrivez, pendant que
vous avez du génie, pendant que c'est le dieu qui vous dicte, et non
la mémoire."[11]

IV

As prose came to dominate the age, the inevitable finally happened
when men like Balzac and Stendhal stopped to consider what they
were doing and, consequently, modified the old recipe so radically
that a new art form, the modern novel, resulted from their subsequent
revision of ancient practice and theory. Not that the romance is
necessarily inferior to the novel; it should be understood only that
it differs in intent and, consequently, in structure.

The change came gradually and was of such a nature that it could
come more easily from Balzac and Stendhal than from the members
of the Cénacle. First of all, these two men were not committed to the
adoration of verse and, secondly, unlike their poetic colleagues, they
did not subscribe to the organic theory of genius. They took their
work every bit as seriously as did the poets, with as much regard
for form as for content; and, as they wrote, they began to develop
consciously a series of principles, to search wonderingly for the
aesthetics governing their prose. There was, of course, no sudden
break with the past yet nonetheless they were to establish a new
kind of artistic structure. Their work actually stemmed from the
romance but contained changes of considerable importance which the
age itself suggested. Writing for a practical middle class of low in-

tellectual curiosity, with little feeling for the niceties of verse, they adjusted their art to fit modern conditions and modern audiences.

For one thing, their work had a time-perspective and a sense of development unknown in the romance. A nation that had enjoyed comparative internal peace for many generations saw an old dynasty disintegrate bloodily, then plunged into civil war while it held all Europe at bay. France spun dizzily through a succession of governments before it fell helpless at the feet of the great dictator. Under Napoleon, the national ego expanded with the country's elastic boundaries only to collapse suddenly after Waterloo. As the French painfully regained their self-respect during the Restoration, they began to wonder what had pushed them into such a whirlpool of history. Puzzled men sought reasons for the course of events, convinced that a logic existed behind them, and, in their consciousness of how yesterday had created today and tomorrow, they went in quest of patterns and motivating causes. Out of this would come modern history, with the wealth of explanatory philosophies that sprinkled the Restoration. In terms of literature, however, these same events left a generation aware of the great force time exerts on things and personalities. Lamartine caught this feeling in *Le Lac*, as did all the romanticists, for whom it furnished a theme they polished into a cliché.

Since Balzac and Stendhal lived in the same intellectual climate as the romanticists, both understood the power of Scott's formula and chose to write in terms of historical scenes. But their understanding of the past did not go so deep as Scott's, only to the recent maelstrom of a generation past. Balzac's recognition of historical perspective had appeared with the first signs of the Human Comedy, in *Les Chouans*. His sense of time and events led him to announce to Gosselin in 1833 a plan to conceive a contemporary history that would embrace all phases of French society. From then on Balzac worked with desperate urgency to paint his age in realistic colors. In so doing, he made certain shifts from the pattern of the romance which formed the basis for a new art form : he changed the focus of the historical romance from the remote and distant to the recently past. With him, the novel moved away from the romance, or what Ramon Fernandez called the recital.[12] Balzac shifted the romance's center of gravity to the immediate evocation of events with his intention to reveal the rhythm of episodes at the moment they were happening, not as something dead and gone. The author thus became a participant in the drama which he unrolled.

Like the historians, Stendhal, too, recognized that precise detail was necessary. As he scribbled on January 4, 1821, in a copy of William Cox's book, " Il faut que l'imagination apprenne les droits de fer de la réalité."[13] Since many of the novelists' readers could be expected to challenge the accuracy of contemporary settings, the romantic theory of local color had to be adjusted to match the new background. This meant the inclusion of detail drawn from life, and, since both Balzac and Stendhal used principally bourgeois characters, a realism of surrounding fact which had meaning and verisimilitude for the largest segment of the French reading public. Hence Balzac situated his plots against carefully delineated backgrounds like the pension Vauquer or the town of Saumur. He lavished a wealth of detail on characters and settings which made them familiar to his readers, all for a purpose which he summed up in a letter to the Countess Hanska in October, 1834 : " Les Études de Mœurs représenteront tous les effets sociaux sans que ni une situation de la vie,... ni une manière de vivre, ni une profession, ni une zone sociale, ... ait été oublié.... Ce ne seront pas des faits imaginaires; ce sera ce qui se passe partout."[14]

Similarly Stendhal considered his work as " un miroir qui se promène sur une grande route." The *Rouge* carried the subtitle of *chronique du dix-neuvième siècle ; Armance* consisted of scenes from contemporary social history; and the *Chartreuse* revolved around precisely defined historical and social settings. Even before 1818, Stendhal had initiated the method of collecting anecdotes from the newspaper for use in his writings. In fact he planned to announce in the second edition of *Rome, Naples et Florence* (1818) : " Les anecdotes que je transcris dans mon journal sont vraies pour moi et mes amis, et les circonstances recueillies avec la plus religieuse exactitude."[15] Actually, both Balzac and Stendhal wrote in terms of the total atmosphere of a milieu into which they placed characters who, for the first time in France, perhaps, became the subject of serious literary representation.

The ordinary citizen inevitably replaced the more heroic personages of previous ages as authors came to deal with the average and the daily. Balzac and Stendhal now faced the problem of integrating time-perspective, the historical attitude which demanded all the realistic detail, trivia, and petty vulgarity involved in contemporary life, and accounts of the lives of the small people who crowd the earth. They found themselves turning to a study of men and manners as they manipulated the real and the ordinary because, far more than the romancers, they dealt with personalities as manifest in society. Plot became subordinate to behavior as both Balzac and Stendhal focused on character analysis or social results rather than pure action. Not only did Balzac " faire concurrence à l'état civil," in terms of his personages, he turned them loose within the confines of a specific series of facts, then watched them react to each other and to their environment. In all cases, the motivation was familiar to readers. A kind of determinism runs through Balzac's works which explains, defines, and sets in relief the relationship of the characters to each other.

As a result, the novel began to assume a coherence unknown to the romance. Though Hugo never attained this kind of unity, he outlined it in a letter to Frédéric Morin on the *Misérables* : " Ce livre a été composé du dedans au dehors : l'idée engendrant les personnages, les personnages produisant le drame, c'est là la loi de l'art."[16] Balzac's great novels move in such a fashion, though at times somewhat jerkily. *Père Goriot* begins with the delineation of a setting into which the characters are plunged and then permitted to move about under conditions pre-determined by the author as characteristic of contemporary society. Further unity of composition was achieved when Balzac borrowed Geoffroy Saint-Hilaire's " théorie des analogues," while at the same time he accepted the scientist's affirmation of the determining action of exterior agents on forms.

Stendhal arrived at similar conclusions by a different route. Early in the century he had written his sister Pauline that the romance of adventure was fit only to forget. What he wanted to produce was a book without interminable stories within stories, the characters of which could be remembered. This he certainly achieved, for his *Rouge* became not merely the relation of Julien's odyssey but a comment on life itself as the hero moved through a series of episodes propelled by the logic implicit in the original premises. The *Rouge et le noir* and the *Chartreuse de Parme* are, then, *summa*, however incomplete. Stendhal portrays Julien and Fabrice as young men seeking an accord with themselves and the world, not in haphazard,

picaresque fashion or wandering along the enormous meanders of the
romance of adventure, but with all the dignity of men in essentially
tragic circumstances. Their life stories take place as the direct rendition
of event, in contrast to the romances, which run their course in a
verbal and psychological past. Events are born, not brought to life
by the magic of a ubiquitous and omniscient author.

Given these shifts, the relationship of the author to his creation
necessarily changed. In the romance, the point of narration lay outside
the story. Writers told stories out of the past to their readers, but
regarded their work as from a distance, alien to, and separate from,
themselves. Romancers did not hesitate to interrupt their tales to
discuss either the characters or the meaning of an incident. The
pressure of the didactic urge led them to interject chatty lectures
on love, morals, or literature. With the shift to a realistic account
of an average contemporary life, Balzac and Stendhal moved the point
of narration to within their plots. Whereas in the romance, the writer
admittedly manipulated characters, the novelist depended on the
characters themselves to make their own story as they reacted to each
other. The author established the original circumstances for motivation,
then withdrew to allow them to lead their own lives. As Balzac set
down the rule : " Dès que, dans un ouvrage, l'auteur se montre et
vous parle de lui, l'illusion cesse."[17] Time became a continuum,
always in the present, and occupied at a given moment by only one
person. Coincidence as a transfer between episodes was thus replaced
by a transition furnished by fact or the verisimilitude of personality.

Since Balzac and Stendhal both practiced this technique, they found
themselves restrained by the resistance of their material from inter-
posing themselves to any extent between reader and story. To be sure,
Balzac still managed to moralize, as did Stendhal. Didacticism continued in their works, but it became implicit, not explicit as in the
romance. Stendhal, for instance, came to depend on what Jean Prévost
calls a " monologue intérieur " to reveal the complexity of his characters
and to establish a rapport between the character and the reader, who
was suddenly gifted with omniscience.[18] Both men depended more
than their predecessors on permitting the story to expose ideas, and
each assumed to a larger extent than ever that the reader had sufficient
intelligence to grasp meaning from situation. Thus it was with some
cynicism that Stendhal dedicated the *Rouge* to the happy few.

V

Not only did the structure of the old romance and its time-sanctioned techniques alter under the pressure of new circumstances, but the characters, now conceived as people as well as vehicles for ideas, changed slightly in respect to their function of porte-paroles. In this regard the works of Balzac and Stendhal, especially those of the latter, established another essential distinction between the novel and the old romance. The romance worked in terms of allegory, whereas the novelist now thought in terms of symbols. As Albert Thibaudet explained, allegorical art rested on a rational framework which had to be made as visible as possible.[19] Allegory presents a series of characters, each of whom represents one thing : vice, virtue, or any given single idea. It becomes immediately apparent that the personages signify values and that the romance can be read on two levels, for the story and for the interplay of ideas. Characters thus tend to flatten the more they are utilized to maintain the author's logic. To avoid confusion, minor personages are rarely delineated; they appear in the plot like shadows, serve as needed, then vanish. Thus Des Grieux and Manon moved before a large number of faceless people as they acted out Prévost's Jansenist thesis. Even in the *Princesse de Clèves*, Nemours functioned as the Tempter, the Princess as Honor Assailed, and her mother as Wise Experience. Human activity envisaged in this way assumes a vaguely intensified significance as a part of the explicit didacticism.

However, the novelist, particularly Stendhal, found himself largely unable to exploit the possibilities of allegory. The techniques he utilized, a different attitude toward his material, meant that the use of allegory would hinder the presentation of average people in life situations. Emphasis had to fall on realistically motivated action, and any attempt to establish a clear and obvious intellectual parallel would present almost insuperable technical obstacles. The didactic aim, so intimately related to the 17th- and 18th-century use of flat, allegorical characters, is still present in the works of Balzac and Stendhal, but their major characters assume multi-faceted personalities and become " round " by virtue of their relationship to plot. Julien is a young man lost in a hostile world, as is Rastignac. Both Balzac

and Stendhal consider their characters in terms of symbols, or as
suggestions of a complete outlook on life.   Where the allegorically
intended protagonist consistently meant one thing, their personages
may signify several at once, or may express any one of their possible
total meanings in different situations.   Fabrice before and after the
battle of Waterloo suggests two different things, as does Julien in
prison and Julien in the Rênal household.   Rastignac vis-à-vis Vautrin
is not the same person as Rastignac sympathizing with Père Goriot.

Similarly, since the realistic approach to the novel prevented in-
forming the reader overtly of the author's purpose, Balzac and Stendhal
had recourse to ancillary symbols or signs planned to focus attention
on a fact or an event, or to give warning that the artist's intent could
be grasped by close consideration of the use of an object or a color.
The minute description of the Maison Vauquer, the carefully outlined
geography of Saumur, the constant reference to the color yellow, are
examples of what Balzac termed " des présentations matérielles que
les personnes donnent de leur pensée."[20]   In Stendhal's *Rouge et le
noir*, each episode in Julien's career carries with it some reference
to an object or to a color.   Not only do the red and the black of the
title suggest an attitude toward contemporary civilization, but the red
holy water, the blue uniform, the broken Japanese vase, and the
constant concern with ladders, constitute additional examples of the
same technique.   More so even than in Balzac, this particular use
of symbol runs through the *Rouge* almost as a counterpoint in the
manner in which other authors have used allegory.   Stendhal depends
on this practice to alert the reader to some of his meaning though,
obviously, such a symbol can carry but a small part of what he has
in mind.   Flaubert would later place more emphasis on this technique.
Beside such minor cases, the ironical references to the keyhole and
the fish in the marriage scene of *Madame Bovary*, there is the appearance
of the blind beggar in the last part to point up the complex symbolism of
the novel.

Curiously, the two men in question happened to exchange opinions
on their work that contain a wealth of information about their personal
theories.   In 1840, Balzac published in his *Revue parisienne* the " Études
sur M. Beyle," and Stendhal answered in a series of friendly letters
that constitute an exchange of trade secrets with his critic.   Balzac,
perhaps still smarting from treatment accorded him by the reviewers,

maintained that the utility of criticism was in the indication of the principles of modern art, and he adopted this point of view when he considered the *Chartreuse de Parme*. It was, he thought, the master-piece of the literature of ideas, though he had some honest reservations concerning Beyle's often incorrect style. But it is interesting to note that Balzac reaffirmed a principle necessary to the novel : " la loi dominatrice est l'Unité dans la composition." Stendhal's work con-formed to his conception of form, a compliment he could not pay to M. de Latouche's *Léo*, too full of unrelated episodes, overtly didactic, and without any character portrayal.

Stendhal answered from the consulate in Città-Vecchia with the defensive remark that he had never considered the *art* of writing a novel.[21] Making plans bored him. One night he wrote about twenty-five pages; on the next he reread the last four, then proceeded with his story. However, his next sentences betrayed more of an interest in technique than he apparently cared to admit. He advocated a simple, direct style, a natural approach to subject matter; as he pointed out, the wordier the book, the less part form played in it. And then he outlined the same theory of realism espoused by Balzac : " Le public en se faisant plus nombreux, moins mouton, veut un plus grand nombre de *petits faits vrais* sur une passion, sur une situation de la vie."

It would be gratifying to be able to show that Balzac and Stendhal created the form of the 19th-century novel in all its new and varied techniques, suddenly deviating from the old pattern in a literary miracle brought about by the facts of the new age. Unfortunately, no such claim can be made. As Northrup Frye has pointed out, it is rare to find a pure novel, free from all influence of romance theory.[22] Until Flaubert appeared, France could not boast of a prose writer who consciously probed most of the possibilities of the genre he was using, to arrive at a carefully considered aesthetics.

In the case of Balzac, not even the pious defence of Laure Surville can make masterpieces of all his novels. True, he planned his books, sometimes slaved over them, but many were hastily written, some acknowledgedly pot-boilers. *L'Héritière*, *Jean-Louis*, the *Vicaire des Ardennes*, all the earlier works, in addition to such later ones as the *Peau de chagrin* are frankly romances, lacking unity, with little, if any, character development and emphasizing principally the delights

of adventure.   Even the *Médecin de campagne* scarcely qualifies as
either novel or romance, being without any intrigue or dramatic
content.   However, *Père Goriot*, *Eugénie Grandet*, and the *Cousin Pons*
reveal a new form, still very much in the transition stage, half novel,
half romance, but definitely developing toward the true novel.

To this last Stendhal made a great contribution.   Though he had
tried to convince Balzac of his cavalier attitude toward the art of the
novel, his letters to Pauline show the contrary.   Actually, he had
been a close student of technique since the age of 17.   As Maurice
Bardèche has pointed out, the very digressions in the *Rouge et le
noir* form a kind of counterpoint to the action.[23]   The episodes in
both the *Rouge* and the *Chartreuse* are too carefully laid out, the
tone too consistent, to have been written on the spur of the moment.
Nevertheless, Stendhal held as loose a rein on his imagination as
Balzac.   Since he worked largely within the circle of his recollections,
he was constantly tempted to follow the will-o'-the-wisp of memory.
Furthermore, his aim of writing contemporary " history " also dictated
to some extent the structure of the work.   Both books, particularly
the *Chartreuse*, are close to the *mémoire* form, with overtones of the
picaresque.

Not until Flaubert, would the novel free itself of the romance.
But the novel would remain too complex, too new, for most 19th-
century authors, almost all of whom felt more at home in the familiar
confines of the romance.   The novel, exacting a blending of character
into setting and demanding a unity based on the logical motivation
of the personages, with theme and symbol subservient to the analysis
of characters living under modern conditions, was more difficult to
write and less easy to read.   Few professionals could afford to spend
the time needed on writing something so little understood by the age.
Romances continued to pour off the presses until the Académie des
sciences morales et politiques began to worry.   In 1857 this august
body proposed for a prize essay the topic : " Exposer et apprécier
l'influence qu'a pu avoir en France, sur les mœurs, la littérature
contemporaine, considérée surtout au théâtre et dans le roman."
Eugène Poitou won, but he obviously misunderstood and disliked
contemporary fiction.[24]   So few people really did comprehend the
novel that even in 1857, Loménie defined it in the *Revue des Deux
Mondes* as :

une fiction en prose donnée comme fiction par l'auteur, acceptée comme telle par le lecteur, et néanmoins composée toujours avec des prétentions à la vraisemblance, ayant généralement pour but d'exposer des faits imaginaires, mais naturels, de peindre des mœurs et des situations appartenant à la vie privée, où les évenemens de l'histoire ne figurent qu'accessoirement et où les personnages publics agissent surtout en tant que personnes privées; — ... enfin on s'arrête sur ce qui fait d'ordinaire le principal sujet d'un roman, sur cette peinture éternellement renouvelée de l'amour avec toutes ses nuances...

The modern novel was destined to remain scarce during the 19th century, but a new genre was being elaborated for the next century under the pressure of the same factors that had caused the shift from poetry and the vogue for the romance.

NOTES

1. Georges Duval, *Histoire de la littérature révolutionnaire*, Paris, Dentu, 1878, p. 147.

2. *De l'amour*, Paris, Mercure de France, 1911.

3. *Op. cit.*, p. 3.

4. New York, Facsimile Text Society, 1930, p. 111.

5. George Edward Smock, *Sir Walter Scott's theory of the novel*, unpublished doctoral dissertation, Cornell University, 1934, p. 56.

6. Paris, Pigoreau, 1821, preface.

7. Troisième supplément, Paris, Pigoreau, 1822

8. L.-J. Avigon, *Les Débuts littéraires d'Honoré de Balzac*, Paris, Perrin, p. 105.

9. *Mélanges de philosophie*, Paris, Guimbert et Dorez, 1830, VI, 3.

10. *Correspondance*, ed. by Léon Séché, Paris, Mercure de France, 1907, p. 60, à George Sand, 30 avril 1834.

11. *Correspondance*, Paris, Calmann Lévy, 1883, I, 300, mai 1835.

12. *Messages*, New York, Harcourt Brace, 1927, p. 68.

13. Jean Prévost, *La Création chez Stendhal*, Paris, Mercure de France, p. 274.

14. Quoted in Erich Auerbach, " In the Hotel de la Mole, " *Partisan Review*, XVIII, (May-June, 1951), p. 290.

15. Prévost, *op. cit.*, p. 152.

16. H. J. Forest, *L'Esthétique du roman balzacien*, Paris, Presses Universitaires, 1950, p. 238.

17. Quoted in Forest, *op. cit.*, p. 238.

18. *Op. cit.*, p. 100.

19. *Réflexions sur le roman*, Paris, Gallimard, 1938, p. 28.

20. Paul Bourget, " L'Art du roman chez Balzac, " *RDM*, 15 février 1926.

21. *Correspondance inédite*, Paris, Calmann-Lévy, n.d., II, 293, CCLXI.

22. " The four forms of fiction, " *Hudson Review*, II (1949-50).

23. *Stendhal romancier*, Paris, Table Ronde, 1947.

24. *Du roman et du théâtre contemporains et de leur influence sur les mœurs*, Paris, Durand, 1857.

CHAPTER 12

DECLINE OF CRITICISM

PROSE THE PEOPLE apparently wanted, and prose they got, as the presses clanked continuously to produce almost uncountable volumes of heady adventure stories. Critics complained loudly and often, but their very insistent hostility to prose was to break any hold they might have over the formation of reading tastes and ultimately to precipitate their own downfall.

I

When the editors of the new penny press discovered that there was a limit to the number of subscribers to be shared, they almost despaired until one by one they came to understand the fascination the romance held for the French public. Once the editorial mind grasped this fact, a diabolical marriage took place between the newspaper and the thriller. And curiously, professional writers of the utilitarian school loudly applauded the mésalliance. The newspaper offered a lucrative way to fortune and reputation, and the kind of story wanted, the roman-feuilleton, was an easy type of recipe literature to produce. In fact, the old romance structure contained all the ingredients needed.

The first tentative use of the roman-feuilleton produced results astonishing even to the most optimistic. Serialized versions of popular novels attracted subscribers in droves. Alexandre Dumas' *Capitaine Paul* brought Girardin's *Siècle* 100,000 new subscribers in three weeks. Women went so mad over his works that the success of *Les Trois Mousquetaires* and *Vingt Ans Après* startled even the most cynical competitors. Since the other papers had lost readers to the *Siècle*, they retaliated by offering feuilletons of their own. The new public reigned as king of contemporary literature, the satisfaction of its whims and fads spelling the difference between fame, fortune, and literary failure. Vigny sadly recorded in his *Journal* the coronation of the Paris bourgeois, to whom the newspapers daily offered a selection of serialized stories.

But an opposition was forming. Even Balzac, the entrepreneur, publicly repented. The *Illusions perdues* struck so close to home with its portrait of the new trade that it infuriated the press. However, the principal objection to the " industrial " literature was raised by the critics. In 1840, Alexis Dumesnil even went so far as to blame the romance for all the moral difficulties of the age.[1] Five years later, Alphonse du Valconseil concluded from an analysis of current production that the feuilleton had grown powerful enough to make or break newspapers.[2] The *Revue des Deux Mondes* added its statement of disgust at the trend when one of its critics, F. de Lagenevais, reported in " Le Roman dans le monde " that the novel had so compromised itself that it was becoming a secondary genre that smelled rankly of the atelier.[3] Paul Limayrac followed this inquiry with an article " Du roman actuel," that mournfully repeated the same charges : the romance had prostituted itself to the people; the feuilleton, an evil thing, sowed such corruption that the critic dreamed of the day when the public itself would reject the literary monster.[4] The *Revue* felt so strongly about the feuilleton, particularly Sue's *Juif errant*, that it unleashed a tame poet against the menace. Even the editors of a strongly established magazine felt that the dubious alliance of newspaper and romance had produced a dangerous child. Amédée Pommier, therefore, was instructed to castigate the " traffiquans littéraires," in classical Alexandrines. In poetry far from deathless, he barked awkwardly at the opposition, using the time-honored technique of multiplied invective :

> Soldats (C'est à mes vers que je parle en ces termes),
> Soyez plus que jamais et résolus et fermes.
> La circonstance exige un vigoureux effort.
> Nous rentrons en campagne, et nous allons d'abord
> Faire une charge à fond sur les auteurs sans style,
> Sur la littérature infime et mercantile.
> Chauds encor du courroux dont vous avez frémi,
> Attaquez bravement ce nouvel ennemi.
> Au roman-feuilleton quand vous livrez bataille,
> Ne jugez pas sa force en raison de sa taille,
> Et que de l'art français ce fils adultérin,
> Par vos coups abattu, reste sur le terrain.[5]

One by one the better-known contemporary critics echoed the complaint. The defenders of literary purity and the status quo welcomed all aid and comfort, even such indignant complaints as the "Lettre d'un habitant de Vendôme à M. le Directeur de la Revue de Paris." Its author, one Emile de la Ripopière, moaned that such trivia was addling his wife's pate and, even more horrible, threatened to desecrate all literature.[6] Jules Janin had tried earlier to stem the tide with a satire on the terror novel, *L'Ane Mort et la femme guillotinée;* but when even this proved of no avail, Désiré Nisard published a "Manifeste contre la littérature facile," an attack on all the literary hacks who indulged in recipe art.[7] Nisard admitted that a depression had encouraged authors to fly into the tainted arms of the penny press, but he begged his colleagues to choose artistic death to pecuniary dishonor.

Born with a pugnacious nature, Gustave Planche could not help joining the fray. Time and again he flailed happily at factory literature with all the lusty zeal of an unregenerate defender of the national tradition. With a curious intuition that industrialization somehow was involved in the change that had obliterated the old literature, he prophesied such a mechanization of talent that the future would see the marketing of a machine for inventing dialogue and plot. The acid-tongued Planche delighted in emphasizing the banality of the feuilleton, each of which imitated its predecessor in complete disregard for simplicity or any semblance of *vraisemblance.*

But Planche showed real anxiety over the state of affairs. Since he considered it the function of the critic to unite art and morality, he worried about the social effects of the newspaper and the industrialization of literature. The critic of the *Revue des Deux Mondes* would have preferred the old days, when readers paid close attention to what an arbiter of literary taste proclaimed. During his apprenticeship on the *Débats,* he had learned well the lesson of every budding critic, so well, in fact, that the only books he was permitted to review were those which the editors felt could be attacked with impunity. But any that bore famous names were kept from falling into his harsh hands. Despite this precaution, his savage honesty made the proprietors of the *Débats* request that he honor some other journal with his strange talent.

Planche left, and he took with him the conviction that his own colleagues were somehow at fault for the sorry state of contemporary literature. In an article in the *Artiste* (1837), he exposed the lack of intellectual integrity in the members of his profession.[8] There were at the moment, Planche thought, only two kinds of critics, the " indifférens," and the " passionnés." The former lived in fear of offending anybody; the latter gleefully insulted all comers, rubbing their hands in sadistic pleasure at the screams of rage wrung from sensitive authors. The existence of these two groups explained the chaos on the literary scene : writers swore allegiance to the *indifférens* and vowed vengeance on the *passionnés*. As for himself, Planche demanded a new kind of criticism, one that would disinterestedly seek the truth and convert it into action on the masses.

However serious his remarks, Planche was indulging in wishful thinking; the reign of the objective critic was still far in the distant future of some never-never era. He came to this realization slowly but, many years later, in 1852, when he asked rhetorically if criticism had done its duty, he could only reply sadly, " je ne le crois pas."[9] He made the same tart comments on his confrères, but he still could not bring himself to believe in the kind of passionately complimentary criticism which the romanticists wanted. Another way had to be found short of burning incense before every self-appointed genius.

Though Planche and his colleagues tried to stem the tide, the roman-feuilleton rose steadily in popularity until even the Olympian Sainte-Beuve cried halt. But the angriest shouts of all came from the tart and testy ultra-conservative, Alfred Nettement. In a series of essays on the feuilleton, this starchy critic adopted a tone of heavy sarcasm.[10] All the scorn of an unreconstructed classicist was heaped on the principal sinner, Eugène Sue, though fundamentally Nettement was defending the reign of the bourgeoisie against all who dared challenge the status quo in either politics or literature. Nettement found Sue's work based on a series of clichés that pandered to popular illusions. Thiers had once pointed out that every revolution needed a Jesuit or a Carlist for daily immolation. Sue prospered by giving the people the Jesuit it needed and resurrected Bonapartism to flatter a latent sense of nationalism. He employed all the cheap tricks of the melodrama to paint a picture of the people as good, honest, infallible, and completely free of any responsibility for thoughtless acts which, n the last analysis, could be blamed either on the rich or on society itself. Nettement castigated the feuilleton as a union of police court and newspaper, a kind of black market in which money-hungry authors hastily ground out insipid prose. Merchants, he sneered, seekers after fool's gold, whose very prosperity seduced honest young writers. Even the old familiar characters were disappearing in favor of monsters spawned in the diseased imagination of psychopathic writers.

For all Nettement's asperity, he could not match Louis Reybaud. The latter had noted that satire ricocheted harmlessly and therefore he turned to a surer weapon : caricature. To combat the pestilence, he summoned forth Jérôme Paturot on the traditionally French theory that it is easier to laugh something out of existence than to try to argue with it. Consequently his hero, a perfect specimen of the naïve and gullible young man, blundered from one impossible situation into another while he sought a social position more befitting his genius than selling nightcaps.[11] Jérôme burned to join the literary revolution, to confound the Philistines with 18,000 lines of verse in the Babylonian manner, or a bristling romance of adventure. When these genres did not fall within the scope of his talent, Jérôme sought the advice of a veteran who promptly cast pearls at him.

To succeed, the veteran advised, a writer had to understand the importance of the feuilleton to the entire middle-class, second only to the pot-au-feu and the loaf of bread. Some writers had abused their position to propound radical social doctrines, but the old veteran saw his mission as one to relieve France of some of its ennuis. Therewith the feuilletoniste gave a sure recipe for success with the newspapers, the ancestor of the Hollywood serial. Most important of all, he considered the construction of the chapter to distinguish the master from the amateur. Each had to end on a note of suspense calculated to entice anxious crowds to the stands for the next installment. Art, for the feuilletoniste, meant manœuvering Arthur, the perennial hero, until he hung desperately in an untenable position, only to be saved in the next chapter. Poor Arthur suffered incredible punishment to keep subscribers on edge until the next issue of the paper arrived.

Once launched in this fashion it behooved the neophyte to follow the accepted standards. Take one female, young, innocent beyond belief, and persecuted. Let her be hounded by a brutal and cruel tyrant, preferably an uncle. Add a hero, simple to the verge of nausea, but with all the virtues esteemed by an adoring mother. Thus the stage is set for a comfortable and reassuring duel between vice and virtue. The heroine might suffer a few bad moments as the villain pursued her, but the reader could always remain pleasantly comforted by the knowledge that right finally triumphed over wrong, even though the author had to resort to a tour de force to accomplish the socially acceptable. The only problem for the author was to maintain the heroine in jeopardy either of life, or worse, for the appropriate number of installments. Add a few horrors, blood stains or sliding panels, season slightly with a supposedly moral aim, applied while the heroine panted hopelessly in the toils of the leering villain, and Jérôme could hope for European success and a profitable career.

Jérôme found that the prescribed pattern made for such mechanical work that, under the pressure of the necessity to produce, all thought of art disappeared. The essential fact was to move quickly, to invent readily, and then spin out the tenuous thoughts over weeks of daily papers. Pressure on him became so great that, adopting current practice, he asked his beloved Malvina to resurrect authors from the peace of literary Limbo. All went well until he made the great error of robbing Ducray-Duminil. Poor Jérôme had committed the one sin for which a feuilletoniste could not be pardoned.

II

Reybaud tried hard but even his witty satire failed. The romans-feuilleton poured off the presses to the delight of subscribers. Newspaper sales boomed and everybody seemed happy but the critics. They might well be sad, for, ironically, the same set of circumstances that had conspired to permit the feuilleton was to push criticism from the high position it had once enjoyed. In retrospect, it seems that such a fate almost had to come. The spread of education, cheap books made possible by the new industrial technology, the tremendous growth of the urban proletariat and, finally, the merger of the newspaper with the romance, all combined to create a climate hostile to the traditional powers of criticism.

The change came gradually, after years of glorious reign. Malherbe and Boileau had raised the critic's banner high, and all through the 17th and 18th centuries critics had remained merciless judges from

whose sentences there could be no appeal. They were men entrusted
with the task of keeping French literature true to tenets laid down
during the golden age. Even the Revolution seemed to leave untouched
this one vestige of an otherwise well-trammeled past. At the dawn
of the century, when the professors had come to join the ranks of the
critics as embalmers of tradition, the combination seemed unconquerable. The old and the cherished were sheltered in the temple of Aca-
deme, from which brash young innovators were ruthlessly scourged.
Stalwarts like La Harpe were backed by Guizot, Cousin, and Villemain,
all dedicated to keeping the faith of the *juste milieu*.

Until about 1830 the critics met no great challenge. During the
Empire men like Joubert, connoisseurs of acknowledged taste, acted
as " directeurs de conscience littéraire " for the whole nation. Under
them several generations of readers were warned that literary salvation
lay in keeping the commandment

Le vrai, le beau, le juste !

Dussanet likewise preached " healthy " doctrines, aided by the wasp-
tongued Abbé de Féletz, a man who would have been conservative
in the 17th century. Everything seemed serene during the Restoration,
when Sainte-Beuve entered the brotherhood, so much so that in
1829, when Jules Janin wrote a preface to *L'Ane mort et la femme
guillotinée*, he smugly extolled the power of the critic : " à cette question
que la Critique adresse nécessairement à un livre nouveau : Où allez-
vous ? c'est non seulement pour l'auteur un devoir de répondre, mais
encore une bonne précaution à prendre."

But hard times were approaching, and they were shaped in part
by the romanticists. In the past, literary judgment had been relatively
easy for a man of taste and education : one either wrote according
to Boileau, or one was not a writer. Recently, however, Mme de
Staël's doctrine of the relativity of taste had seriously affected the
young. In fact, the new school dared contend that a writer was free
to create as he wished, and some of these upstarts even suggested
that France needed a new criticism. Perhaps Janin remembered
Aloysius Bertrand's famous anecdote about the unfortunate M. Paul
Foisset. Admitted to the intimacy of the Cénacle, M. Foisset had
naively proffered a suggestion to Hugo after a reading from the master's

work. Hugo silenced him with a gesture. " Voyez-vous, mon cher M. Foisset, nous autres, nous ne critiquons jamais, parce que la critique nuit à l'originalité. D'ailleurs, la critique est une chose impie, car c'est Dieu qui a fait le poète."[12]

Hugo's attitude was exaggerated but, certainly, the romanticists were far from content with the manhandling they had been receiving from the professional critics ever since their movement first gained public recognition. The Cénacle not only insisted on a new start in literature but also on a renovation of critical attitudes. What they fervently desired was a criticism liberal enough to understand the new without automatically indulging in a stream of frantic invective. Hugo had prayerfully asked for this point of view in the preface of *Cromwell* at a time when romanticism still remained the target of any fledgling conservative. But soon, he trumpeted, the Philistines would be confounded. The 19th century would see a criticism based on the sensible premise that writers must be judged according to " les principes immuables de cet art et les lois spéciales de leur organisation personnelle." Modern critics would penetrate the very mind of the author to grasp the creation through the eyes of the creator. Hugo spoke loudly, perhaps to comfort himself, for at that moment romanticism had great need of understanding.

But Hugo spoke too soon and too provocatively. Old-line critics smiled at his brashness and continued hacking away, gleefully uncovering breaches of the rules or a chronic inability to remain within the limits of a genre. Therefore, in the preface to the *Orientales*, Hugo returned to the attack. His outline of the theory of art for art's sake was calculated to confound the enemy; it warned both writers and critics that art existed only for the artist, that public and critic participated in his creation only on sufferance. Hugo was later to retract when he had climbed beyond reach of hostile shafts but, for the moment, he bitterly resented antagonistic remarks. Once more he roundly scored the critics who had dared mock the very book that sought to instruct them.

Hugo reacted differently from Janin : a critic had no right to question a creative writer; no one could ask why a given subject had been chosen. Criticism should be limited to but a single question : was the work good or bad ? No praise, no reproaches, just a discussion of the author's purpose and the means used to attain it. The

critic was thus transformed into a mere commentator on techniques.

The critics, however, refused to be convinced; in fact they disagreed vigorously. Since the men of the Cénacle had attained national reputations by 1830, and many were, in fact, far better known than their judges, they felt less vulnerable to the ruin that carping attack can often bring. Moreover, by that time, they had even charmed a few critics into their circle. Traditionalists still sniped energetically at the elders, but they fell on the unprotected youngsters of the Petit Cénacle with abandon. The *Figaro* jeered at their mannerisms, while other papers warned of the menace to society implicit in the doctrine of art for art's sake. The *bousingo* became a favorite whipping boy, an object of mixed fear and contempt. The young men scratched back, particularly Gautier, who denounced these Bossuets of the Café de Paris as literary assassins paid by the line to murder talent. The morality of the people, the amelioration of society, the edification of cultured young ladies, none of these was the business of the poet. Only form and style, image and rhyme, were of any consequence.

However great the breach between writer and critic had been during early romanticism, it widened noticeably with the advent of the daily paper. Critics had pontificated at their ease during the Restoration, writing for a comparatively small elite with great respect for tradition. Thus their opinions had carried tremendous weight in proportion to the number of potential readers. But the appearance of the newspaper seems to have altered this position. As Sainte-Beuve pointed out in his essay on industrial literature, a change occurred when the newspapers reacted to the heavy taxes imposed by the Martignac law of 1828.[13] Whereas editors had previously permitted a small number of announcements, they now encouraged them for income to supplement funds received from subscriptions. As the habit of reading newspapers spread, advertising became even more important to the financial health of the journals, with the result that the advertiser tended increasingly to be treated with the respect due his bank account.

Since, at this time, a great deal of space was reserved for book ads, publishers were treated gingerly, in exact proportion to the amounts they fed into newspaper treasuries. The power of the franc began to limit the power of the critic and the latter, sometimes instructed by employers to handle carefully the popular writers of the big houses, found their positions untenable.   Literary principles and the feelings of the advertisers did not mix well.

Thus the penny press signalled the end of the reign of the all-powerful judges.   First of all, the function of the critic changed.   The subscribers to the *Presse* or the *Siècle* had had little to do with aesthetics, felt, in fact, completely unawed by such ideas.   Few cared anything about Boileau's precepts and the sanctity of poetry.   Therefore a critic was under pressure to adopt the same utilitarian attitude as the men of the Cénacle if he hoped to reach the new audience.   But he had to abandon all discussion of the fine points of prosody, to hold in check an ever-present desire to sparkle on some obscure point of literary history. Rather his new position demanded that he limit himself to the simplest kind of observations, to ideas easily grasped, to points of morality or to a discussion of plots.   In fact, the modern newspaper transformed the critic into a new phenomenon, the book reviewer. Sainte-Beuve, as usual, put his finger on the problem when he wrote to Charles Monnard :

La plus grande difficulté est de fixer l'attention d'un public léger et saturé, et même celle des journalistes encore plus légers et plus saturés eux-mêmes. Dans l'état où est tombée la presse, il est peu d'indications à vous donner. Le sceptre de l'opinion littéraire n'est nulle part; il n'y a plus de sceptre. La critique, à proprement parler, n'existe plus dans les journaux quotidiens; ce n'est guère que commercialement et par argent qu'on obtient non seulement des annonces mais des articles, lesquels sont d'ordinaire de peu d'effet.[14]

The only alternative open was for the critic to persist in writing for the élite, disregarding the newspaper readers as unqualified for such discussions.   This became the attitude of the proud few who had already attained some measure of reputation, of Saint-Beuve, for instance, who refused to change his standards.   In a sense, it was another kind of art for art's sake, a proud but unpopular stand, as the Petit Cénacle could testify.   Now that public opinion counted more than discerning judgment, many an author felt he could dispense with the good will of the critics.   In December, 1833, Désiré Nisard already sensed the growing separation between both critic and reader and critic and writer.

Quant aux deux autres manches de la littérature facile qui ont nom *roman* et *conte*, on peut voir que les critiques dont l'opinion est la plus comptée se refusent depuis longtemps à analyser tout livre qui porte la marque de cette fabrique. Mais aussi voilà tous les grands hommes qui accusent les critiques de déserter l'art, et s'en vont semant par le peuple des bruits d'injustice inouïe, d'ingratitude criante. Ingrats de quoi ? — Les critiques ne se souviennent-ils donc plus que les grands hommes leur ont dit : *Mon cher ami !*[15]

In turn, each critic raised his hands in horror at the turn of events. Sainte-Beuve cried out against industrial literature; Nisard and Janin fought a violent rear-guard action against the use of recipes. Most often it was the romanticists who felt their anger. Because of their early insistence on a new kind of criticism, the professionals blamed them for the threat to their very existence. Inevitably, too, the feuilleton received its share of the blame. Critics resented its dominance over the press since it not only appealed to a huge mass beyond their reach but also robbed them of space in the journals. By 1845 even the dullest knew that the peculiar combination of technological advance and democratic education had pushed an objecting body of critics to a position almost akin to art for art's sake. Thus it is not surprising to find the irascible Nettement swiping vigorously at the roman-feuilleton, the newspaper, the new literature, and anybody who refused to accept the authority of criticism. All he hated seemed symbolized in Eugène Sue's *Juif Errant,* by the printing of which he claimed that the *Journal des Débats* relinquished any claim to moral and intellectual leadership. For principled critics faced with a generation of authors more hungry for money than for glory he had a solution : they should pledge never to mention the works of industrial writers. It might seem like cutting off his nose to spite his face, but Nettement felt that, in any case, criticism had been killed.[16]

This strange situation produced a new kind of critic, one interested more in *what* was said rather than in *how* it was said. Most of these men adjusted their art to write specifically for the middle class, as apostles of bourgeois standards. Like Nettement, Saint-Marc Girardin worried so much about morality that he scarcely ever discussed litera-ture. During the years 1827-1830, while he was supposed to be writing literary criticism for the *Débats*, he rarely ever found time for it, preferring to review books on history, education, or voyages. When Saint-Marc became an academic, he brought to the Sorbonne a dedication to the task of safe-guarding French morals. By teaching students to seek *le beau* in *le vrai* and *le bien*, he expected to serve both the current government and the cause of " sane " writing.

He was not alone, to be sure. Villemain, Nisard, Cuvillier-Fleury, Sacy, Janin, Labitte, Vitet, Ampère, Pontmartin, Mazade, and Lément, all said about the same thing. But Saint-Marc seems to fit almost too perfectly the slogan " médiocre avec éclat." In fact he freely admitted that " toutes les fois qu'un jeune homme me vient confier qu'il veut être homme de lettres, je le détourne de cette carrière."[17]

Curiously, some writers also resented the change from the old to the new. Of all people, George Sand argued against tame critics who jumped at the command of the treasurer. When a reporter for the *Figaro*, she had felt the heavy hand of the editor on all her work. As she complained to Jule Boucoiran in 1831, M. de Latouche peeped over everybody's shoulder to impose his whims and prejudices on all. Here she first learned of a criticism tied to the purse strings of advertisers and in the preface to *Indiana* Sand joined the growing host who complained of the hirelings. " Cette race," she called them, and in 1835 she complained to the editor of the *Journal de l'Indre* that it was discouraging to write for people who couldn't read, and worse to write for people who didn't *want* to read. She cynically recalled that during the July Monarchy one could have said " Dis-moi dans quel journal tu écris, et je vais te dire quel artiste tu vas louer ou blâmer."[18]

Balzac, of course, welcomed the debate. In the *Monographie de la presse parisienne*, he repeated all the previous insults, even managed to add a few of his own. Having antagonized most Paris editors, Balzac was considered fair game for all critics, for him they reserved their choicest insults. Consequently, he indicted these scribblers for soiling their own profession. The contemporary critic was only an impotent author, unable to create and unwilling to let others create. Like his confrères, Balzac sensed the great change. No longer did it matter to have ideas, since a sharp tongue substituted for a sharp mind. Criticism had reached such a low point that its practitioners worked only to perpetuate their own positions, decent only to mediocrity or that scribbler known as the feuilletoniste.

Chose étrange ! les livres les plus sérieux, les œuvres d'art ciselées avec patience et qui ont coûté des nuits, des mois entiers, n'obtiennent pas dans les journaux la moindre attention... tandis que le dernier vaudeville du dernier théâtre... enfin les pièces manufacturées aujourd'hui comme des bas..., jouissent d'une analyse complète et périodique.

NOTES

1. *Histoire de l'esprit public en France depuis 1789*, Paris, Pagnerre, 1840, p. 90.

2. *Revue analytique et critique des romans contemporains*, Paris, Gaume, 2 vols.

3. 15 mai 1843.

4. 1 septembre 1845, p. 957.

5. Décembre 1844, pp. 893-94.

6. *Revue de Paris*, février 1840.

7. Essay published in December, 1833, reprinted in *Essais sur l'école romantique*, Paris, Calmann Lévy, 1891, pp. 173-4.

8. " Du rôle de la critique, " X.

9. " La Poésie et la critique en 1852, " *RDM*, XVI, 1852, p. 928.

10. *Études critiques sur le roman feuilleton*, Paris, Perrodil, 1845, 2 vols.

11. *Jérôme Paturot à la recherche d'une position sociale*, Paris, Dubochet, 1846.

12. Cargill Sprietsma, *Aloysius Bertrand*, Paris, Champion, 1926, p. 124.

13. *Portraits contemporains*, II.

14. *Correspondance générale*, Paris, Stock, III, 398, ce 15 Xbre 1840.

15. " Manifeste contre la littérature facile, " in *Essais sur l'école romantique*, Paris, Calmann Lévy, 1891.

16. *Études critiques sur le feuilleton-roman*, Paris, Perrodil, 1845, I, 62.

17. Laurence Wylie, *Saint-Marc Girardin*, Syracuse University Press, Syracuse, 1940, p. 161.

18. *Histoire de ma vie*, IV, 239.

CHAPTER 13

THE NEW MYTHOLOGY

THE NEW ERA, however, did more than limit the power of the critic; it directly affected what an author wrote. The early 19th century saw the tremendous expansion of the bourgeoisie because of the machine which, though it may have spread misery and squalor, also created new sources of wealth. As the Orléans monarchy matured, men of property became the idols of the day, money the measure of success and social standing. This attitude most writers could understand since, with the passing of the patron, an author necessarily had to furnish his own support. Consequently, however dedicated to the Muses a man might be, he also had to consider the monetary value of his talent. The writer became a business man and, as the reading public expanded, he increasingly dealt with the economic aspect of a book. Literature became property, cherished and defended as such, though this last the authors had learned the hard way. At first naïve in the marts of trade, they had literally been robbed by pirates. Editions of Parisian best sellers appeared all over France while their enraged authors helplessly tried to protect their incomes. It took constant vigil and countless lawsuits to restrain the hordes of trespassers.

Being for the most part " utilitarians " in the full sense of the word, authors and editors had to protect a major investment in time and talent. Royalties meant security to the authors; sales were the economic blood of the publishers. Each in his own way was vitally interested in the preservation of literary property, the author more than the publisher since adequate returns might free him from the bondage of tyrants like Buloz. The latter drove his writers mercilessly, then shrugged when they stamped out of his office in revolt. " Bah! ils reviendront, il y a de l'argent à l'auge."[1]

Ironically enough, a group of authors united with Louis Desnoyer,

director of the *Siècle*, to defend author and publisher from pirate
and plagiarist. Unlicensed borrowing had become so general that
few men received even a small fraction of the money their books
earned in France, to say nothing of the rest of Europe. Balzac, one
of the most injured by unethical practices, took an eager part in the
formation of a mutual protection alliance to be known as the Société des
Gens de Lettres. So earnestly did he labor that his colleagues jealously
accused him of an exaggerated tendency towards " la fiscalité littéraire."
With so many prima donnas the society's first years were stormy,
but its foundation established an important fact : writers had agreed
to share in the scramble for the sacred franc. Their banding together
symbolized, in a sense, the highest triumph of the middle class.
Creative artists had finally accepted contemporary values; Mammon
ruled supreme and the bourgeoisie could exult that at last it had
brought art to heel.

II

But the age set its brand on literature in other ways. The Industrial
Revolution so permeated the era of Louis-Philippe that the very
language of the writer changed. The fact that an increasing number
of poets turned to prose for a decent living tended to raise stylistic
standards but, conversely, the aim of both novelist and romancer to
describe contemporary society in terms meaningful to the great masses
made literary prose, and to some extent the vocabulary of poetry,
conform to that of the age. New words crept in, from the factory,
technical words with a music magical to writers. Hugo rolled them
around his tongue, savoring their evocative power before he used them
in sonorous prose or poetry.

To a lesser degree other writers followed this trend, but the most
revolutionary change came from the introduction into literature of
argot, the slang peculiar to the underworld. Many an author aped
the pithy expressions of the *Memoires de Vidocq;* Hugo or Balzac,
especially, had occasion to put into the mouths of characters the
idioms of the sea, a province, or a specialized trade. *Enfin Malherbe
partit.* As Georges Matoré has shown in *Le Vocabulaire et la société
sous Louis-Philippe*,[2] the vocabulary of the writer expanded enormously
as authors began consciously to make the language of their books

approximate more closely that of the average man, or to pluck special-ized phrases from the various trades and professions. Neologisms flooded the French language, some of them the gift of the machine age. In this respect the romance reduced many a phrase to the status of cliché as authors ransacked the language for effects.

More than that, the Industrial Revolution offered writers a whole series of images and similes, references to the puffing machine, the clanging presses, or the dirty nakedness of the factory. At first only the more spectacular aspects of the change were evident : the snorting locomotive contrasted to the miraculous steamship. Poets preferred the clean, quiet grace of the balloon, Gautier's favorite image, while novelists tended to use the more ugly aspects of the era. Though most poets rejected the Industrial Revolution on aesthetic grounds, nonetheless they utilized its possibilities. In fact the concern of writers with the new provoked a wrangle over the use of technical terms which Planche summarized in the *Revue des Deux Mondes* of 1837.

Surprisingly early a few writers began to pluck images from in-dustrialization. At the beginning of the Restoration Rouget de Lisle composed a *Chant des industriels* more notable for its ideas than its poetry:

> Déployant ses ailes dorées,
> L'industrie au cent mille pas,
> Joyeuse, parcourt nos climats
> Et fertilise nos contrées...[3]

Not to be outdone, Madame Amable Tastu likewise celebrated *La France et l'industrie* in unimaginative *vers de circonstance* intended to extol an exhibit of cloth at the Louvre put on by French imitators of Albion.[4]

Most romanticists, however, came more slowly to acknowledge the new imagery. Prior to 1830, poets fiercely defended their purity. They were still full of youth and theory, too intent on their right to perfect freedom of art to lift their eyes to the new mountain. The Middle Ages attracted fledgling royalists, particularly since nascent industry was obviously accompanied by the continued rise of the constitutionally-minded bourgeoisie and the pushing newly rich. Though industrial capitalism, sprawling, ugly, and terrifying, had some of the attractions of the monsters they loved to describe, they failed at first to recognize the analogy. Only hesitantly, after 1830, did they grant it room in their poetry. Since prose came second with most of them, the machine age here made its most important conquest.

A break in this early prejudice came in 1830 when Jean-Jacques Ampère, a member in good standing of Madame Récamier's coterie, published two poems in the *Heures de Repos*, " La Flotte " and "La Democratie," both built around the image of the steamship. The next year Vigny was struck by the fact that Paris, from an elevation, resembled a gigantic bubbling factory cauldron, as full of latent power as the new industries. In part III of the *Illusions perdues (Les Souffrances de l'inventeur)*, Balzac went closer to the heart of the matter. The story of David Séchard tells of a search for methods of making cheaper paper to feed the now ravenous presses. The inventor symbolized the urge to mechanize, to simplify old procedures for greater profit. Lamartine, as a politician, made many a speech about the machine; but as a poet he excluded the Industrial Revolution from his verse until he came to write *La Chute d'un ange*. At that time he became so entranced with the possibilities of industrialization that he set a pattern for Jules Verne. A curious combination of the balloon and airplane, loaded with soldiers, landed in the wilderness to seize Cédar and the old prophet. As for Hugo, in 1832 he began *Les Misères*, later better known as *Les Misérables*, and his manuscript catalogued many of the phenomena that marked the age. Hugo discussed the obvious contemporary ills in an effort to show how the factory system could be made to work for the good of all under the guidance of benevolently despotic employers. In a sense *Les Misérables* was a treatise on the organization of a modern, mechanized society.

To be sure, not even all the romanticists could agree with Hugo. Some joined the art for art's sake group in its condemnation of industrialization as anti-human and anti-poetic. Auguste Barbier jibed at the English factory system in both " Lazare" and " La Machine." Musset concurred when he celebrated the completion of the St. Etienne-Lyon railroad on August 15, 1833 by publishing part IV of *Rolla* in the *Revue des Deux Mondes* :

> Les monts sont nivelés, la plaine est éclaircie;
> Vous avez sagement taillé l'arbre de la vie !
> Tout est bien balayé sur vos chemins de fer;
> Tout est grand, tout est beau, — mais on meurt dans votre air.

Vigny agreed " qu'un monde tout nouveau se forge à cette flamme,"
but did not generate any particular hostility toward it until he heard
the grim news of the Versailles railroad catastrophe of May 8, 1842.
Privately he warned the Marquise de la Grange that the accident
was a warning that the machine might eventually conquer man.[5]
Publicly he displayed in the *Maison du berger* a hostility to the devasta-
tion the locomotive left in its smoky wake. About the same time,
Amédée Pommier attacked the grey materialism of technological
progress in a book with the curious, though apt, name of *Colères*.
The attitude became almost a fashion, a sign to the aesthetically
pure that differentiated the literary sheep from the goats.

Certainly Gautier seemed to think so. In the *Charte de 1830*, he
expressed the same contempt for the " rails-way" that was implicit
in the preface to *Mademoiselle de Maupin*. Peering judiciously into
the future, he ventured a prophecy that the railroad was a scientific
curiosity destined to disappear once industrialists tired of their toy.
Why save so much time? Why the need for speed? Only a fool
could believe that miserly businessmen would move mountains and
fill valleys only to have the monsters consume the earth's meager
supply of coal. Gautier was of the same mind as those Chinese who
fired on any steamships they saw: " Ils ont raison, le bateau à vapeur,
c'est la prose; le bateau à voiles, c'est la poésie."[6]

The debate waxed so furious that it even came to the attention
of the Académie.   In its bumbling way it decided in 1842 to set the
discovery of steam as the subject of an essay contest. But the topic
proved so unappetizing that the prize was not awarded until 1847.

III

If the Industrial Revolution had merely influenced literature to the
extent of expanding vocabulary and, to a lesser degree, the contemporary stock of imagery, its impact could be called negligible.
But evidence points to a deeper, more important change that seems
to mirror the shifts in society : new allegorical and symbolical figures
appeared as a part of the literary shorthand accepted by the age.

To a certain extent each age reflects change by rebuilding the myths
and symbols it inherits from the past to fit the new conditions. Changes

in society affect those living at any given time; and their experiences,
if sufficiently general in character, tend to be expressed in the form
of allegorical or symbolic figures. As Ernst Cassirer pointed out
" a conception is fixed and held only when it has been embodied
in a symbol." Susanne Langer refined this theory when she wrote
in *Philosophy in a new key* that human experience is constantly being
wrought into symbols, non-discursive or presentational forms which
contain complex combinations of attitudes.[7] " These artistic symbols...
are untranslatable; their sense is bound to the particular form which
it has taken. It is always implicit and cannot be explicated by an
interpretation."[8] A peculiar characteristic of these presentational forms
is that they may be merged into a single expression without being
presented in their constituent parts. They constitute a kind of literary
shorthand whereby hopes, fears, aspirations, or beliefs may be clothed
in human form for incorporation in a story.

As the generations pass on to each other their legends or anthropo-
morphic expressions of concepts, some of these presentational forms
tend to die, no longer capable of expressing anything valid for their
inheritors. Others, more elastic, can be stretched to cover modern
conditions. But always there seems to be a necessity to create new
forms for what is completely personal to an era. And along with
any great social shift there appears to go a greater than normal need
to create additional personifications of complexes of ideas and emotions
to express what is peculiar to a given age.

Obviously, the use of allegory, symbol, or archetype serves as an
aid to the author. Any writer, even a Horatio Alger, puts more into
his story than a plot. To his work he brings an attitude toward life
in terms of which he consciously or unconsciously manipulates situation
and character. And since the writer is also communicating his sense
of values to a group of unknowns, he naturally plans to express himself
in terms meaningful to his audience.

But the artist faces a particular problem : confined within the limits
of a genre, he cannot possibly explain logically, among other things,
all the background of his characters, their relationship to each other
in either intellectual or emotional terms, or their social significance,
while at the same time he develops a plot and controls the meaning
which he expects story development to convey. The difficulty is
most apparent in the case of the secondary characters. For them,

as well as for most, if not all, the primary characters, the author finds himself in need of a kind of shorthand. As a part of his technique he uses presentational forms, or symbolic personages, incorporating, not intellectual concepts, but emotional attitudes towards society, personifications that sum up all the truths and falsehoods concerning a given subject. And, obviously, the larger the audience the author expects to reach, the more he tends to reach into popular myth-making potential for the generally accepted symbols of what he is trying to express.

Any age finds itself gifted with legacies from the past, presentational forms, or symbolic figures that once functioned as commonly accepted literary currency. To an extent that depends on its literacy, each generation can draw on the experience of the past: it can delve into Greek and Roman mythologies for situations, characters, or symbols bulging with accreted meaning. But given the sudden spurt in the tempo of French civilization at the end of the Revolution, the 19th century suddenly found itself in a dismal position. Whereas the 17th and 18th centuries had been able to utilize the mythologies of antiquity to express contemporary opinions and desires, the 19th found itself embarrassingly in need of a more adequate mean of communication. Learned in antiquity, the 17th century had been satisfied with the old, adding, among others, the myth of the Sun King, the Universal Man, the "honnête homme," the Cornelian hero and the Racinian heroine. The 18th century generally agreed with its predecessor but it, too, embroidered on the past with the legend of the Noble Savage, El Dorado, the Best of All Possible Worlds, the Natural Man, and the *philosophe*.

Unfortunately for literary stability, the Revolution smashed the old mythology ruthlessly. For a while, stern originators of the great revolt counted on antiquity to replace the Catholicism they expected to discredit, but their hopes suffocated in the smudge fires that blackened the Goddess of Liberty on the Champs de Mars. Apollo, Jove, Aphrodite, and their relatives vanished forever from the murky heights of Olympus with the first flush of the 19th century. Somehow these whimsical and capricious gods seemed worn and heavy with years in the cold light of the world of Robespierre and Napoleon. Quietly they withdrew to see what creations man would dare raise in their places.

The 19th century had a hard time replacing the old gods. They and their legends, with a curious admixture of Catholicism, had functioned admirably during the 17th and 18th centuries. An author lacking a frame of reference merely reached casually into his memory for a reference from a tale oft told and, as educated people, all his readers understood the meaning of his symbolism. Sisyphus or Antigone, Oedipus or Andromaque, could be used to express Christian or pagan thoughts, so elastic were their presentational possibilities. But the gods could live only with people who understood them. During the 17th and 18th centuries, the élite had studied Greek and Latin as the prerequisites for entering the state of gentlemanliness. Hence, to them, knowledge of such references formed part of the necessary social graces, to be understood without benefit of footnote.

Under pressure of the Revolution, the old order passed and, with it, the old education. For a time some remnants of the past survived the early days of the holocaust, but these soon shriveled under the general suspicion of things ancient and aristocratic. Modernity became the touchstone and, by the time Napoleon pushed his way to prominence, the old regime had irrevocably vanished. The suppression of the universities and the famous schools almost obliterated classical learning except for those oldsters who remembered their Latin or Greek. The young who escaped the draft and who managed to enjoy the advantages of higher education never did attain the polish and the classical grounding of their forebears. They had lost the fine art of living delicately, to say nothing of their literary heritage.

Given such a state of affairs, the generations educated after the Revolution felt the urgent need of a new mythology not apparent to their elders. During the entire struggle between pseudo-classicism and romanticism, one of the great points at issue was precisely that of a frame of reference for the budding literature. Chateaubriand attempted to introduce Christianity as a substitute for a bloodless neo-paganism, but the parade of saints and holy men attracted the attention of few writers. For one thing, Catholicism was still protected by too many tabus. There could not be the same free and rollicking familiarity with its saints as with the gods of antiquity. Furthermore, tales from the New and Old Testaments lacked the flexibility of the myths of antiquity. Few dared dally with figures so important to their contemporaries, especially since the Christian God had tended to become a god of vengeance ever since '89. Because Catholics had rarely studied the Bible, any attempt to speak in terms of its wisdom would almost automatically surpass the ken of the average Frenchman. And, as the 19th century aged, it became increasingly important to the author not to confuse or antagonize the ordinary citizen.

Hence, the 19th century witnessed a major shift from the literary frame of reference previously used. To be sure, the 17th and 18th centuries had not accepted ready-made mythologies, but they had filled in around an inheritance from antiquity. And some of their particular creations passed unscathed through the Revolution. The Wicked Jesuit, the Noble Savage, the Heartless Nobleman, or the Avaricious Tax Collector managed to survive the ruin of their creators. To these the Revolution added some of its own, notably the Pure and Heroic Son of the Revolution, the Camp Follower, the Dastardly Reactionary, Perfidious Albion, the modern Spartan warrior, the Sans-Culotte, and the ever-present vulture of all wars, the Profiteer who sold cardboard boots to Courageous Patriots. Needless to say the advent of the Consulate and the Empire added a few new faces, but they were essentially the same old presentational forms in new uniforms and bright frogging.

By the time Napoleon assumed power, the nymphs and dryads had been consumed in the hot flames of civil war. Some memory of them found refuge abroad with the emigration, but the bulk of the population, semi-literate at best, felt no sentimental or academic ties with Jove and his nectar-drinking cohorts. Life was too earnest for modern man to worry about the grandeur that was Greece. Robespierre tried, but encountered only the indifference of apathy. For a time, after the outlawing of the Church, it seemed that France would have to be satisfied either with atheism or a clandestine religion.

Consequently, at the time when romanticism was first becoming an issue, French literature also sensed a desperate need of renewing its mythological structure. The old and the stable bitterly resented the modern and the experimental. Young men found that their language could barely express the thoughts of the new century. Those who had heard the Te Deum sung for victories of the Empire could scarcely be thrilled by tales in a minor key from the century of Louis XIV. The petty troubles of the past, even the Fronde, could scarcely measure up to the frightening majesty of the Revolution or the spectacular drama of the Emperor's return. Since society had changed so radically in recent decades, politically, socially, and economically, communication in the old terms no longer seemed possible. New ideas needed new expressions: the machine, the stock market, the voter, and, most startling of all, the people. To convey all the overtones associated with these, they had to fashion new figures on whom to drape their thoughts.

The religiously minded, but not quite orthodox, filled their verses with paeans of praise for a pantheistic god. Progress, of course, was unquestioned : the world moved smoothly toward a perfection guaranteed by the universal consent of two centuries. Yet, despite this, the Cénacle could not shake off a vicarious sadness. When it contemplated the ruins of past glories, it wept crocodile tears on what might have been.

Fumblingly, early romanticism sought a path through the tangle of contemporary events, to end up in a welter of philosophies of history. Quinet went in one direction, Michelet in another. Obviously, such creation came painfully. The romanticists had to glean from their own age the stuff for myths, legends, and presentational forms which make literature more than a sequence of words. Consequently, the new school begged, borrowed, and stole from all sources to establish literary conventions more meaningful than those vaunted by its opponents.

At first the romanticists departed only timidly from the ways of their forebears, then, emboldened, struck out along divergent paths. But strong echoes of the 18th century persisted. The nature known to Jean-Jacques Rousseau and to Bernardin de Saint Pierre, usually friendly and apprehended tactilely, played a large part in early verse. The sea roared in approved fashion; the night closed in classic darkness over the bleakness of a realistic day; the stars shone coldly or warmly depending on whether the lovers had quarreled or were on the verge of melting into each other's arms. Young swains and their maids sat beside rushing torrents near a lightning-struck oak close by a fresh grave, while they tearfully meditated on the passing of time. Thomson, Haller, Rousseau, and Bernardin de Saint-Pierre all left bequests that enriched the next century. The concept of change, of yesterday, today, and tomorrow struck the first romanticists as a great discovery. All things appeared in movement; man seemed to walk on the shifting sands of time where no human could leave a permanent mark. Hence the plaintive plea of Lamartine in *Le Lac* and the constant repetition of the theme of ruins and death, the focus on moving water as a symbol of life.

To some extent, Atala and René made an impression on the French, but the " good " primitive always remained an academic theme. Because of Chateaubriand, the French never compared the American Indian with the ill-smelling, painted savage who ran amok through captured villages. The " good " savage, scrubbed and deodorized for public appearances, somehow seemed anodyne and fit only for political purposes.

Religion may have provided an infertile field for symbols of good, but it furnished a striking example of a presentational form of evil in the person of Satan. Vigny created Eloa, the angel of pity, from one of Christ's tears; Hugo exalted the faith of the Middle Ages as frozen into the architecture of Notre-Dame de Paris; and occasionally Lamartine prayed in his own way in the *Méditations*. But the material was too resistant, the results often insipid. On the other hand, the Prince of Darkness presented no such difficulties. Quite the contrary, he seemed to invite attention in literature, particularly since the romanticists found him so exploited in the medieval tales they avidly copied prior to 1830. Magic of the blackest kind, sorcery to chill any spine, became almost a sine qua non of early romanticism. And in the midst of this reared the figure of His Satanic Majesty. For a while the devil's popularity rose to such heights that it became almost de rigueur for a young man to decorate his bachelor apartment with a black and white picture of Milton's Satan.

Actually, Satan appealed less as a religious figure than as a symbol of the romanticist's own lot. He epitomized the act of rebellion against impossible odds at the moment when the young writers felt themselves to be in exactly the same position. Since they could appreciate both the magnitude of his sin and the incredible courage it implied, they portrayed him from both points of view. As an extension of the same idea, romanticism also favored such lesser practitioners of social revolt as Lara or Don Juan. Byron himself they elevated to the rank of demi-god.

They were so conscious of the presence of evil that their first works abound in presentational forms of the ugly and the wicked. A minority group perhaps felt an affinity with the outcasts they created; at any rate, they lavishly sprinkled both prose and poetry with moral or physical monsters, strange creations almost Freudian in conception. England exported a good many when the Gothic novel entered France after the Revolution to enjoy an immediate vogue.   Monk Lewis, Anne Radcliffe, and Clara Reeve, to mention only the masters, apparently offered an exciting diet of adventure that attracted readers then living the epic of the Revolution and the Empire.   For them evil was menacing, virtue more pure than verisimilitude actually permitted, but their characters summed up many a superstitious belief of long standing.   For a Catholic nation, nothing could express more complete wickedness than monks or nuns who betrayed their vows and sold themselves to the Prince of Darkness for a mess of the world's pottage.   And around these traitors formed a substantial cast which time had consecrated as the supporters of evil : witches, black cats, and the whole paraphernalia of the supernatural.

To be sure, the French romanticists were not naive enough to trap themselves into complete identification with such primitive beliefs.   But it is curious to note that when they abandoned such obvious forms, they had to create others to replace them.   Claude Frollo epitomized for Hugo the powers of darkness; to a lesser extent the same could be said of Bug-Jargal or the unbelievable Hans d'Islande. Balzac preferred the more human Vautrin for symbolizing an easily understood view of good and evil.

These forms, however, all came from literature.   In addition, the romanticists had at hand another ready-made series of symbols from the popular literature and imagery.   Here again the past gave richly, but of a more plebeian fare than came from the sophisticated classics. Lustucru, Crédit est mort, Grattelard, the henpecked husband, le Bonhomme Misère and Ahasvérus, or the Wandering Jew, came to their attention as symbols endowed with considerable meaning and prestige.

Of them all, Ahasvérus seemed to fit best a generally felt need. Fascinated by the Revolution and eager to find an explanation for the present in the past, the romanticists developed a fondness for philosophies of history.   To the theory of progress adopted from the 18th century, each added his own particular beliefs, some seeing 19th-century democracy as the final perfection of mankind, while others prophesied an indefinite ascent toward the perfect good. Michelet, Quinet, Hugo in the preface of *Cromwell*, Vigny in *Cinq-Mars*, all had their word to say on the present and future as an extension of the past. But it was one thing to write long and learned introductions for academics, to translate Herder or Vico, and quite another to know how to dilute a philosophy for general consumption. Thus Quinet realized that he could make his thesis more readily understandable to a wider audience through the story of the Wandering Jew. Others followed his suit, and the figure of the lonely little man helplessly trapped in the web of time became a commonplace. Through this reappearing character, the romanticists hoped to express the epic feeling they sensed in their age. Moreover, Ahasvérus had already been properly introduced by Béranger, a writer with a sure sense of popular feeling. Therefore it was with complete confidence in the clarity of his meaning that Lamartine used an altered version of the wanderer as the central figure of a projected many-volume epic, only two parts of which were published, *Jocelyn* and the *Chute d'un ange*. Similarly Balzac introduced a modified form of the Wandering Jew in the *Peau de chagrin* in the antiquarian who furnished Raphaël with the ass's skin.

IV

When romanticism passed 1830 and the test of *Hernani*, to reach a confident maturity, it found its literary shorthand still far from satisfactory. What had seemed apposite under the Bourbons now scarcely fitted conditions during the Orléans monarchy. The helpless orphan, that lost heiress to a magnificent fortune, finally fled from her wicked uncle right off the printed page. The panoply of the Middle Ages, false troubadours, pages, witches' sabbaths, vanished in the smoke of new factories.

Most curious of all, the misunderstood poet left the Cénacle to join Bohemia. Whereas France felt convinced politically of her manifest destiny, young writers acted with far less confidence. As Musset wrote in the *Confession d'un enfant du siècle*, they felt that life had cheated them of the opportunities it had lavished on the men of the Empire. As a minority with an apparently bleak future, they wrapped themselves in a dark cloak and enjoyed their loneliness. They were misunderstood poets. So often, in the early years, had they smarted under the sting of critical bastinados, that they justifiably felt themselves struggling against insuperable odds to bring artistic truth to obtuse minds. Vigny's *Chatterton* summed up the feelings of many who despaired at stinging critical reviews, or whose poetic optimism had run headlong into the indifference of publishers. The first romanticists felt a supreme contempt for the earth-bound condemned to prose, and they could not understand that the great day of verse was passing. Their lack of recognition they imputed to the calculating materialist who, himself, was to become a familiar figure in literary mythology. The Lord Mayor of London who scorned Chatterton's talent symbolized for them the cold, unemotional side of life that threatened to extinguish the spark of creative genius. This was the same feeling that gripped Musset's poet in the *Nuits*.

As France passed into the industrial age, its urban centers swelled prodigiously with the jamming of the industrial proletariat. New ideas and thoughts crowded forward for expression. The entire social pattern was now being woven around a dominant middle class that had elbowed aside the old nobility. And its reign brought the supremacy of the values which the bourgeoisie thought inalienable, irrefutable and immediately obvious to all enlightened people. From 1830 on, the French ruling class smugly announced to the less fortunate that salvation lay within its ranks, acceptance into which was accomplished only by the diligent practice of such virtues as thrift, dedication to the *juste milieu*, established religion, and the principle of nationalism. So firmly was the righteousness of these concepts embedded in their minds that members of the middle class believed they had constructed a perfect society based on economic, political, and artistic conservatism.

In terms of literature, however, the romanticists could not agree. And since about 1830 the Cénacle had split into utilitarianism and art for art's sake, at least three groups faced the problem of renovating symbolic forms. As a result the same presentational figures could be used by all with different overtones of expression. Thus to the Petit Cénacle the Banker was a figure of derision, to the Cénacle a person of either good or evil possibilities, whereas the bourgeois writers treated him as a man of solid merit.

Paradoxically, the Petit Cénacle seems to have had the least need of new symbols. After *Hernani* the young romanticists, even fiercer poets than Hugo's friends, found themselves in much the same situation as had the rebels of the previous generation. Aware that they were continuing the great revolution, they now felt they had two sets of enemies : the bourgeois and those who had abandoned the cause of a modern art. They heartily despised Louis-Philippe and all he represented. But these youngsters had surpassed the timid experiments of the Cénacle. Since they intended to create a poetry for their own kind that primarily emphasized technique, they felt less in need of new presentational forms. Innovation in rhyme and form was what most attracted them, and since content assumed secondary position in their scheme of values, the old symbols could be made to do. Consequently, with them the myth of the misunderstood poet still enjoyed a restricted vogue. Similarly, they retained a con- servative interest in the Middle Ages. Thus, Alphonse Rabbe drew heavily on his classicial studies for the chapters of the *Album d'un pessimiste*, " Sisyphe " and " Le Centaure." Aloysius Bertrand satisfied a penchant for the past with messires Hugues, archers, the gallows, and other bits of medieval exoticism. Philothée O'Neddy dreamt of succubi and skeletons, while Pétrus Borel wrote within just as limited a frame of reference, though he did portray a rabid Republican when sketching himself as a lycanthrope. Alfred Le Poittevin faithfully entitled one of his poems " Satan," another " Ahasvérus," in *La Bacchante*. Théophile Gautier unoriginally leaned heavily in *Albertus* on such trite effects as witches, black cats, magic coaches, and a reincarnation of the bloody nun. A rich sense of color, a sharp sense of irony, and a dedication to the task of enlarging the possibilities of poetic expression seem the principal attributes of these latter-day Renés, the dispossessed of the machine age.

Men like Hugo and Balzac, Lamartine or Sue, however, had a different problem to solve. They had accepted the changes and, as self-appointed Messiahs, found it almost essential for communication to rely on new presentational forms drawn from the world around them, summations of popular reactions to contemporary civilization. The most obvious symbols were old friends in new clothing. The noble savage, once happy in war paint, became Toussaint-Louverture or Lamartine's peasant friends. The Black Monk continued his frightening way but after the founding of the July Monarchy he

joined the Jesuits, became a pillar of the Congrégation or metamorphosed into the Macchiavelian Julien Sorel.   The Bloody Nun
crept back to her grave, but Satan, Lara, or Don Juan turned into
Hernani, the good outlaw, and later, when the bloom rubbed off
romanticism, into Vautrin, the many imitations of Vidocq, even Jean
Valjean.   The villain of the melodrama and the terror novel abandoned
a fruitless attempt to bilk frail heroines for the more sedentary and
profitable manipulation of the stock market and the foreclosing of
mortgages.   A far more sinister portrayal, the Wicked Capitalist, a
Gobseck or a Nucingen, meant more than the old fermier-général
to members in good standing of the National Guard and firm believers
in the sanctity of a savings account.

New conventions and forms inevitably made their appearance.   A
survey of French comedy 1815-1848 reveals that the people were
busy inventing the figures needed by authors.[9]   The pursuit of money,
social climbing, love, of course, but also illegitimate children, the
condition of women, slavery, capital punishment, political intrigue,
and journalism, all were topics that enjoyed high favor.   The public
became accustomed to such figures as the Minister, the Artisan, the
Capitalist, the Convict, the Jesuit, and the Stockholder.   But most
of all, they came to know the Worker, the Deputy, the Stock Market
Manipulator, the Boss, the Inventor, the Journalist, and the Politician.
A host of lesser lights surrounded them : the Travelling Salesman,
Robert Macaire, the Swindler, the Poet, and the Bourgeois.

But by far the most stupendous legend of them all was bequeathed
by the little corporal, whose legend had begun to grow almost with
his first appearance.   Once a consul, Napoleon encouraged all to
sing his praises, and soon the constant peal of the Te Deum, the confident parade step of the grognards year after year impressed on France
that a hero had been born.   France believed him, for, between 1797
and 1899, playwrights mounted some 596 plays dealing with the great
conqueror.[10]

To the people of France, the Emperor forever remained the great
savior of their pride and glory, even after Waterloo.   For the veterans,
of course, but, more important, for the peasants and the first proletariat,
he attained the stature of a demi-god.   Some of the Restoration
goguettes made him their sole hero, chanting hymns to his glory in
preference to all other songs.   Then, Barthélemy and Méry, two

acidulous pamphleteers, set the pattern for the new legend. Imbued with the religion of the conqueror, they seized every occasion to vaunt his superhuman qualities. Behind them they could always feel the support of Béranger or Casimir Delavigne, both early converts to the new religion of the Superman.[11]

The result was that the people never really accepted the Emperor's defeat, neither the peasants nor the few workers then in the factories. Through them the Napoleonic legend took such hold during 1815-1830 that even after the announcement of Bonaparte's death, Béranger could announce confidently, " Il n'est pas mort." France believed that the Emperor had gone into hiding and would reappear when the condition of the country required his services.

Under Louis-Philippe, the myth assumed even greater proportions. The bourgeoisie became the little corporal's strongest support, particularly those bellicose pacifists who sported the uniform of the National Guard, and the strength of this opinion forced the replacement of a Greek imitation of the general on the column of the Place Vendôme on July 28, 1833. Curiously, a violent spirit of revenge played an important part in this change of heart. During the last days of the Empire the middle class had believed itself victim of the dynastic and imperialistic dreams of its ruler, but once he had been driven to Elba, a drab present made them regret a past made even more glorious by the distortion of time. France entered days economically golden, but dull and without savor; France seemed a second-rate military power, a position painful to the vicariously warlike merchants. The bourgeoisie reacted against this inferiority by making the erstwhile enemy a symbol of their hopes and dreams. He became nationalism incarnate, the perfect representative of middle-class chauvinism. Consequently, from 1830-1851 there unfolded a period of unbridled admiration, not only on the part of the devoted *demi-soldes*, but almost all except the royalists.

In line with the trend, writers began making obeisance to the colossus. Hugo recalled that his father had risen to the rank of general under the Empire, could, in fact, boast that he had never surrendered to the Allies. Quinet, Dumas père, Balzac, Thiers, even the republican Armand Carrel, added to the legend. Stendhal translated a personal devotion into the hero worship that motivated the tremendous drive and ambition of Julien Sorel. To join him, though not for the same

reasons, came the supercilious Musset, the grave Vigny, Quinet, and
the fledgling Brizeux. In fact, all who wrote between 1830-1848 did
so under the shadow of the little corporal, and to them he epitomized
their various hopes and dreams : the great rebel, the misunderstood
genius, the Messiah of France, manifest destiny personified, and the
glory that once was, and perhaps again could be, France.

The romanticists themselves furnished part of the material they
were seeking. The furious newspaper debate over the unities and the
freedom of the artist had ruffled the tempers of only a small group,
but the din of battle was louder than the number of participants would
indicate. The dramatic climax of *Hernani* focused attention on the
Cénacle beyond the wildest dreams of the young rebels. They became
models for the dissatisfied type called the Poet, and later, when the
art for art's sake group continued the revolution, they attracted even
more attention. But by now the bourgeoisie suspected them of sub-
version. Consequently, to the Poet was added the Bousingo and the
Jeune-France. The former lived lustily in the first literary Bohemia,
mocked the bourgeoisie, and delighted in playing jokes on the
Philistines. The latter, much more dainty, epitomized what the
average citizen understood romanticism to mean. The young man
dressed in dark clothes, lived in an apartment filled with such exotic
articles as Indian relics, Greek fire, or tomahawks. Gloomy beyond
belief, he was addicted to long walks or standing rapt on deserted
headlands. He could be writer, sculptor, or painter, but he was always
the blood brother of René.

Beside him stood the Romantic Heroine, a composite of types
ranging from pure angels like Doña Sol and Kitty Bell to the more
energetic Lucrèce Borgia or Dumas' Adèle. Beautiful but weak, the
young lady suffered from circumstances beyond her control. Often
she fainted from the stress of too-easy emotions; but at all times she
lived above the prosy concerns of the world, a fit companion for the
Jeune-France.

They, of course, were not the result of the new age; in fact they
existed almost in spite of it, and tended to fade somewhat after 1830,
when new heroes and heroines replaced them. Balzac, as a careful
social historian, reflected the change. His work contains an almost
unbelievably complete catalogue of these gifts of the industrial era
and no writer, perhaps, has utilized so many presentational forms.

They were, in fact, an integral part of the novel as he conceived it.

Since Balzac dipped into the reality of his day for his portraits, it is not surprising that he fixed on the figures of the Banker, the Stock Market Player, and the Confidence Man as major figures of an age which revolved around the Bourse. The Bureaucrat, the contemporary Caspar Milquetoast, the Social Climber, all found a place in the *Comédie Humaine*. Closer to the Industrial Revolution, even, were Lucien Rubempré, the Commercial Writer, and the illustrious Gaudissart, Travelling Salesman par excellence. Balzac himself an incorrigible builder of fortunes, seems to have tried to find a way to make cheap paper, perhaps his inspiration for the last part of *Un Grand Homme de province* with its portrait of David Séchard, the Inventor, bent on simplifying life through the possibilities of the machine. One after another Balzac used the new presentational forms : Gobseck, the Moneylender; the Journalist with all the power of the press; César Birotteau, the Shopkeeper, half Babbitt, half M. Jourdain, trying to make a fortune; the Bourgeois, confident in his adoration of the marvels of progress.

Balzac, however, made little mention of the 19th century's greatest contribution to literature's gallery of presentational forms : the urban worker. The People had become a favorite of the romanticists, but in large groups, fluid mobs pushing blindly and irresistibly, capable of tremendous power for good or evil. This was a political view, and it was matched by the picture of the Proletarian, the factory worker living the barest of lives in a slum area. Normally the romanticists treated him as inherently " good," as Hugo did, first as the man of the people in *Ruy Blas*, then as Jean Valjean, the poor worker of *Les Misérables*. Sue made a fortune with the convention in the *Mystères de Paris* and the *Juif Errant*. Even Alfred de Vigny, supposedly above the mêlée, planned a sequel to *Eloa* in which the angel of pity would successively appear as the slave of antiquity, the medieval serf, and the salaried worker. The aloof Gérard de Nerval became so interested in the plight of the worker that he sketched a *Doctrine Sociale*, only a few notes of which remain.[12]

Around this contemporary exemplification of the factory system formed a ring of supporting characters. The Prostitute, long known in French literature, became a victim of society, forced by circumstances to sell herself to exist. Thus Cosette and her sisters made their entrance into literature, wicked only from necessity and always available for regeneration by the love of a good man or as a sacrifice for an illegitimate child. These worthy descendants of Marion Delorme and the Dame aux camélias were the Poor Working Girls of the age, often burdened with a love child. George Sand, in particular, dedicated herself to the task of trying to rehabilitate these seduced and misunderstood women.

Similarly, the romanticists well knew that the melodrama and the terror novel had firmly fixed children in the French heart, especially the Orphan. Behind them lay the dreary slum, spawning evil around its factories. Men like Lamartine recognized this as they poured forth speech after speech in the Chamber of Deputies, talking " out the windows " to the Workers and the People. It was, perhaps, too soon for other figures to appear clearly, the Union Organizer or the Huckster, but many were forming. The Striker was taking shape, immortalized by Daumier in the Massacre of the Rue Transnonain, Louis-Philippe's punishment for industrial rebellion. And the fact that cartoonists like Daumier were able to portray the new presentational forms in easily recognized fashion testifies to the great myth-making capacity of the age. Along with the writers they were shaping the personality of the Boss, the harsh Foreman, the Salesman, and, as an inevitable result of the labor-management clash, the Socialist.

The power of these forms was such that no matter how the artist or writer viewed the social scene, they came to his mind as shortcuts to communication. Conservatives might paint the Worker as bad, liberals as good. Reybaud mocked Jérôme Paturot, others imitated him. Even Gautier poked fun at the Jeune-France and the *bousingo* he had helped originate. Almost all the forms could be treated either favorably or unfavorably, but one fact remained clear : they symbolized the aspirations and fears of that day, and many of them, the new ones, were grounded in the conditions of the Industrial Revolution. As Alfred Nettement, arch enemy of the modern, admitted, " Tous représentent cet être multiple qu'on appelle le peuple, ils le représentent avec un visage à la fois douloureux et terrible."[13]

NOTES

1. Sainte-Beuve, *Correspondance générale*, Paris, Stock, 1936, II, 388.

2. Genève, Droz, 1951.

3. Georges Friedmann, " Faust et Saint-Simon, " *Europe*, XXVI, 16.

4. *Mercure du XIXe siècle*, II (1823), 529-33.

5. *Lettres inédites de Alfred de Vigny au Marquis et à la Marquise de la Grange (1827-1861)*, Paris, Conard, 1914, p. 97.

6. *Musée des familles*, janvier 1842.

7. Cambridge, Harvard University Press, 1951, pp. 60-61 : " Symbols are not proxy for their objects, but are *vehicles for the conception of objects.* To conceive a thing or a situation is not the same thing as to " react toward it " overtly, or to be aware of its presence. In talking *about* things we have conceptions of them, not the things themselves; and *it is the conceptions, not the things,* that symbols directly " mean. "

8. *Ibid.*, p. 260.

9. Sylvia England, " The characteristics of French comedy during the period 1815-1848, " *RHL*, XLI, 1934.

10. Jules Deschamps " La Légende de Napoléon et la littérature comparée, " *RLC*, April-June, 1929, pp. 285-307; L.-Henri Lecomte, *Napoléon et l'Empire racontés par le théâtre*, Paris, Raux, 1900.

11. Jules Garson, *Les Créateurs de la légende napoléonienne*, Paris, Fischbacher, 1899.

12. *Mercure de France*, 1 septembre 1950.

13. *Op. cit.*, II, 41.

CONCLUSION

ROMANTICISM, IT SEEMS, can be divided into at least two distinct periods, with the division coming roughly about 1830. Prior to then, the movement was apparently held together by a negative attitude, by what the young men objected to, not what they stood for. During all the years of the early debate with the classicists, the proponents of the modern had somehow failed to present a manifesto acceptable to all the literary rebels. Thus, while they objected to perpetuating mummified themes, they came to few conclusions on firm proposals for what might fill the void their reaction had created.

Consequently, at first they wisely took Madame de Staël's advice and from their neighbors enthusiastically borrowed plots, themes and symbols, or invoked the magic names of foreign masters to bolster a position weak in the prestige of ancestry. However, progressively as they won their argument for the right to create as they deemed fit, they felt less and less need for foreign aid and, by 1830, they had learned the lessons other nations could teach and belatedly turned their gaze back to France. But all this time, the romanticists had given careful attention only to poetry and the theater. Prose, particularly the novel, had not yet earned their approval, though many of them had dabbled sporadically in this medium.

By 1830, then, the romanticists had freed themselves from restraints but, unbeknownst to them, they were about to be plunged into a strange new world, one far less comfortable than the bumbling and slow-moving Restoration. The Industrial Revolution had crossed the Channel in the wake of Wellington; and by the time Louis-Philippe came to power, industrial capitalism was much in evidence. The sudden, even explosive entry of the machine, with all its social consequences, struck the nation just as the romanticists were seeking material to continue their revolution.

Coincidentally, the position of the professional author changed drastically. For the first time writers had the means to reach a mass

audience with inexpensive literature. By virtue of the technological
advances in printing which it brought, the Industrial Revolution gave
them the possibility of a more profitable living than ever, provided
they could satisfy the public. Meanwhile, too, this public had been
experiencing the effects of the first attempts to introduce mass education
in France, experiments which broadened tremendously the potential
reading audience. And given the contemporary crisis in the book
trade, authors did not have to be told where lay the butter for their
bread.

Perhaps to their sorrow, the modernists soon discovered how radically
the public had changed, even since the first skirmishes over romanticism. The age belonged to the bourgeoisie, but writers concerned
with large editions had also to calculate on the tastes of the peasant
and the proletariat, the latter a strange new class that seemed to spring
from the sowing of cogwheels. The urban workers did not at first
weigh too heavily in the literary balance, though they later would,
but from the start they attracted attention because in the conditions
of their existence could be seen the violent social effects of the Industrial
Revolution and the difficulties the nation faced in adjusting to them.
This class and its problems would furnish the young writers with
much of the material they used after 1830.

This, then, was the new public. Its low literacy and incapacity
for the subtler forms of writing, particularly for any demanding
sophistication of taste, had lowered the standards set by the elite
of the 17th and 18th centuries. The spread of elementary schooling
had made France, not just Paris, the audience to be faced. And this
audience had wants far different from those of its intellectual leaders.
The upper bourgeoisie might still be classically minded by taste or
hostility to change, but the rest of the nation, including both the
peasants and the industrial workers, belonged completely to the present.
Their outlook was far more practical, since they could not afford
to live vicariously in other times, no matter how intriguing the past;
and only prose, not poetry, enticed them to spend their hard-earned
sous, for this they could grasp as the medium of story-telling.

None but the dullest could escape the fact that the day of prose
had come, even though critics still considered it an illegitimate child
of the muses. About 1830 poetry had slid into a decline despite the
vociferous mourning of its practitioners, immediately to be replaced

in the public favor by prose. Publishers shed a delicate tear but no longer considered its existence justified because it did not sell. Economics had conquered the Alexandrine and no respectable professional writer missed the signs pointing to prose.

Just as these facts became obvious, the modern newspaper rose full-formed from the fertile brain of Emile de Girardin. This, too, had been made possible by the Industrial Revolution and it was to have a major effect on literature. In their mad race for subscribers, editors conscious of the habit-forming effects of the feuilleton enticed novelists to their aid. Since the alliance proved profitable to both parties, it tended to become permanent, but it meant that the feuilletoniste, even more than the independent writer, had to submit himself almost completely to the domination of a public given to sudden whimsical shifts in taste. The average man became the arbiter of literary success.

As the preceding series of facts dawned on the romanticists, their revolution changed sharply, almost abruptly. The movement split into factions as its proponents reacted to contemporary events, and literature developed along lines unperceived and undreamed by the men of the Restoration. One segment, dedicated to art for art's sake, rejected the machine and all it represented. These men, a second generation of romanticists, created the myth of the modern avant-garde poet. Leftist in politics, hostile to " bourgeois " values, they continued the experimentation implicit in the preface of *Cromwell* to produce the prose poem and rare and exotic verse forms. But they paid the price in full : their work tended to become increasingly obscure to the layman, with the result that they divorced themselves almost completely from the public as different coteries battled over fine points of prosody.

The other group, the " utilitarians," decided to face contemporary civilization, its factories, slums, and the social problems that followed the advent of an urban proletariat. As self-appointed Messiahs, putative politicians and leaders in a dozen different faiths, they expected to direct the course of their age. Consequently, they sponsored a worker's literature as one of the responsibilities of their position. To their amazement, they found that though some of their protégés meekly repeated advice on accepting one's lot to store up treasures in heaven, others wanted heaven on earth. From the latter would come the rumblings of dissent that presaged the first signs of a socialist literature.

Unlike their younger colleagues, these utilitarians accepted grudgingly the prose which the age craved, particularly the old and hoary romance. But new conditions made some of them consider the medium in which they were working and out of this meditation men like Balzac or Stendhal would see the basis of a new art form, the modern novel. Historically-minded, they would change the romance's point of narration, drop story into the present, and make the analysis of psychologically motivated characters their chief concern. How society made people act on each other interested them more than plots built of incidents strung haphazardly in bead-fashion.

But the novel gave the old romance little competition; the latter flourished in sturdy fashion when the penny press adopted it in the form of a feuilleton designed to attract subscribers. Professional writers, very much business men now that the patron had disappeared, reduced the romance to a recipe for easy serialization. The resultant concoction of stock characters, conventional situations, weary plots, and conversational clichés may have disgusted aesthetes, but the great mass of new readers loved it. And since the latter constituted the source of a writer's bread and butter, artists accepted the mésalliance of romance and newspaper as a fact of life. Critics might howl at the literary changes, but their position merely forced them into a different kind of art for art's sake. They, like the Petit Cénacle, wrote more and more for an elite, and their former glory fell to a new breed, the reviewer.

Both victors and vanquished, however, seemed to react similarly in one way to the nascent machine age. All felt the need for a more expressive language, an imagery closer to reality and presentational forms tailored for modern conditions. Each in his own way helped rejuvenate in this manner the literature of the nineteenth century. To be sure, they were still adjusting to the effects of the Industrial Revolution but what they did was in some ways a forecast of things to come. In this respect, perhaps, the change in society left its deepest mark.

That the course of Industrial Revolution and the development of romanticism in France are contiguous is beyond question, and, likewise, the fact that they are inextricably intertwined and specifically related is beyond doubt. Yet, to demonstrate a determinism or a causality in any direction, however enticing, would lead beyond the safety of the facts. Nevertheless, it is possible to conclude that the Industrial Revolution opened the way for a mass literature, and that the very machines which fashioned that age split romanticism into two factions, one of which continued the poetic revolution that the first generation had begun. To the other it presented new possibilities for artistic expression. It helped focus attention on prose, thereby aiding the shift from the romance to the novel and further contributed to the novelist a modern set of characters and themes; to both prose and poetry it gave new and striking images. In short, it was a major factor in the development of French romanticism.

81-10694

840.   GEORGE, ALBERT JOSEPH
914   THE DEVELOPMENT OF
GEO   FRENCH ROMANTICISM